POETRY IN EXILE

A study of the poetry of W.H. Auden,
Joseph Brodsky and George Szirtes

Michael Murphy

GREENWICH EXCHANGE
LONDON

Greenwich Exchange, London

First published in Great Britain in 2004

Printed and bound by Q3 Digital/Litho, Loughborough
Tel: 01509 213456
Typesetting and layout by Albion Associates, London
Tel: 020 8852 4646
Cover design by December Publications, Belfast
Tel: 028 90286559

Cover: 'Window' by Merilyn Smith

Greenwich Exchange Website: www.greenex.co.uk

ISBN 1-871551-76-5

for Bob Hornby

"So as to say for certain I was here
Or somewhere else."

Robert Frost, 'The Wood Pile'.

Acknowledgements are due to the editors of *Miscelánea: A Journal of English and American Studies, Symbiosis: A Journal of Anglo-American Literary Relations, English: The Journal of the English Society* and *The Cambridge Quarterly* where excerpts from this book have been published in essay form.

I would like to express my sincere gratitude and appreciation to The Nottingham Trent University for the award of a Trent Editions Research Bursary, George Szirtes for letting me see unpublished versions of his poems and for responding to my many questions, Matt Simpson for permission to quote from his correspondence with George Szirtes, and Dimitris Tsaloumas for his hospitality on Leros and the many insights his poetry and conversation provided into the experience of exile.

Thanks, too, to the following for their encouragement and support: Brenda Breen, Dick Ellis, Paul Leahy, Terry and Gladys Murphy, Bernard O'Donoghue, Judith Palmer, Deryn Rees-Jones, Monika Simpson, Merilyn Smith, and Stan Smith.

Above all, I would like to acknowledge the invaluable part played by John Lucas in the writing of this book. For his advice and enthusiasm – both of which were inspirational – much thanks.

Contents

Introduction

Europe and America After the Lights Went Out

> [W]riting a poem you can read to no one
> is like dancing in the dark.
>
> Ovid, *Black Sea Letters*: IV.2

I

My aim here is to examine the poetry of W.H. Auden (1907-1973), Joseph Brodsky (1940-1996), and George Szirtes (b.1948) in relation to their differing experiences of exile. In doing so I want to suggest that there are similarities and distinguishable patterns in their writings which tell us important things about the ways in which exile has come to be a defining feature of, and give a precise identity to, aspects of European and American poetry. Underpinning this is a reading of modernism and post-modernism that sees both as representing a crisis of subjectivity characterised by Fredric Jameson as an historical shift "in which the alienation of the subject is displaced by the fragment-ation of the subject".[1]

Throughout the 20th century decisive changes in global history, commerce and politics, the ensuing emphasis on nationalism and ethnic division, and the migratory movements of tens of millions of people, subjected the individual's concept of identity to specific and insistent pressures. This resulted, as Helga Geyer-Ryan has said, in "the need for alternative modes of identity which would be constructed in such a way as to include from the start the notion of alterity, the place of the other".[2] Such a place, such an engagement with the 'other', is, for these three poets, the literary text, with their identities becoming mediated and negotiated through, and defined by, the freedoms and limitations of language. Accordingly, exile is a condition that straddles, and in many important ways defines, the claims of modernism and postmodernism to speak of and for the modern world. Indeed, the emphasis placed by both 'movements' on the figure of the exile, émigré or nomad, and the challenge s/he offers to social stability is itself a direct product of particular historical events. There is a clear sense, then, in which we cannot grasp the identity of 20th century exile apart from these social and political upheavals; and we cannot fully understand the continuing course of history or developments in culture without reference to exile.

"It is one of the unhappiest characteristics of the age," Edward Said has written, "to have produced more refugees, migrants, displaced persons and exiles than ever before in history".[3] And in his essay 'The Condition We Call Exile' Joseph Brodsky commented that "Displacement and misplacement are this century's commonplaces".[4] But as the experience of the poets discussed here demonstrates, exile is neither uniform in kind nor predictable in its outcome. Neither does it always mean the same thing. As Susan Rubin Suleiman says:

> Émigrés, exiles, expatriates, refugees, nomads, cosmopolitans – the meanings of those words vary, as do their connotations. Expatriates can go home any time that they like, while the exile cannot. Cosmopolitan can be a term of self-affirmation, straight or postmodernly ironic, or else an anti-Semitic slur. Over and above their fine distinctions, however, these words all designate a state of being 'not home' (or of being 'everywhere at home', the flip side of this same coin), which means, in most cases, at a distance from one's native tongue.[5]

Historically, exile has assumed many different forms. There is the Russian model of the internal émigré, the alienated individual ostracised even while living within his own country. This is the tradition to which Brodsky, at the beginning of his writing life at least, belonged. There is also the writer who out of economic necessity or psychological compulsion moves from the small town to the city, from the province or colonised country (we might think of Joyce leaving Ireland and history as nightmare for continental Europe) to the metropolitan centre. The latter, as we will see, is a theme on which Auden provides a series of fascinating variations. Then there is exile as a violent fracture of the self as it locates itself in terms of history, geography and language. This is exile as a line drawn in the sand, cutting off the past from the present in such a way as to threaten to turn history from continuum to stasis. This is exile as experienced and written about by George Szirtes.

At its simplest, though, exile has a literal meaning. Derived from the Latin *exsilium*, meaning banishment, it is the result of having transgressed a societal norm or broken some taboo. It is a condition that always implicates its opposite: to be settled, to be a citizen, to belong, to be at home in the world. In these terms exile is always and primarily a political act, one that means redefining the relationship between self and society, the private imagination and the public narrative. It also, of course, means to become alienated, psychologically and economically, in both Marxist and Freudian senses of the word.

Whether of their free will or not, the exile is someone who has – or is seen to have – overstepped the mark, necessitating their removal if society is to function as before. This clearly involves something other than geographical estrangement, though that is important. In all probability it will mean a separation from family, native language and that complex web of influences we call culture – those laws, traditions and superstitions by which we understand our relationship with, and towards, other members of society. It means leaving those familiar places by which we learn to orientate ourselves. There are the seemingly mundane losses exile brings: the patina on familiar objects among which we live our lives; those things which, ordinarily, we take for granted but once removed from begin to assert enormous symbolic importance. Such are the things which the writer in exile returns to and writes about in order, as Walter Benjamin said, to "vaccinate himself ... against the homesickness that exiles experience ... attempt[ing] to limit it by becoming conscious of the irremediable loss of the past, due not to biographical contingencies but to social necessities".[6] And as the quotidian is that which occurs or recurs daily, then exile (as a fracture of this pattern) involves not only displacement in space but in time. As a result, it causes a crisis of subjectivity: divorced from these familiar places and things – and the names we learn to give them – how can we know ourselves? In short, exile means a realignment of those boundaries and landmarks by which, however precariously, we seek to define and delineate the world we inhabit.

While Ovid can be seen as providing a model for the exile as political refugee, the 'recording angel' of a more subjective – and, it should be stressed, metaphorical – aspect of exile, is Proust. For Proust's Marcel each day begins with an experience as psychologically hazardous as Odysseus' ten-year wandering: waking up in bed and trying in those moments during the return of consciousness to piece together the clues as to not only where but who he is. Life, or consciousness, is thus mediated between the Scylla and Charybdis of memory and forgetfulness. But by locating his narrative in the world of dressing tables and mirrored bookcases rather than the classical topos of myth, Proust is saying that exile is in some way integral to how we all experience ourselves. Central to this retrieval and reconstitution of the self is language. As Christopher Prendergast points out in his General Editor's Preface to the 2002 translation of *In Search of Lost Time*, Proust's novel "defines a position of incurable exile not only for the hero of the narrative but also for the artist [who,] remarks [Proust's] narrator, 'is the native of an unknown country'".[7]

It is this aspect of an exile's experience that George Szirtes discusses in relationship to his own preoccupation with verse forms:

> Poetry is always local. It is just that in [my] case – and in the case of other writers ... used to moving about from place to place without a secure notion of belonging – the notion of the local is rooted in the incidental. ... Hence also, at the same time, the conscious attempt to break against that form, to run sentences against lines, but to keep rediscovering the line, the rhyme, the integral pattern against which the sprawl of experience can be mapped.[8]

As with Proust's narrator, Szirtes locates himself in terms of the incidental, the fragment. This has important consequences for Szirtes' poetry, particularly the role of montage. It is not to say that the wider currents of culturated meaning and determinancy can be ignored, only that the writer in exile, at the point of writing, cannot take them for granted. Tradition, that sense of oneself as existing in time and space, is something that has to be searched out. The pain of not belonging, to qualify Wittgenstein's phrase, has *always* to choose the mouth with which it speaks. Clearly this becomes exaggerated, as in the cases of Szirtes and Brodsky, when the language in which they write is a second language and where both a literal and metaphorical translation has occurred. Even in the example of W.H. Auden, however, these structures cannot be taken wholly for granted. The main difference between Auden's case and that of Brodsky and Szirtes is that he welcomed this. Wanting to re-define the relationship between himself and England, he did so by adopting an American idiom. The opening lines of 'September 1, 1939' – "I sit in one of the dives/ On Fifty-Second Street" – show Auden having 'gone native', attempting to dissolve certain aspects of his relationship with English culture and history. In so doing he can be seen as reiterating something Proust wrote in *Contre Sainte-Beuve*: "Beautiful books are written in a kind of foreign language."

II

"The detached observer," Adorno wrote, "is as much entangled as the active participant; the only advantage of the former is insight into his entanglement, and the infinitesimal freedom that lies in knowledge as such".[9] The years leading up to the outbreak of full-scale war in September 1939 saw Auden attempting to gain just such a degree of detachment; a process figured in those many images and vantage points in his poetry to do with observing events from the air. In poems such as 'Dover', 'Spain' and 'Musée des Beaux Arts' the timbre of Auden's poetic voice works hard to build up an illusion of objectivity, one that convinces us of the authority of the speaker not just because of the tone of voice but the fact that he seems to be speaking at a clear remove from the events described. This reached a crisis with the decision at the end of 1938 to leave Britain and to settle in the States. It is the poems written in the years immediately preceding and following this move, and subsequently collected in *Another Time* (1940) and *The Double Man* (1941), that form the subject matter of Chapter One, 'The Boundaries of a Common World: Exile and the Just City in the Early American Poetry of W.H. Auden.'

In examining Auden's concern for how we establish the Just City, Chapter One discusses the subtle inter-textual relationships between Auden's poetry and other exilic texts: Anglo-Saxon poetry; the blues and calypso; Lorca's *Poet in New York*; the writing of German refugees such as Ernst Toller and Thomas Mann; and the myth of Orpheus. The chapter also looks at the immediate influence of Marianne Moore on Auden's developing poetics, how it facilitated a looser, more discursive form of writing, and provided him with a model with which to write about the death of Freud. The purpose throughout the chapter is not only to understand why Auden decided to leave England and Europe, but to recognise the impact the decision had on his poetry.

As we might expect, the reasons for Auden leaving Europe and becoming a voluntary exile are complicated. For while the poetry he wrote throughout the 1930s searched for a clear vantage point from which to view contemporary events, another motif was that of the relationship between the individual poet and wider society. Auden returns to this theme time and again in poems that mirror his growing anxiety about negotiating for himself a course between his private life and his public role. Not that the two were always distinct. We might argue, for example, that the 'lonely impulse' which took him to Spain in 1937 was prompted as much by the need to test himself and his art against the experiences of earlier generations of young men who had seen active service, as it was a gesture of support for the Republic. What is clear, however, is that Auden's poetry charts a gradual disillusionment with the occupation and practical benefit of the poet within British and European culture.

In important respects Auden's departure for the States was an act of solidarity with Europe's displaced millions. And what better place to prove it than in the nation which, in the words of Emma Lazarus' poem 'The New Colossus' inscribed on the Statue of Liberty, declared herself to be "Mother of Exiles". We might see this as smacking of hubris on Auden's part, or simply an acknowledgement of those doubts expressed by writers on all sides of the political division that the artist had any role to play in the coming war. As Louis MacNeice put it: "We envy men of action/Who sleep and wake, murder and intrigue/Without being doubtful, without being haunted".[10] Or as Evelyn Waugh said in a letter from 1943: "I wrote ... very early in the war to say that its chief use would be to cure artists of the illusion that they were men of action".[11] Perhaps it also hints at the diminished and diminishing role Britain was to play in the world, and where the best that a British poet could hope was, as Auden wrote in the mid-1960s, to "become, if possible, a minor Atlantic Goethe".[12] What we cannot deny is that exile provided Auden with the space necessary to write about those wider currents of economic and psychological alienation from the Just City defined by Hegel, Marx and Freud.

Another perspective is offered by Auden's writing about those people throughout history who had been denied a safe house within the *polis*, and who were then fleeing Europe to escape the rise of fascism, anti-Semitism, homophobia and anti-Communism. Increasingly, and in a variety of ways, Auden's poetry after his arrival in the States shows a marked concern with such groups. Whether writing about the plight of German-Jewish refugees or the alienation of American workers migrating from city to city, Auden attempted to gain an historical perspective on contemporary events. What is more, by using forms derived from Europe and America's legacy of colonialism and the slave trade, Auden articulated the relationship between current events and the legacy of the Enlightenment. It was a critique, and subject matter he continued to develop in 'New Year Letter'.

In many ways 'New Year Letter' is a poem in which Auden scrutinises a predicament described by Hans-Martin Lohmann:

> The proletariat is more and more replaced by a small group of intellectuals or even by the 'solitary' intellectual who doesn't see himself as subject to progress but rather as a critical institution of remembrance and reflection which recognizes and digests the conditions of defeat and ruin of the former revolutionary class.[13]

As the title suggests, the poem implicitly raises questions about the relationship between the private and the public. Poems such as 'Refugee Blues' and 'Calypso' do much the same thing by utilising popular art forms, while 'New Year Letter' harks back to the high art of the 17th and 18th centuries. Is the poem an admission, then, that poetry cannot speak for and to all people, but only some 'ten persons'?

Along with figures such as Joyce or Beckett, Auden is a model for a certain kind of literary exile. As with Joyce and Beckett it is highly unlikely that he would have become the writer he did had he not chosen voluntary exile. With its sympathetic references to German art and philosophy, 'New Year Letter' would surely have been a dangerous poem to publish while living in a Britain at war with Hitler's Reich. Likewise, criticism of the part played by British imperialism in provoking the war which was unfolding across much of the surface of the planet was at least implicit in poems such as 'September 1, 1939' and 'Refugee Blues'. Poems like these would have put Auden in an untenable situation had he remained in Britain. It is in this context and in these specific terms, the chapter proposes, that we are justified in calling Auden an exile. For though his situation cannot be compared to that of those other artists who were compelled to leave Europe following Hitler's rise to power, he was deeply alienated from many aspects of English culture and politics. Not least among these was the growing tide of nationalist fervour aimed against a country with which he felt close personal ties. Auden's decision to emigrate brings him close to Adorno's assertion that "For the intellectual, inviolable isolation is now the only way of showing some measure of solidarity".[14] Despite the sniping accusations of cowardice, Auden's was a mightily brave decision. His leaving provoked anger and critical hostility, a hostility that continues to echo today among those who would have it that nothing he wrote after 1939 was any good. I hope that what I have to say about the work Auden wrote in the immediate years after his docking in New York goes some way to proving such comments tin-eared and wrong-headed.

While Auden's exile was voluntary, Joseph Brodsky's seems fated. Tried for 'social parasitism' in 1964, Brodsky was challenged by the judge to justify his calling himself a poet. He replied by saying it was a right that came directly from God. Implicit in the judge's question was the fact that if Brodsky did not hold the appropriate post within the Soviet literary establishment then he had no right to call himself a writer. Explicit in Brodsky's response was a direct challenge to the authority of the State.

The trial resulted in Brodsky receiving a sentence of five years hard labour – later commuted to 20 months – to be served in the small village of Norinskoya in Russia's frozen north. It was here that he first began reading and translating the poet who was to have such a decisive impact on the rest of his life: W.H. Auden. And it was Auden who, following Brodsky's expulsion from Russia in 1972, took the then 32 year old poet under his wing.

Julia Kristeva has pointed out with specific reference to the Soviet Union that "any society may be stabilized only if it excludes poetic language". And she continues: "The poet is put to death because he wants to turn rhythm into a dominant element; because he wants to make language perceive what it doesn't want to say".[15] It was a conflict of interests encountered by those generations of Russian and then Soviet poets to which Brodsky, even before his banishment in 1972, was regarded as the heir. From Nabokov back through Tsvetaeva, Mandelstam, Dostoevsky and Pushkin, Russia's history of exile – internal or abroad – joined it to the wider currents of Europe's literary past, where it met with figures such as Heine, Byron, Mickiewicz, Dante, Petrarch, Ovid and the writers of the Jewish diaspora. And this sense of a continuum was of increasing importance within the Soviet Union at a time when writers felt both artistically and geographically isolated. It also provided Brodsky with a number of exilic personae through which to voice his dissent against the state. More importantly, it allowed him to graft an isolated and threatened Russian poetic tradition back onto the main branch of European history and literature. And it is this essential hybridity of Brodsky's poetry that forms the main argument of Chapter Two.

'Here and There: Exile as Homecoming in the Poetry of Joseph Brodsky' focuses on an aspect of Brodsky's writing which he inherited primarily from Mandelstam: namely, a belief that the Russian language and its poetry is hybrid, "growing out of the self-perpetuating interplay of its own devices".[16] Mandelstam also believed that the word – Logos – is where the material and the spiritual, form and content, merge. Concerned with exile as an essentially metaphysical, rather than biographical condition, this chapter argues that Brodsky's poetry is continually directed towards that point where, entering language, the material world is translated into metaphor, becoming both uniquely itself and the wider connotations of itself as text. And in that metaphor, like a journey by train, unites, in Proust's words, "two distinct personalities of place, taking us from one name to another name"[17], we can see how, in poems such as 'Elegy for John Donne' and 'Lithuanian Nocturne', Brodsky's use of metaphor literally enacts his sense of alienation, first within the Soviet Union and later in his exclusion from its language and culture. In so doing Brodsky can be regarded as adopting and adapting Shklovsky's Formalist theory of *ostranenie*.

As well as considering those aspects of his poetry that have their origins in the cosmopolitan aesthetics of Mandelstam, the chapter focuses on what Brodsky gained from a prolonged engagement with the Anglo-Irish and Anglo-American traditions. As I said earlier, it was while in Norinskoya that Brodsky began reading and translating Auden. And it was Auden's elegy for Yeats that provided Brodsky with a model for his own 'Verses on the Death of T.S. Eliot', a poem which, in significant ways, re-imagines Auden's elegy for Yeats within a Russian context. Later, in an elegy for Robert Lowell, we see Brodsky engaging in a subtle dialogue not only with the deceased poet but also, through him, Elizabeth Bishop and W.D. Snodgrass.

Jaqueline Chénieux-Gendron has written that the situation of any artist is by definition one of an 'interior exile'. "Any writer," she says, "is exiled in language itself, in the language of communication; he creates a space in which he can write *his own* language".[18] While the body is bound in time and space, poetry allows the ability to restructure and reconstitute these elements within language. The boundaries Brodsky crossed, therefore, were both geographical and linguistic – with the accent placed on the latter. What the shift of emphasis achieved, to Brodsky's way of thinking, was to make his exile less a political than a semantic act.

George Szirtes has admitted that the sense of being at home nowhere not only defines his writing but, in all likelihood, made him a writer. Though he no doubt means it in more of an historical than metaphysical sense, exile for him, as for Brodsky, is a defining feature of humanity. "We live in a world," he says, "which is full of people in transit, full of people living in fragments, moving from place to place and somehow or other, although we don't necessarily all speak the same language, nevertheless there ought to be certain elements in our experience which are common".[19]

Szirtes was born in Budapest in 1948, and his family was among the large number of refugees that left Hungary following the 1956 uprising. After crossing the Austrian border on foot, the family spent three days in an Austrian refugee camp before being offered a flight to London. At the time only Szirtes' father spoke English. It was therefore out of necessity, as Szirtes writes in his Preface to *The Budapest File*, that the family disciplined themselves to speaking English at home. It is a discipline that Szirtes has now maintained over a career stretching back to 1979, resulting in the publication of over twenty collections of poetry and translations.

Szirtes has consistently examined how the objective events of history become intermingled with the private material of memory. Balanced as it is between description and reflection, his poetry enacts the dramatic tension between the stories we are told and subsequently re-tell ourselves to explain our presence in the world, and the significant objects and places that govern the provinces of the imagination. His poems thus become, as Szirtes has described them, "intimate spaces arising from the no-man's-land of childhood memory".[20] What complicates Szirtes' writing about historical events is his awareness that memory is an unreliable witness. This is not to say that the vision of history it presents is invalid. On the contrary, what is often most significant in his poetry are the ways Szirtes finds of resolving the different ways we experience the past. And from among these it is his continued use of photographs and photography as a means of restructuring identity that forms the basis of 'A Brightness to Cast Shadows: Photographic Memory and the Poetry of George Szirtes'.

Using a technique that has parallels with montage, Szirtes focuses, in Walter Benjamin's words, "on hidden details of familiar objects, … exploring commonplace milieus [and] extend[ing] our comprehension of the necessities which rule our lives".[21] And while montage is particularly suited to writing about the relationships between photography, memory and identity – themes explored in sequences such as 'The Photographer in Winter' and 'For André Kertész' – it also provides Szirtes with a means of coherently structuring the essentially unstable material of his family history in the long poem 'Metro'.

Memorably defined by Susan Sontag as a "featherweight portable museum", the photograph is a portmanteau of memories and lost objects. As an intermediary between absence and presence, life and death, biography and history, identity and anonymity, silence and speech, photography provides a uniquely powerful subject matter for the writer in exile aiming to realise a sense of a personal past and a cultural identity. This is doubly so for Szirtes as many of his Jewish relatives died in the concentration camps or 'disappeared' in the persecution of 'asocials' which followed the Nazi take-over of Hungary in 1944. Any attempt by Szirtes to reconstruct the past – both personal and cultural – necessarily involves an engagement not just with memory but with the memorial, an aspect of his poetry which is read alongside the work of the French artist Christian Boltanski.

Szirtes has written how "The process of writing continually modifies and re-directs intention".[22] It is a process that parallels the condition of exile itself in that, unsettled in and by language, the exile must constantly renegotiate a fixed position, however temporary, from where to identify themselves as a speaker. For Szirtes this means recognising that the language he uses will always have "an air of the synthetic" which speaks from a position of "inbetween-ness". His writing is also a synthesis in that it lends a "structure to disparate experiences [he] cannot flavour with the vibrancy of a local diction". Therefore, this concluding chapter also examines Szirtes' synthesis of form and content, and how an engagement with metre and rhyme underpins his continuing search for, and engagement with, poetic form as a kind of homecoming.

III

Surveying the wreckage of wartime Europe from his exile in the States, Adorno wrote that "the house is past. The bombing of European cities, as well as the labour and concentration camps, merely proceed as executors".[23] Thus homelessness became a – if not *the* – defining feature of modern life, epitomised by the exile or émigré who, like Poor Tom, stands for the quintessential human being: "bare, unaccommodated man." Although the negative aspects of such a condition are obvious, Adorno saw in its virtues a possible path to the redemption of, in his own admittedly stringent terms, a disabled culture. Unburdened by the past, the exile is able to discover in his or her marginality that "a gaze averted from the beaten track, a hatred of brutality, a search for fresh concepts not yet encompassed by the general pattern, is the last hope for thought".[24] A fragment of a dispersed cultural unity, the exile becomes, like the splinter in one of Adorno's aphorisms, "the best magnifying glass" for seeing and understanding the causes of the catastrophe. What is more, Adorno believed that art, in its withdrawal from society, can function as the unconscious writing of history.[25] Thus the exiled writer is doubly important: while his or her experience is determined by the objective forces of politics and economics, their writings, drawn from the subjective world of the imaginary, offer a reading that provides a form of resistance against those forces which advocate and initiate destruction. The émigré writer – or, rather, their writings – becomes the epitome of what Adorno meant when he said: "He who wishes to know the truth about life in its immediacy must scrutinise its estranged form ... even in its most hidden recesses".[26]

In placing the emphasis on "universal social and economic determinants instead of national ones"[27] Adorno offered a critique of those nationalist forces which led to the material conditions of exile in the 20th century. It is a position Albrecht Wellmer has summed up in the context of Adorno's relationship to German culture:

> Critical Theory proved to be a position from which it was possible on the one hand to analyze those aspects of the German cultural tradition that were reactionary, repressive, and hostile to culture, and to do so more precisely than from any other standpoint; and on the other hand to reveal the subversive, enlightening, and universalistic features of the same tradition. I would say that Critical Theory was the only theoretical position represented in postwar Germany that made a radical break with fascism ... without entailing a similar radical break with the German cultural tradition, that is, with one's own cultural identity.[28]

This last statement is important to each of the poets included here. For while they offer a critique – or re-reading – of history, they are each attempting to do so within the context of a cultural identity and tradition that, while specifically American, British or Russian, is also cosmopolitan. Rather than assuming the position advocated by postmodernism, that the subject is irrevocably fragmented or de-centred, each of these poets reintegrates their writings within cultural boundaries, while also recognising that these boundaries are necessarily porous.

Adorno's influence has also proved decisive in that he is concerned with the ways in which identity can be made to inhere within the writing and written subject. As with a photograph, for example, truth and semblance can be found co-existing, a condition Adorno calls "aesthetic coherence". If this coherence is to be possible, "art must turn itself against aesthetic illusion, against everything that is illusory about it".[29] The means by which it can do this is to subject aesthetic illusion to the scrutiny of philosophical reflection: "only philosophical reflection can inform aesthetic experience about what it experiences; only philosophy can decipher the mirror-writing of the absolute in the semblance of artistic beauty".[30] Only then, as Auden puts it in 'September 1, 1939', will we be able to understand the underlying historical condition "That has driven a culture mad".

The other theoretical keystone to this study is Walter Benjamin. As with Adorno, Benjamin's experience of cultural dislocation was a formative (and ultimately terminal) influence on his writings. A refugee from Germany following Hitler's rise to power in 1933, Benjamin's life was shaped by a *wanderlust* that took him from the Berlin of his childhood to Riga, Naples, Munich, Danzig, Moscow, Florence and finally Paris. Rarely did he settle anywhere for more than a couple of months. And it was at a border crossing between France and Spain where, in September 1940, he committed suicide. Susan Sontag has called him 'The Last Intellectual'. 'The Last European' is how he thought of himself, imagining the life he would lead as a circus exhibit if, as many friends suggested, he emigrated to the States.

Benjamin's theories are situated between a range of disciplines relevant to this book: philosophically and intellectually he was influenced by Marx and Freud (both of whose writings, it is worth remembering, were spread by the stateless, marginalised, or exiled); he studied the cabbala, deriving a theory of language expressed in 'The Task of the Translator' that has much in common with Osip Mandelstam's writings about the Logos; and an early critic and advocate of Surrealism, he wrote about its use of photography. A writer and collector of fragments, his 'Theses on the Philosophy of History' proposes the retrieval and redemption of history through an engagement with civilisation's off-cuts, its detritus. Like Adorno, his writings are consistent in that they display a preoccupation with issues concerning the nature of, and relationship between, art and philosophy.

Benjamin therefore offers a vision of the relationship between the individual and history analogous to, though not identical with, Proust. For while Proust advocates a recovery of the self from the feral material of memory, Benjamin's angel of history – the *Angelus*

Novus of the 'Theses on the Philosophy of History' – sees any such redemption of identity in terms of cultural history:

> Where we perceive a chain of events, he sees a single catastrophe which keeps piling wreckage upon wreckage ... The angel would like to stay, awaken the dead, and make whole what had been smashed. But a storm is blowing from Paradise; it has got caught in his wings with such violence that the angel can no longer close them. The storm irresistibly propels him into the future to which his back is turned.[31]

Here then, somewhere between Proust's narrator and Benjamin's angel, on a floating island of memory and history, is where we might discover the exiled writer: retrieving and redeeming through memory and culture not only their own identity, but that of the artistic estates to which, like Prospero, they are the dispossessed heir.

Notes

[1] Fredric Jameson, 'Postmodernism, or the Cultural Logic of Late Capitalism ' in *Postmodernism: A Reader*, ed. Thomas Docherty (Hemel Hempstead: Harvester Wheatsheaf, 1993), 71.

[2] Helga Geyer- Ryan, *Fables of Desire: Studies in the Ethics of Art and Gender* (Cambridge: Polity Press, 1994), 2.

[3] Edward Said, *Culture and Imperialism* (London: Chatto and Windus, 1993), 402.

[4] Joseph Brodsky, 'The Condition We Call Exile' in *On Grief and Reason: Essays* (New York: Farrar Straus Giroux, 1995), 23.

[5] Susan Rubin Suleiman (ed. with an Introduction) *Exile and Creativity: Signposts, Travellers, Outsiders, Backward Glances* (Durham and London: Duke University Press, 1998), 1.

[6] See Rainer Rochlitz, *The Disenchantment of Art: the Philosophy of Walter Benjamin* (London: The Guildford Press, 1996), 181.

[7] Marcel Proust, *In Search of Lost Time*, General Editor Christopher Prendergast, 6 vols. (London: Penguin/Allen Lane, 2002), Vol. 1: xix-xx.

[8] George Szirtes, *The Budapest File* (Newcastle-upon-Tyne: Bloodaxe, 2000), 15-16.

[9] Theodor W. Adorno, *Minima Moralia: Reflections from Damaged Life* (1951), trans. E.F.N. Jephcott (London: Verso, 1974), 26.

10   Louis MacNeice, *Collected Poems* (London: Faber and Faber, 1979), 131.

11   See Adam Piette *Imagination at War: British Fiction and Poetry 1939-1945* (London: Papermac, 1995), 82.

12   W.H. Auden *Collected Poems* (London: Faber and Faber, 1976), 693.

13   Hans-Martin Lohmann, 'Adorno's Aesthetic Theory' in *Adorno: an Introduction* (Philadelphia: Pennbridge Books, 1992), 74.

14   Theodor W. Adorno, *Minima Moralia*, 26.

15   Julia Kristeva, 'The Ethics of Linguistics' (1974) in *Modern Criticism and Theory: A Reader*, ed. David Lodge (London and New York: Longman, 1988), 236.

16   See David M. Bethea, *Joseph Brodsky and the Creation of Exile* (New Jersey: Princeton University Press, 1994), 57.

17   Marcel Proust, *In Search of Lost Time*, Vol. 2: 223.

18   Jaqueline Chénieux-Gendron, 'Surrealists in Exile: Another Kind of Resistance' in *Exile and Creativity*, 164.

19   George Szirtes, 'Losing Our Identities' in *The Independent on Sunday*, (28/5/2000), 16.

20   George Szirtes, *The Budapest File*, 12.

21   Walter Benjamin, 'The Work of Art in the Age of Mechanical Reproduction' (1950) in *Illuminations*, trans. Harry Zohn (London: Fontana Press, 1992), 229.

22   George Szirtes, *The Budapest File*, 15.

23   Theodor W. Adorno, *Minima Moralia*, 39.

24   Ibid., 67-68.

25   See Robert Hullot-Kentor, 'The Philosophy of Dissonance: Adorno and Schoenberg' in *The Semblance of Subjectivity: Essays in Adorno's Aesthetic Theory*, ed. Tom Huhn and Lambert Zuidervaart (Cambridge, Massachusetts, London, England: The MIT Press, 1997), 313.

26   Theodor W. Adorno, *Minima Moralia*, 15.

27   Albrecht Wellmer, *Endgames: The Irreconcilable Nature of Modernity* (Cambridge, Massachusetts, London, England: The MIT Press, 1998), 254.

28   Ibid.

29   Ibid., 156.

30   Ibid.

31   Walter Benjamin, 'Theses on the Philosophy of History' (1950) in *Illuminations*, 249.

1

The Boundaries of a Common World:
Exile and the Just City in
W.H. Auden's Early American Poetry

Outside a surfeit of 'planes.
Inside the hunger of the departed
to come back.

'All Soul's Night' by R.S. Thomas.

I

In his essay 'American Poetry', written after he had left Britain for
the States in 1939 and subsequently become a US citizen in 1946,
Auden remarked that "the only British poets who could conceivably
have been American are eccentrics like Blake and Hopkins".[1] Where,
then, does this leave Auden in relation to the poetic traditions of his
adopted homeland? Is he suggesting that at heart he remained British,
rooted within its traditions and bound by its conventions, failing to
adapt his métier to the rhythms of American life and speech? If we
stress the fact, however, that Auden says poets "*like* Blake and
Hopkins" we see that he has cannily left the door ajar so as to be
able to slip away and join their party. The inclusion of the word
"eccentric" pushes that door a little wider open. Derived from the
Greek, it means 'to depart from the centre'. And it is the nature of
this eccentricity that I want to consider.

 Auden's voluntary exile has been variously and often venomously
interpreted. This began almost as soon as he and Christopher

Isherwood were known to have docked in New York, with one Tory MP proposing in the House of Commons that, as "British citizens of military age", they should be "summoned back for registration and calling up".[2] Though hardly an impartial judge, Joseph Brodsky has summarised the case thus:

> His departure caused considerable uproar at home; he was charged with desertion, with abandoning his country in a time of peril. Well, the peril indeed came, but some time after the poet left England. Besides, he was precisely the one who, for about a decade, kept issuing warnings about its – the peril's – progress ... What's more, his decision to move to the United States had very little to do with world politics: the reasons for the move were of a more private nature.[3]

With the benefit of hindsight and the evidence of those poems collected and published as *Another Time* in 1940, we can see that rather than being a sudden decision there was a certain inevitability in Auden's actions. Dominated by images of the sea and troubled leave-takings, and engaging as they do with the complex relationship between the writer and society, the poems Auden wrote in the immediate years leading up to his leaving for the States articulate not only that sense of personal isolation indicated by Brodsky but a growing awareness that, given the political situation on the continent, to be a poet was at best a marginal occupation, at worst a retreat from reality. At the same time, therefore, as the political map of Europe was being redrawn by the emergence of repressed historical grievances, Auden was clearly undergoing a profound personal and artistic crisis.

This is not to suggest that the decision to leave England was a purely negative one. As early as 1887 Yeats, living in London, was planning "a school of Irish poetry", the chief tutor of which was to be Walt Whitman. What Whitman and America offered Ireland, in Eamon Grennan's words, was "a literary direction, away from colonial provincialism towards imaginative independence."[4] Something of this same enthusiasm remained alive in Yeats when, twenty years later, and looking to remake himself as a poet, he put himself to school under Ezra Pound. As we will see, it was a need to re-fashion and re-define himself as a writer that Auden came to share.

And as with Yeats, the influence of America was decisive.

Central to an understanding of Auden's poetic relationship with Yeats are the intertextual borrowings from, and references to, Yeats' work which sustain the structure and argument of Auden's great elegy, 'In Memory of W.B. Yeats'. Written in the weeks following Auden's arrival in the United States, the poem is an implicit response to Yeats' doubts and self-questioning in 'Man and the Echo' where he refers to events in Ireland during Easter 1916 and the possibility that his nationalistic drama, *Cathleen ni Houlihan,* had played some part in determining the actions and subsequent deaths of the leaders of the uprising: "Did that play of mine send out/ Certain men the English shot?" Writing in 1939, Auden can only have had in mind those more immediate political upheavals which were threatening a second world-wide conflagration.

In his essay 'Auden's Oedipal Dialogues with W.B. Yeats', Stan Smith provides arguably the clearest and most detailed account of the nature of these textual exchanges. Charting their advent from the publication of Yeats' '[The] Man and the Echo' in *The Atlantic Monthly* and *The London Mercury* in January 1939, the month of Yeats' death, Smith notes the relationship between this poem and Auden's elegy. Begun in February, 'In Memory of W.B. Yeats' was first published in the *New Republic* on 8th March, without what we now know as the middle section of the poem's triptych (the revised version appeared in *The London Mercury* in April). It is a dialogue which culminated in Auden's prose obituary 'The Public v. the Late Mr William Butler Yeats', published in the spring edition of *Partisan Review.*

Smith begins his essay by quoting an extract of a letter Auden wrote Stephen Spender in 1964. It is a letter which shows Auden acknowledging Yeats as a poetic father-figure while at the same time demonising him, in Smith's words, as the "devil of rhetoric and political propaganda":

> I am incapable of saying a word about W.B. Yeats because
> through no fault of his, he has become for me a symbol of my
> own devil of unauthenticity, of everything which I must try to
> eliminate from my own poetry, false emotions, inflated rhetoric,
> empty sonorities.[5]

What Smith doesn't comment on is the significance of the word "symbol" in this paragraph. Not only does Auden say that he was still struggling to come to terms with aspects of Yeats' influence, but the very language in which this struggle is described is itself an implicit acknowledgement of the importance he attached to Yeats' art. Consciously or not, Auden is admitting that he has used Yeats as a symbolic foil for his own demons, just as Yeats used figures such as Maude Gonne, Lady Gregory and James Connolly in the symbolic drama of his own poetry. This is clearly the case in 'In Memory of W.B. Yeats', where Auden mines the occasion of Yeats' death and voices those anxieties which so powerfully animated his own poetry at this time.

The elegy is not an isolated example. For if, as Stan Smith suggests, the relationship between Auden and Yeats is Oedipal – with Auden playing the role of Oedipus to Yeats' Laius – then Spain and Fascism is the crossroads at which they fall out. While 'In Memory of W.B. Yeats' integrates themes and images from Yeats' poetry, thus signalling the debt Auden owed the older man, it also points the reader back in the direction of Auden's 'Spain', written in early 1937, and that wider group of poems he wrote prior to arriving in the USA in January 1939. Furthermore, it also prepares the way for certain key themes and influences which were to dominate Auden's poetry in the months after his arrival in New York, and which consistently take issue with aspects of Yeats' politics and writings. These poems can be read as Auden's cohesive and imaginative response to the political crisis in Europe, the artistic crisis prompted by Yeats' death, and the crisis of his own voluntary exile. Central to all three concerns was a fascination with how human beings determine the ways in which they live in relation to one another. And Auden's symbol for this, as it was for Sophocles, is the Just City.

II

The only new poem of Auden's to be included in the double-issue *New Verse* published in November 1937, and dedicated to a discussion of his work and influence, was 'Dover'. Written in August 1937, the eponymous town serves as locus (or symbol) for ambivalent feelings, a watery crossroads of arrivals and departures, of idealistic hopes and the onset of harsher realities. It also serves to remind us of historical intersections between England and continental Europe: 'the dominant Norman castle' and 'Georgian houses'. In one sense 'Dover' is only the latest incarnation of those troubled and troubling landscapes which haunted Auden's imagination throughout the late 1920s and early 1930s. What is different is that these earlier locations – mine shafts and dams, washing-floors and tramlines – though they might be man-made, were either abandoned or uninhabitable. 'Dover' finds Auden more specifically engaged with the urban and how we construct an environment in which to live moral and ethical lives. He has come down from the hilltops and entered the polis. Or almost.

The opening stanzas provide a view not as it would be experienced from the ground but as from the air. The poem moves at tremendous pace, first showing us the approaches to the town – "Steep roads, a tunnel through the downs" – before hurrying on to a "ruined pharos", a "constructed bay" and an "almost elegant" sea-front. The tone of voice – cool, detached, descriptive – comes from one of the documentary films Auden worked on during the 1930s, as does the camera-like movement of the poet's eye. It works hard to build up an illusion of objectivity, an objectivity that convinces us of the authority of the speaker not just because of this tone of voice but the fact that he seems to be speaking at a clear remove from the events described. Countering this realism are details alerting us to the fact that Auden is concerned with exposing a reality that, like the town itself, has "a vague and dirty root".

Throughout the poetry Auden was writing in the 1930s he provides insights into the economic realities of a contemporary England in steep economic decline, about to become the world's first post-industrial nation. Though a "constructed bay", Dover manufactures nothing. It is a place of faded elegance and diminishing economic importance. Any short-term use it may continue to have is to help shore-up a British Empire already in retreat. The vision of England granted to Auden, like Gloucester's in *King Lear*, is one of preparedness for war, spies and civilian informers, disputed inherited wealth, and fear and ignorance of the world 'without'. Only later does the poet show us the view from ground level: "The eyes of the departing migrants are fixed on the sea,/To conjure their special fates from the impersonal water". Both the individual images and the point-of-view are significant.

The roll-call of foreign countries Auden visited between 1934 and 1939 provides us with a list of the world's political hot spots: Belgium and Czechoslovakia in 1934; Spain and France in 1937; and, in 1938, Hong Kong and China. A pattern emerges in Auden's travels, one that sees him gravitating to places where the political map was being re-drawn. Just such a process is at work in 'Dover', charting as it does the decline of England as a world power, and figured in the image of the aeroplane superseding the ship:

> Above them, expensive and lovely as a rich child's toy,
> The aeroplanes fly in the new European air,
> On the edge of that air that makes England of minor importance[.][6]

It is an image to which we will return. The town also functions as a symbolic arena for the struggle between Auden's idealism and his awareness of pragmatic reality; between, as Auden portrays it, the migrant convinced that his or her fate will be special, and the wiser tears or thanks of the returning traveller, grateful that "The heart has at last ceased to lie, and the clock to accuse."

Auden's personal experience of these states was both recent and painful. Other than a brief visit to Paris in April 1937, his previous journey abroad had been to Spain to join the International Movement in support of the democratically elected government. What exactly Auden did in Spain is still subject to conjecture. Throughout the rest of his life he remained curiously reluctant to discuss the experience.[7] The effect it had upon his poetry, however, was to become more and more clearly defined.

In a letter to E.R. Dodds on the 8th December 1936, Auden wrote: "I so dislike everyday political activities that I won't do them, but here is something I can do as a citizen and now as a writer, and as I have no dependants, I feel I ought to go." "Please," he added, "don't tell anyone about this." Dodds wrote back asking for further explanation, to which Auden replied:

> I am not one of those who believe that poetry need or even should be directly political, but in a critical period such as ours, I do believe that the poet must have direct knowledge of

the major political events. It is possible that in some periods the poet can absorb and feel all in the ordinary everyday life, perhaps the supreme masters always can, but for the second order and particularly today, what he can write about is what he has experienced in his own person. Academic knowledge is not enough.[8]

Auden's letter can have left Dodds in little doubt that the primary reasons for his going to Spain were less to do with supporting the Republic than his needing an opportunity to test himself as a poet against the "supreme masters" and to discover a social role for himself as a writer.

Yeats' response, meanwhile, to the deepening European crisis was, to say the least, capricious. In his infamous introduction to *The Oxford Book of Modern Verse* in 1936, as well as dismissing the poets of the First World War ("passive suffering is not a theme for poetry") he made slighting reference to the politics, and by extension the poetry, of Auden and his followers: "Communism is their *Deus ex Machina*, their Santa Claus, their happy ending, but speaking as a poet I prefer tragedy to tragi-comedy."[9] The anthology did little to placate those looking for an excuse to marginalise Yeats further and to dismiss his poetry as old hat.

Yeats' stewardship of the anthology would seem a critical point in marking him out as the antithesis of everything the Auden Generation stood for. Louis MacNeice, however, in his important 1941 study of Yeats' poetry, while prepared to acknowledge these differences, argues that there were deep affinities between Yeats and some of the younger poets. He writes:

> The earlier Yeats had been too remote from [the younger English poets of the 1930s], subsisting on *fin de siècle* fantasies. But now he had broken into the twentieth century; *he had been through the fire.*
>
> It must be admitted that there was a certain snobbery in our new admiration, a snobbery paralleled in Yeats' own remark: 'I too have tried to be modern.' The word 'modern' is always relative. What did Yeats' modernity – a quality which in his youth he had violently repudiated – consist of? As far as content goes ... Yeats was 'modern' in the following respects.

He had widened his range ... was now dealing fairly directly with contemporary experience, some of it historical, some of it casual and personal. As well as admitting contemporary matter into his poetry, he was also admitting moral or philosophical problems. And he was expressing many more moods, not only the 'poetic' ones. He was writing at one moment as a cynic, at another as an orator, at another as a sensualist, at another as a speculative thinker ... But on the whole it was Yeats' *dryness* and *hardness* that excited us. T.E. Hulme, in an essay on Romanticism and Classicism written some time before the Great War, prophesied an era of dry hard verse in reaction against the Romantic habit of 'flying up into the eternal gases'. Yeats, who had flown up there himself, had managed – on occasions, at least – to come down again. Therefore, we admired him.[10]

"Dryness and hardness": the mixing of poetic registers and modes of discourse; the admittance of the personal and the political, the contemporary and the historical; a willingness to try to keep his poetic feet on the ground. MacNeice's summary of Yeats the Modern can also serve as a description of Auden's techniques in a poem like 'Dover'. Where the two men fundamentally differ, of course, is in their reading of and response to historical events. According to Yeats' apocalyptic vision, war could only help bring about "Heaven blazing into the head:/Tragedy wrought to its uttermost," with history a stage on which all "perform their tragic play". It was the artist's role, Yeats believed, to pick up the pieces and begin again from scratch. And to do so joyfully: "Out of Cavern comes a voice/And all it knows is that one word 'Rejoice.'"[11]

Though not without its ambiguities, Auden's response was altogether less confident. Along with the tens-of-thousands of other men and women who made the journey, Spain offered him the opportunity of intervening personally and of doing something not only as a writer but also as a citizen.

III

"FAMOUS POET TO DRIVE AMBULANCE IN SPAIN". Readers of the *Daily Worker* picking up their morning newspaper on 12th January 1937 might have been forgiven for wondering whether the sit. vac. column hadn't been moved onto the front page.

The nearest Auden came to describing the banality of war in verse is 'Musée des Beaux Arts'. It is a poem that takes Yeats' tragic vision of human suffering and does to it precisely what he accused the younger poets of: turning history into a tragi-comedy:

> ... the dreadful martyrdom must run its course
> Anyhow in a corner, some untidy spot
> Where the dogs go on with their doggy life and the torturer's horse
> Scratches its innocent behind on a tree.[12]

Not only are human actions deprived of the redemptive power of Yeats' "tragic joy", they are removed from the scene completely. In many ways, though, we can see the poem as an example of MacNeice's insistence that poetry take its head out of the clouds – literally so when we remember that the painting which is the subject of the second stanza is Brueghel's *The Fall of Icarus*.

While 'Musée des Beaux Arts', written in Paris and Brussels during the winter of 1938/39 can be read as Auden's considered reflections on the realities of war, his more immediate response was 'Spain'. Begun almost immediately after returning to England in March 1937, the poem was first published in pamphlet form by Faber on 20th May, with royalties donated to the work of Medical Aid in Spain.

There are some interesting parallels to be drawn between the response to Auden's poem and those that greeted Picasso's painting of the bombing of Guernica when it was first exhibited in England at the New Burlington Gallery in October 1938. Both poem and painting divided their critics, causing some who had previously admired Auden and Picasso to question these latest developments in their work. One of the acutest of those who responded positively was Stephen Spender. Replying to André Gide's criticisms of Picasso, Spender picked up on the fact that Gide saw the failure of *Guernica* in terms of its having become "*excentric* [sic], it breaks away from its centre, or has no centre".[13] Spender had isolated a similar eccentricity in Auden's work a year earlier when, in 'Oxford to Communism', his contribution to the Auden issue of *New Verse*, he offered a quizzical reading of Auden's work based on the tensions between Auden's middle-class, High-Church Anglican background and his intellectual and political commitment to the Left. These opposing tensions, Spender claims, fuelled the energy of Auden's poetry. His great gift was to be able to find a vantage point allowing him to see and judge clearly:

> The subject of his poetry is the struggle, but the struggle seen, as it were, by someone who whilst living in one camp, sympathises with the other; a struggle in fact which while existing externally is also taking place within the mind of the poet himself.[14]

And the poem that most clearly articulated this position, Spender wrote, was 'Spain'.

As with *Guernica*, 'Spain' can in no way be read as reportage. Humphrey Carpenter has noted that it begins with one of Auden's "hawk-like" views, the subject being not a place, as it was to be in 'Dover', but time or, more properly, history. Carpenter also points out that one stimulus to Auden's writing the poem was his having read *Illusion and Reality: A Study of the Sources of Poetry* by the young critic Christopher Caudwell, killed in Madrid in February 1937. In his book Caudwell discusses the radical changes affecting the modern world as a result of economic forces. "These changes," he wrote, "do not happen 'automatically', for history is made by men's actions, although their actions by no means always have the effect they are intended to have. The results of history are by no means willed by any men."[15] Caudwell clearly pre-empts the central concern of Auden's elegy for Yeats, that "poetry makes nothing happen". But in March 1937 Auden was still very much concerned with the belief that poetry *could* and *should* effect change. There were, however, hard choices to be made: "The conscious acceptance of guilt in the necessary murder", as he bluntly puts it in 'Spain'. Though he later changed this line to "The conscious acceptance of guilt in the *fact* of murder" [my emphasis] and, in 1965, omitted the poem altogether from his *Collected Poems*, the fact remains that on his return to England Auden saw what was happening in Spain as a decisive point in Western history, one which would determine how the past could be read and the future shaped. The decisive influence in this 'struggle', however, would not be the appearance of some *Deus ex Machina* but active human involvement:

The stars are dead; the animals will not look:
We are left alone with our day, and the time is short and
                    History to the defeated
May say Alas but cannot help or pardon.[16]

As Valentine Cunningham says in relation to Auden's poem, Spain became "all things to all men (and women), it respond[ed] to whatever subjective needs the observer [brought] to bear on it [becoming] very like Hamlet's cloud formations, in fact, very like a whale".[17] The problem, then, lay in determining what exactly was being fought for. The ideals of the young were easily manipulated, and reports of events in Spain were not exempt from being economical with the truth: "To you I'm the/'Yes-man, the bar-companion, the easily-duped:/I am whatever you do.../.../ I am your choice, your decision: yes, I am Spain."[18]

"[I]f Spain's necessities," Cunningham writes, "tested thirties writers in their lives, it also provided tests for their writing. Bluntly put, thirties writing's preoccupation with questions of war, action, pacifism and the possibility of heroism ... came suddenly very sharply and nastily to life in Spain ... Auden, for example, found it difficult to go on praising bombing planes and helmeted airmen after his Spanish experiences."[19] There is every possibility, however, that as a 'FAMOUS POET,' Auden was protected from seeing much real front-line action. His experiences in Spain, then, might not have been such as to cause the changes in his poetry Cunningham suggests. What would undoubtedly have shaken him was the aerial bombing of Guernica on 20th April 1937 by German Junker 52s and Heinkel 111s. Used, as Goering admitted in 1946, as a "testing ground"[20], Guernica proclaimed the future of modern warfare: the systematic terrorisation and destruction of civilian populations. If the Just City remained an ideal, Guernica, a small market town with a population of some 7,000 people swelled by upwards of 3,000 refugees, demonstrated the latest threat to its fragile existence.

Auden's poetry continued to show a fascination with towns and cities. Between finishing 'Spain' and starting 'In Memory of W.B. Yeats', he was to write about Dover, Oxford, Hongkong and Brussels. Images of the city also appear in other poems, always associated with the figure of the artist. Rimbaud is located in a landscape of "railway-arches"; A.E. Housman is linked to Cambridge and North London; Voltaire is found in exile in Ferney; and in 'Matthew Arnold' it is the poetic "gift" itself that is "a dark disordered city". This relationship between the poet and the community where he or she lives, works and writes, was later analysed by Auden in 'The Poet & The City'. Some of his conclusions are among the most iconoclastic he ever wrote:

> A society which was really like a good poem, embodying the aesthetic virtues of beauty, order, economy and subordination of detail to the whole, would be a nightmare of horror for, given the historical reality of actual men, such a society could only come into being through selective breeding, extermination of the physically and mentally unfit, absolute obedience to its Director, and a large slave class kept out of sight in the cellars.[21]

Auden's distrust of artists and their Utopian dreams also occurs in one of the aphoristic paragraphs that make up *The Prolific and the Devourer*. Written in the spring or summer of 1939 and left unfinished, the book was to be Auden's first attempt at coherently expressing those ideas which were to form part of his elegy for Yeats and which, as we will see, were later developed in 'New Year Letter'. The title, taken from Blake's *The Marriage of Heaven and Hell*, explores the relationship between artists and politicians, and the contribution they make to the building of a Just City. Rather than resolving the conflicts between the two, Auden, like Blake, sees the necessity of their opposing views existing in a kind of creative tension or friction. The proper function of both artist and politician, he proposes, is to "seek to extend their experience beyond the immediately given".[22] In many ways, then, his decision to leave England can be seen as simply taking his own beliefs to their logical conclusion.

IV

Auden and Isherwood arrived in New York, via Paris and Brussels, on 26th January 1939. Ice blocks floating on the Hudson greeted them. "There they stood in the driving snow," Isherwood later wrote, " – the made-in-France Giantess with her liberty torch, which now seemed to threaten, not welcome, the newcomer".[23] The afternoon of their arrival brought news that Barcelona had fallen to Franco.

Two days later, Yeats died in the South of France.

Despite its stark vision of a city in the grip of winter, the opening section of Auden's elegy for Yeats immediately alerts the reader to the fact that, like 'Spain', the poem does not mean to be taken as realism. Indeed it must have struck contemporary readers as having much in common with the pictures of de Chirico. What is also striking about the opening stanzas, as with 'Spain', 'Dover' and, to a lesser extent, 'Musée des Beaux Arts', is the poet's physical detachment from what is being described. Where exactly is he speaking from, able to command this sweeping view of brooks and airports, public statues and evergreen forests, rivers and "fashionable quays"? It is an aloofness that can in part be seen as dramatising a deliberate attempt at objectivity on Auden's part, one that withdraws from an emotional response to Yeats' death, thereby allowing the reader to consider the event in the light of its wider significance.

The effect is also remarkably similar to the experience described by Auden in 'American Poetry'. Analysing the differences between European and American writers, he focuses on the changed relationship between the individual and landscape; a change, he suggests, which can best be judged from the air:

> It is an unforgettable experience for anyone born on the other side of the Atlantic to take a plane journey by night across the United States. Looking down he will see the lights of some town like a last outpost in a darkness stretching for hours ahead, and realize that, even if there is no longer an actual frontier, this is still a continent ... where human activity seems a tiny thing in comparison to the magnitude of the earth.[24]

A strange amalgam of primeval forests and the contemporary world of airports and suburbs is the setting for Auden's opening stanzas. What we have, then, is a literal representation of the Greek polis, where "the city was merely the focal point of an area made up of both city and countryside".[25] It is also a city where, as George Szirtes has commented, "The political ghosts of the age haunt [the] buildings and streets".[26] Like the figure encountered by the poet in Eliot's 'Little Gidding', Auden's vision of the city is "a familiar compound ghost/Both intimate and unidentifiable." The city has become a Necropolis, and the poem, in its movements through, over and around that city/body assumes the clinical air of an autopsy. The poet's seeming disinterestedness is also reminiscent of the airman in Yeats' elegy for Robert Gregory, who, "Somewhere among the clouds above," looks down and declares: "Those that I fight I do not hate,/ Those that I guard I do not love". It is not difficult to imagine Auden sympathising with Gregory's reason for taking part in the war – "A lonely impulse of delight/Drove me to this tumult in the clouds" – nor that these lines of Yeats' may have prompted the images of helmeted airmen that populate his own poetry.

News of Yeats' death and the defeat of Barcelona seem to have fused in Auden's imagination. The vision of the dying man's stricken body beset by rumours, the failure of electrical supplies, and emptying squares and silent suburbs had a very real correlative in many Spanish towns and cities. While what is most often remembered about the elegy is the phrase "poetry makes nothing happen", we can only grasp the full significance of this if we acknowledge the fact that many of the writers who fought in Spain did so in the belief that their being there could and would make something happen. Though Auden's political ideals may have been irrevocably shaken by the experience, Spain had been an opportunity – perhaps the last – when he might do something as citizen *and* poet. The Fascist victory may simply have confirmed Auden's growing doubts of ever successfully resolving the tensions between the two. In which case 'In Memory of W.B. Yeats' becomes a record of his determination to write free of the illusion that poetry of itself could bring any significant political or social change. Just as the brutal assassination of Lorca in July 1936, only two days after the outbreak of the Civil War, was a warning shot that writers could no longer assume that they had any part to play in the constitution of the Just City, so the fall of Barcelona showed that the youthful idealism of "poets exploding like bombs" could happen all-too literally and still fail to make a jot of difference.

In his biography of Auden, Richard Davenport-Hines describes the poet's mood during the early months after his arrival in the States as "a mixture of apprehension and zest".[27] The elegy for Yeats confirms this. Balanced between affirmation and disavowal, Auden knows he has escaped the stifling, negative influences which England had come to represent for him but, like the free man at the close of 'In Memory of W.B. Yeats', still needed to learn "how to praise".

Three times within the ten-lined second section of the elegy, the word 'survive' appears in connection not with Yeats – who has yet to be mentioned by name – but with poetry in general. Threatened by "physical decay", "hurt", "madness", "isolation" and "grief", it retreats "to the valley of its saying", becoming simply "A way of happening, a mouth." While Auden offers us the example of a poet alienated within a landscape that contains the possibility of tragic suffering, it is also one he firmly locates within an economic, and therefore political, climate. The poet's experience of "the parish of rich women" is balanced by the sense of a wider world in which "the poor have the suffering to which they are fairly accustomed,/And each in the cell of himself is almost convinced of his freedom."

The influence of Lorca on Auden's poetry and his decision to move to New York has received little critical commentary. It is therefore interesting to consider the parallels between Lorca's 'Lament for Ignacio Sánchez Mejías', his elegy for the death of a bullfighter friend, and Auden's elegy for Yeats. It seems highly unlikely that Auden wasn't familiar with Lorca's work by early 1939. Both poets had been published in *New Writing*,[28] and Stephen Spender had translated several of Lorca's lyrics, including 'Adam' from *Poet in New York*. We can imagine Auden being interested in Lorca's treatment of homosexuality, and in hearing of the formative influence New York played in shaping Lorca's political and artistic sympathies. Auden may also have borne in mind the deep sense of unease and alienation that pervades Lorca's 'American' poetry while deciding for himself if and when to leave England.

All this is a matter for conjecture. What is certain is that if we compare the two elegies some interesting similarities do begin to emerge. 'In Memory of W.B. Yeats' begins with specific mention of the time of Yeats' death – "the dead of winter", where "dead" might also mean 'dead-centre', the exact middle – while Lorca's opening stanza insists that the reader remember the time of the bullfighter's death:

> At five in the afternoon.
> Exactly five in the afternoon.
> A boy fetched the white sheet
> at five in the afternoon.
> A basket of lime made ready
> at five in the afternoon.

The rest was death and death alone
at five in the afternoon.[29]

"At five in the afternoon" continues as a refrain throughout the opening section of the poem, just as "O all the instruments agree/ The day of his death was a dark cold day" is repeated at the end of Auden's first and last stanzas. (In both we might see something of the influence of the blues, where each phrase of sung text is normally followed by instrumental improvisation, creating a call-and-response pattern.) There are other incidental similarities between the opening sections, specifically the images both poets use to build up a picture of a city: Auden's suburbs invaded by silence become, in Lorca's elegy, "Silent groups on corners"; and Auden's "in the importance and noise of tomorrow/When the brokers are roaring like beasts" has an equivalent in Lorca's "the crowd was breaking windows". Both poems are also governed by a structure which moves from the urban to the rural, a movement which signals a return to the classical topos of elegy with its traditional setting within an idealised pastoral landscape. What is also striking is that both end with the poet contemplating the absence of the dead person or, more properly, the nature of what it is about them that is now missing. For Lorca's devout Catholicism, the answer is simple: it is the soul. For Auden, it is more complicated. The ambiguous nature of the "vessel" Yeats' body has, in death, become, suggests ritual funerary rites – the burying of amphora stocked with grain and wine, or a ship to help the departed on his journey across to the Other Side. Read in this context, the emptied vessel can be seen as referring to the painted sarcophagi that Yeats admitted a youthful interest in, with the poet's grave becoming another version of the Cavern out of which "Old Rocky Face" speaks in 'The Gyres'. Indeed Auden's imaginative sympathy with the dead poet is now such that he even echoes the 'voice/rejoice' rhyme which Yeats used in both 'Man and the Echo' and 'The Gyres': "Follow, poet, follow right/To the bottom of the night,/With your unconstraining voice/Still pursuadd us to rejoice".[30]

The significant difference between the two poems in which Yeats uses this particular rhyme is that while 'The Gyres' shows the poet greeting the destruction of civilisation with shouts of encouragement, 'Man and the Echo' is full of doubts and hesitations which, as Daniel

Albright has commented, display a mood of "dismal self-interrogation."[31] In his use of this rhyme and its implicit acknowledgement of both Yeats' poems, Auden is highlighting the thin line separating exuberance and despair. Though the poet's voice has the capacity to free us, doubts remain and we are in constant need of being persuaded to rejoice. Lorca acknowledges similar ambiguities in his essay on the *duende*. Great art, Lorca proposes, is only possible when the artist is acutely aware of the presence of death:

> The *duende* does not come at all unless he sees that death is possible. The *duende* must know beforehand that he can serenade death's house and rock those branches we all wear, branches that do not have, will never have, any consolation. ... With idea, sound, or gesture, the *duende* enjoys fighting the creator on the very rim of the well. Angel and muse escape with violin and compass; the *duende* wounds. In the healing of that wound, which never closes, lie the invented, strangest qualities of a man's work.[32]

These parallels shouldn't lead us to conclude that Auden was in any way simply rewriting Lorca's masterpiece. He may well have used it as a model; he may have recognised similarities between his own situation in New York and that of Lorca a decade earlier; he may even have begun the process of reassessing Lorca's assassination in the light of subsequent events in Spain and Yeats' refusal to engage in any significant defence of the Spanish government or to rebuke Fascism. What is indisputable is that for almost two decades Yeats' poetry had provided, in Rilke's words, a "practised distance as the other" for Auden in a way that paralleled Lorca's association of the poet and the bullfighter.[33] By physically removing himself from the Old World to the New, Auden may have hoped to discover a distance that would enable him to slough Yeats' influence. Doing so meant first immersing himself in Yeats' poetic personality to such an extent that, as Joseph Brodsky has commented, the elegy's very structure was "designed to pay tribute to the dead poet [by] imitating in reverse order the great Irishman's own modes of stylistic development."[34]

As Brodsky says, the intertextual references that litter the elegy are not limited to individual lines alone. With its structure like a time-lapse film run backwards, 'In Memory of W.B. Yeats' is seen as a reconstruction of Yeats' corpus through the re-integration of isolated examples of his poetic style. Having become his admirers and been 'scattered' like the pieces of Orpheus' dismembered body "among a hundred cities", Yeats' poetry is reassembled by Auden to create a modified form of meaning, one which allows the poet, again like Orpheus, to continue singing even after death. And in assimilating what Ian Gibson calls "the mythical view", Auden is once again imitating, or modifying, an aspect of Yeats' art. Even dead, it must have seemed to Auden, the old man was dogging his footsteps.

V

"A poem such as 'In Memory of Major Robert Gregory'," Auden wrote in 'Yeats As An Example', "is something new and important in the history of English poetry. It never loses the personal note of a man speaking about his personal friends in a particular setting ... and at the same time the occasion and character acquire a symbolic and public significance."[35] One of the things Auden most admired about Yeats' verse, therefore, was that it restored gravitas to the occasional poem. In doing so it re-enabled the poet to speak about public people and social events. He was to develop the idea further in 'The Poet and the City':

> All attempts to write about persons or events, however important, to which the poet is not intimately related in some way are now doomed to failure. Yeats could write great poetry about the Troubles in Ireland, because most of the protagonists were known to him personally and the places where the events occurred had been familiar to him since childhood.[36]

The third and concluding section of *Another Time* is titled 'Occasional Poems' and contains, as well as the Yeats elegy, a re-written 'Spain' (now entitled 'Spain 1937' so as to draw attention to a specific moment in history and the provisional nature of the original version), elegies for Ernst Toller and Sigmund Freud, 'September 1, 1939' and 'Epithalamion'. By any standard it is a remarkable grouping of poems, one which shows Auden fully engaged with the issue of the poet's freedom and ability to speak on behalf of his or her fellow citizens in times not only of personal grief and celebration but of political and cultural crisis.

Though *Another Time* has Auden acknowledging his debt to Yeats, the collection also contains a measure of rebuke. Yeats' *Last Poems* was published posthumously in 1939 and the collection ends with 'Politics', prefaced by an epigraph from Thomas Mann: "In our time the destiny of man presents its meanings in political terms." Yeats quotes Mann only to dispute with him, arguing that: "How can I, that girl standing there,/My attention fix/On Roman or on Spanish politics." It seems highly unlikely that Auden would not have read Yeats' poem without some wry amusement. Mann was by this time Auden's father-in-law, Auden having married Mann's daughter Erika in 1935 so as to gain her a British passport with which to escape Nazi Germany.

Four years later in November 1939, Erika's sister, Elizabeth, married Guiseppe Antonio Borgese. Auden marked the event by writing 'Epithalamion', a poem that takes Elizabeth Mann's marriage to her Italian husband as an occasion to comment on the altogether less harmonious alliance between Hitler and Mussolini. Individual lives, Auden is saying, are related to, if not coterminous with, wider political events. There is a sense, therefore, in which 'Epithalamion' is a direct refutation of the emphasis Yeats places on human behaviour in 'Politics', where the sexual and political must be kept apart.

The Manns were among Auden's closest friends when he arrived in the States. It was through them that he came into regular contact with a number of other European artists fleeing Hitler's Reich. But Auden had met German refugees before his arrival in the States, among them the poet and dramatist Ernst Toller, whose suicide in May 1939 prompted Auden to write an elegy which, like 'Epithalamion', provides further evidence of his disenchantment with Yeats.

Auden first met Toller in Portugal in 1936, admiring his work sufficiently to agree to help translate the lyrics of Toller's satirical play *No More Peace!* Imprisoned between 1919 and 1924 for his part in the Communist uprising in Bavaria, Toller had been forced to leave Nazi Germany in 1933. After several years spent wandering round Europe, he had emigrated to the States where he suffered a brief unhappy stint as a scriptwriter in Hollywood, before moving to New York where, convinced that his plays were passé, he hanged himself in his Manhattan hotel room.

Unsure of how he would himself be received in the States, Toller's death could not but have struck a chord with Auden. He may also have known of Toller's meeting with Yeats in London in October 1935, when Toller tried to persuade the Irishman, then Nobel Laureate, to support the movement to have the imprisoned German writer Carl von Ossietsky awarded the Nobel Peace Prize. The award would almost certainly have meant that the Nazi authorities would have released Ossietsky, yet Yeats refused, saying that he knew nothing about Ossietsky as a writer and that "it was no part of an artist's business to become involved in affairs of this kind".[37] If Auden did know of this meeting then his use of the 'voice/rejoice' rhyme in the elegy for the disillusioned Toller becomes a damning indictment of Yeats' concern, in 'Man and the Echo', that certain of his actions as a poet may have led to the murder of Irish Nationalists.

Auden's response to Yeats' doubts in 'In Memory of W.B. Yeats' is to affirm the poet's role, no matter how circumscribed. This 'affirming flame' is all but extinguished, however, in the opening lines of the elegy for Toller:

> The shining neutral summer has no voice
> To judge America, or ask how a man dies;
> And the friends who are sad and the enemies who rejoice
>
> Are chased by their shadows lightly away from the grave
> Of one who was egotistical and brave,
> Lest they should learn without suffering how to forgive.[38]

Whispering to Toller that, dead, he could enjoy a world where there is no evil and therefore "no need to write", Death intervenes. Only this time there is no voice straining from the tomb. The poet is silent. It is his enemies who now rejoice. The weather, so sympathetic to the poet in the Yeats elegy, is here 'neutral' – perhaps satirising Yeats' professed objectivity in the case of Ossietsky. In this context, it is difficult not to read the sixth stanza as another sideswipe at Yeats: "Dear Ernst, lie shadowless at last among/The other war-horses who existed till they'd done/Something that was an example to the young." Yeats' example, Auden had come to understand, was riddled with dangerous contradictions. For while he was admitting moral or philosophical problems into his poetry, in his private life he had proved unwilling to take a decisive stand on an issue of precisely this kind.

Toller is just one of the many exiles and migrants who criss-cross the pages of *Another Time*. Poets from earlier centuries – Voltaire, Rimbaud and Edward Lear – find their parallels in the contemporary world: Yeats dying in France, Toller in New York, and Freud – "an important Jew who died in exile" – in London. Among their number sits Auden, "Uncertain and afraid/As the clever hopes expire/Of a low dishonest decade", exiled like Thucydides from the demos. It is therefore not surprising that his thoughts should return to the ideal of the Just City, a place where men and women can live in creative sympathy, and where, as he says in 'Epithalamion', "Though the kingdoms are at war,/All the peoples see the sun,/All the dwellings stand in light". It is a pan-European vision which, in concluding, Auden associates with art and artists:

> Vowing to redeem the State,
> Now let every girl and boy
> To the heaven of the Great
> All their prayers and praises lift:
> Mozart with ironic breath
> Turning poverty to song,
> Goethe ignorant of sin
> Placing every human wrong,
> Blake the industrious visionary,
> Tolstoi the great animal,
> Hellas-loving Hölderlin,
> Wagner who obeyed his gift
> Organised his wish for death
> Into a tremendous cry,
> Looking down upon us, all
> Wish us joy.[39]

In *The Prolific and the Devourer* Auden had written, more than a little tongue-in-cheek, that one of the reasons he knew Fascism was bogus was that it was "much too like the kinds of Utopias artists plan over café tables very late at night".[40] The disparity between these Utopian dreams and the vision with which 'Epithalamion' concludes allows Auden to hand responsibility for the creation of the Just City not to artists but to ordinary 'girls and boys' who, inspired less by the actions of artists than by the vision of their art, will build the City for themselves. Gathered like fairy-godmothers invited to bless Elizabeth Mann's wedding, the litany of musicians, poets and novelists look down from the baroque clouds and provide a counterpoint to the hawk-like airmen who haunted Auden's imagination throughout the 1930s, terrorised the skies above Spain, and were even then preparing for war "in the new European air".

VI

There is a famous anecdote, perhaps apocryphal, about Picasso handing out postcards of *Guernica* to German officers who visited him in his studio during the occupation of Paris. Asked by one bemused officer "Did you do this?" Picasso is reported to have answered "No, you did."

In his influential study of Picasso's art, *Success and Failure of Picasso*, John Berger argues that *Guernica* is less a representation of modern warfare and "the specific kind of desolation to which it leads" than an allegorical painting which protests not against a specific historical event with specific historical causes and effects but against "a massacre of the innocents at any time." The problem, argues Berger, is that "Picasso abstracts pain and fear from history."[41]

With *Another Time*, Auden worked to strike a balance between precisely these tensions. If he observed events from too subjective a position, the historical causes would become blurred and ill-defined like an out-of-focus snapshot; assume too lofty a perspective, and he would become the author of vague abstractions. One of the ways Yeats had handled this same problem was to balance figures such as Cúchulainn and Pearse, the mythical and the historical, not only within the same poem but often within the same line: "When Pearse summoned Cúchulainn to his side,/ What stalked through the Post Office?" The significance of contemporary events is therefore given meaning in their juxtaposition to the mythical. Though Auden's practice is rarely so stark, *Another Time* provides a number of examples of the lessons he learnt from Yeats. As he himself said in relation to poems included in the final section of the collection: "These elegies of mine are not poems of personal grief. Freud I never met, and Yeats I only met casually and didn't particularly like him.

Sometimes a man stands for certain things, which is quite different from what one feels in personal grief."[42] Though hardly unique in recognising the limited claims subjective experience has to being called Truth, Auden stood alone amongst his generation of English writers in the lengths he was prepared to go to gain a vantage from which history and human actions might be read and interpreted. The effort was not without its cost. Ultimately, we might say that Auden was condemned to a position where all he could do was to look back and, like the prophet Jeremiah, lament the loss and destruction of Jerusalem without being physically able to do anything to remedy it.

Only months after docking in New York, Auden was writing home to a friend that America was:

> The most decisive experience of my life so far. It has taught me the kind of writer I am, i.e. an introvert who can only develop by obeying his introversions. All Americans are introverts. I adore New York as it is the only city in which I find I can work and live quietly.

Any return to England was out of the question. "No, God willing," the letter continues, "I never wish to see England again. All I wish is, when this [war] is over, for all of you to come here."[43]

There may well be an element of wish fulfilment in this, as the tone of the letter is markedly different from that of a poem such as 'September 1, 1939', which speaks less of the creative benefits of New York than of alienation and homesickness. It is therefore interesting to return to the example of Lorca and to note the striking similarities between Auden's initial responses to New York and those of Lorca during his stay in the city between June 1929 and March 1930. Like Auden, Lorca's decision to travel to the States was prompted by both a personal and artistic crisis – a failed love affair and the poor critical reception of *The Gypsy Ballads*. Again like Auden, Lorca's decision came at a time when the tensions between his public image as a writer and his private life as a man were becoming ever more painful. "People confuse my life and character," Lorca complained in 1927. "And this is the last thing I want. The gypsies are nothing but a theme. I could just as well be the poet of sewing needles or hydraulic landscapes."[44]

The parallels between the two poets extend to the glowing image of New York painted in letters home and the harsher, lonelier, grittier vision of the city that pervades their poetry. "On arriving in New York", Lorca wrote to his family in Granada,

> one feels overwhelmed, but not frightened. I found it uplifting to see how man can use science and technology to make something as impressive as a spectacle of nature. It is incredible. The port and the lights of the skyscrapers, easily confused with the stars, the millions of other lights, and the rivers of automobiles are a sight like no other on earth.[45]

The city portrayed in poems such as 'Dawn' is notably different, dominated as it is by Lorca's growing sense of personal isolation. This is not to say that Lorca's response was wholly subjective. He saw and condemned the poverty of people struggling to exist under capitalism:

> Those who go out early know in their bones
> there will be no paradise or loves that bloom and die:
> they know they will be mired in numbers and laws,
> in mindless games, in fruitless labors.[46]

And in a number of other poems, most notably 'The King of Harlem', he wrote sympathetically – if idiosyncratically – about the profound sense of cultural dislocation experienced by the country's immigrant populations. The result, again analogous to aspects of Auden's writing in the early months after his arrival, is that Lorca wrote poems that dealt with the loss of an idealised childhood and about Black-America; themes, as we will see, that recur throughout Auden's poetry during this period.

Something of these same feelings entered a later essay on Robert Frost,[47] where Auden compares the American poet's treatment of the theme of human isolation to that of his European contemporaries. The latter are at a disadvantage, Auden suggests, because they inhabit a landscape which:

> thanks to centuries of cultivation ... has acquired human features [and] they are forced to make abstract philosophical statements or use atypical images, so that what they say seems

to be imposed on them by theory and temperament rather than facts.[48]

Read in this context, the opening lines of 'September 1, 1939' become Auden's attempt at defining himself both geographically *and* verbally. With the self-conscious adoption of Brooklyn slang – "I sit in one of the dives/On Fifty-Second Street" – he means to make it clear that he was capable of remaking and relocating himself as a poet. He remained, however, suspicious – not least of himself. In condemning the "clever hopes ... /Of a low dishonest decade", we sense that he is also damning his own ideals, or at least his tendency to write under their influence. Only months after the elegy for Yeats, Auden revisits the third section of that poem and dismisses its graveside affirmations:

> Exiled Thucydides knew
> All that a speech can say
> About Democracy,
> And what dictators do,
> The elderly rubbish they talk
> To an apathetic grave[.]

Europe is portrayed – or rather personified – as a succession of influential men, each representing an aspect of civilisation. America, with all its disparate immigrant populations, becomes a second Babel: "blind skyscrapers use/Their full height to proclaim/The strength of Collective Man,/Each language pours its vain/Competitive excuse".

At home in neither Europe nor 'fortress' America, Auden was hardly alone in his predicament. What marked him out, if not to others then to himself, was the fact that unlike so many of the country's other immigrants and exiles he was there voluntarily. Perhaps it was a later recognition of this that made him disown 'September 1, 1939' for what he came to regard as its intellectual and moral failings.

The months leading up to and following the outbreak of war were later characterised by Auden in *The Age of Anxiety* as a time when "everybody [was] reduced to the anxious status of a shady character or a displaced person, when even the most prudent become worshippers of chance, and when, in comparison to the universal disorder of the world outside, his Bohemia seems as cosy and respectable as a suburban villa".[49] It was a climate of alienation and uncertainty, fuelled in part by the exodus of artists and intellectuals that had been fleeing Germany and Austria for the States. Schoenberg arrived in 1934; Kurt Weill and Lotte Lenya in 1935; deprived of German citizenship because of his attacks on the Nazi regime and his belief that an artist must remain fully involved in society, Thomas Mann landed in 1938; Adorno and Horkheimer arrived the same year; and Hermann Broch, imprisoned in a concentration camp since the Austrian *Anschluss* of 1938, was only allowed to leave in 1940 after pressure had been put on the German authorities by artists including James Joyce. Others, including Brecht, Paul Klee[50] and Robert Musil, took refuge in neutral Denmark and Switzerland. Once full-scale war began, however, even these havens were not always safe. Brecht left Europe to settle in California in 1941, while Musil, impoverished and isolated, died in exile the following year. Yet others were unable to leave. In September 1940, Walter Benjamin was arrested at the Franco-Spanish border, choosing to commit suicide rather than face being returned to occupied France. Reluctant to leave Europe for an America which culturally meant nothing to him, the only future Benjamin could envisage for himself in the States was to be carted up and down the country and exhibited as the "last European".

In a review of Auden's *The Double Man* (published in England as *New Year Letter*) in 1941, Randall Jarrell referred to what he called the "Völkwanderung of the barbarian scholars"[51] alluding to those American writers – notably Eliot, Pound and H.D. – whose arrival in Europe in the years preceding the First World War did so much to spark Modernism in Britain. The tide, as Jarrell noted, had now decisively turned, taking with it to America many of those younger artists considered a part of Modernism's continued vibrancy. It is as a betrayal of these principles that Jarrell chose to view Auden's verse epistle 'New Year Letter', seeing it as a reaction against the kind of poetry that was "experimental, lyric, obscure, difficult, violent, irregular, determinedly antagonistic to didacticism, general statement, science, the public". We will return to Jarrell's argument later. What is interesting to note at this point, however, is that similar criticisms were levelled at Stravinsky when he turned from the rhythmical and harmonic violence of *Le Sacre du Printemps* (1913) to the comparative harmonic stability of *Pulcinella* (1920) based on compositions attributed to the 18th century composer, Pergolesi.

"My instinct is to recompose," Stravinsky wrote in *Memories and Commentaries*. "Whatever interests me, whatever I love, I wish to make my own".[52] It was to Auden that Stravinsky later turned when he wanted to explain the role neo-classicism had played in the development of his music:

> I believe, with Auden, that the only critical exercise of value must take place in, and by means of, art, i.e., in pastiche or parody; *Le Baiser de la fée* and *Pulcinella* are music criticisms of this sort[.] *Pulcinella* was my discovery of the past, the epiphany through which the whole of my late work became possible. It was a backward look, of course [and] I was chided for composing 'simple' music, blamed for deserting modernism, accused of renouncing my 'true Russian heritage'.

A refugee in Europe from the outbreak of the First World War until he left for America in 1939, the social and economic conditions during and after the Great War made it practically impossible for Stravinsky to secure performances for large-scale works. The personal disillusionment and straitened circumstances of these years can be felt in a work like *The Soldier's Tale* (1918) which, to quote Adorno, was written for "a sparse, shock-maimed chamber ensemble. ... The pre-condition of the piece was poverty: it dismantled official culture so drastically because, denied access to the latter's material goods, it also escaped the ostentation that is inimical to culture".[53] It was not just the music of Europe's past that influenced Stravinsky. Jazz, too, was becoming important to him in the immediate post-war years, as shown by compositions such as *Rag-time* (1918) and *Piano Rag-Music* (1919).

Rejecting the overt emotionalism which went hand-in-hand with the nationalism of so much late 19th and early 20th century music, Stravinsky's compositions during the inter-war period were marked by an ever-increasing search for clarity and objectivity. Commenting on this in 1935, Stravinsky wrote that "Music is, by its very nature ... powerless to express anything at all." He continues: "The phenomenon of music is given to us with the sole purpose of establishing an order in things, including, and particularly, the coordination between man and time".[54] It is a view that finds a parallel in Auden's "Poetry makes nothing happen", and it is not difficult to imagine Auden having enormous sympathy with the wider implications of Stravinsky's words. Indeed, his own rejection of Yeats neatly parallels the neo-classical rejection of romanticism; and with titles such as 'Another Time', 'Heavy Date', 'New Year Letter' and 'The Dark Years', we can appreciate how Auden was becoming increasingly preoccupied with what John Fuller sees as "an acute sense of the present moment and its demands upon the individual to justify his way of life."[55] What is more, time as history was central to Stravinsky's thinking about the relationship between the individual composer and the tradition to which he belonged:

> Was I merely trying to refit old ships while the other side –
> Schoenberg – sought new forms of travel? ... The true business
> of the artist *is* to refit old ships. He can say again, in his way,
> only what has already been said.[56]

Understood in these terms, neo-classicism becomes not simply a re-working of old themes but, in as much as it consciously and explicitly utilises the forms of the past, an attempt at thinking and creating historically. There are then some striking similarities between Stravinsky's neoclassical compositions and Auden's 'New Year Letter' (which itself refers back to that most neoclassical of literary forms, the verse epistle), similarities which can be usefully summarised in Robert Craft's comments on Stravinsky: "Living in an age where he could feel no development towards a common style, he was impelled, by an amazing self-awareness, to force his position, to establish his own relation with the maturities of the eighteenth and other centuries."[57]

VII

We have seen that among Auden's closest friends after his arrival in the States were the Manns and the circle of émigré artists who gathered round them, and how references to German art and culture – Mozart, Goethe, Hölderlin and Wagner – entered a poem such as 'Epithalamion'. It was not, however, an isolated example. Neither did it remain so.

Reviewing *The Double Man* in *New Republic* in April 1941, Malcolm Cowley noted that 'New Year Letter' included references or allusions to Goethe, Wagner, Nietzsche, Kierkegaard ("a Dane adopted by the Germans"), Freud, Jung, Thomas Mann, Kafka, Rilke, Groddeck and Jaeger. Cowley ends by drawing the conclusion that Auden's "real interest is in the priests, prophets and healers who were admired in the Reich before Hitler".[58] In many ways this interest in German culture signalled a return to Auden's youth. Germany, and more particularly Berlin, had played an important role in his early adult life. As New York was now providing him with an opportunity to escape the stifling conformities of wartime Britain, so Berlin had fulfilled the same role at the end of the 1920s. And if, as Auden recorded, it was in Berlin that he "ceased to see the world in terms of verse",[59] New York allowed a continued reorientation of the relationship between art and life.

'Epithalamion' and 'September 1, 1939' show how Auden was attaching himself to the wider ideal of a European rather than a more narrowly based English or British culture. In the months after his arrival in America, Auden sought to affirm rather than demonise the role played by Germany in the development of Europe. He was certainly not alone in this. Back in England the arrival of large numbers of Jewish refugees led the composer Michael Tippett to condemn "the view that all Germany was evil".[60] Similarly, E.M. Forster in his *Three Anti-Nazi Broadcasts* of 1940 drew a distinction between the 1914-18 war and the 1939-45 one, making it clear that democratic Europe was less at war with Germany than with the Nazis:

> In the Kaiser's war, Germany was just a hostile country. She and England were enemies, but they both belonged to the same civilisation. In Hitler's war Germany is not a hostile country, she is a hostile principle.[61]

Like Tippett and Auden, Forster draws sympathetic attention to the plight of Hitler's German victims, in particular the vast numbers of refugees fleeing the country. And this led him to see distinct differences from the experience of the First World War:

It is important to remember that Germany had to make war on her own people before she could attack Europe. So much has happened lately that we sometimes forget that during the past seven years she robbed and tortured and interned and expelled thousands and thousands of her own citizens ... The 1914 war was not preceded by ... these floods of unhappy and innocent refugees.[62]

There are ways, therefore, in which it is vitally important to recognise Auden's decision to leave England not as an act of denial and negativity but a renewed commitment to, and demonstration of, solidarity for those suffering persecution. By becoming an exile himself, Auden could not have made his sympathies clearer. Indeed, Forster might almost have been describing Auden's predicament when, in 'Post-Munich', he wrote that:

Sensitive people are having a particularly humiliating time just now. Looking at the international scene, they see, with a clearness denied to politicians, that if Fascism wins we are done for, and that we must become Fascists to win. There seems no escape from this hideous dilemma, and those who face it most honestly often go jumpy ... so that whatever they do appears to them a betrayal of something good.[63]

From the evidence of the poetry, we can see that Auden's sense of empathy with America's migrant population, particularly the blacks and Jews, was as strong as Lorca's a decade earlier. A growing number of influences contributed to this. Obviously there was his own personal situation. There is the fact, as discussed earlier, that many of Auden's closest friends at the time were exiles from Nazi Germany. Though Auden knew about events in Germany, first-hand accounts would have impressed on him the scale of Hitler's Terror. Then there was the persecution of the Jews, rife throughout Fascist Europe but quietly persistent, as Forster wrote, even in the democracies.[64] And while Jews were being physically removed from the modern Germany, so too were they being erased from records of the country's past. Writing in 1937 about the revised edition of *Geschichte der deutschen National-Literatur* [*History of German Literature*], Jorge Luis Borges condemned it as a "perverse catalog", before listing a number of important German writers who had been excluded. Included on Borges' list are Heine, Max Brod, Kafka, Gottfried Benn, Martin Buber, Stefan Zweig, and Brecht. In trying to account for these omissions, Borges draws the following conclusion: "The (unreasonable) reasons for this manifold silence are evident: most of those eliminated are Jewish, none is a National Socialist." Borges continues in a vein with which we can imagine Auden having considerable sympathy:

> Things are worse in Russia, I hear people say. I infinitely agree, but Russia does not interest us as much as Germany. Germany – along with France, England, and the United States – is one of the essential nations of the western world. Hence we feel devastated by its chaotic descent into darkness, hence the symptomatic seriousness of a book such as this.[65]

Two further things complicated Auden's response to events. Firstly, in May 1939 he met and fell in love with Chester Kallman, an American Jew whose family came from Romania and Latvia. Secondly, he became increasingly aware of a cultural guilt and historical responsibility for the persecution taking place in Europe. As he wrote in a Christmas card to Kallman in 1941, he had come to consider himself "a Gentile inheriting an O-so-genteel anti-semitism."[66] In any circumstances we can imagine Auden's sympathy for the persecuted and homeless. Given his personal situation as the 1930s ended and war closed in, exile became for him not only an historical and objective phenomenon but also a metaphor for his own psychological dis-ease.

On 16th March 1939, Auden addressed a meeting of the Foreign Correspondents' Dinner Forum, a group set up to help refugees from the Civil War in Spain. It was his first political speech since arriving in the States. His message was straightforward: The Spanish and Weimar Republics had failed because their leaders "lacked the kind of character which alone makes a democratic form of government possible to run". It was, he continued, a situation that even now threatened the governments of Britain and the United States. If we want to save democracy, he said, "we must first make it more worth saving; and to do this, we must first see to it that we personally behave like democrats in our private as [in our] public lives; and when I look at my own, I wish I had a clearer conscience".[67] It is not Germany or the German people Auden is attacking. Rather, he is making the point that if we value democracy then we must create the conditions where it can flourish. Resentment over Versailles and the crippling costs of paying reparations to the Allies, along with the economic slumps of the 1920s, made such conditions difficult to foster in Germany. Therefore Europe's remaining democracies must shoulder their part of the blame for contemporary events.

'Refugee Blues' – written only a couple of months after his arrival in New York – is also directed at an American audience.[68] Indeed, its very form is one clearly intended to remind America of its own involvement and responsibility for previous waves of forced mass migration and exile. Rooted in various forms of black American slave song, the blues were widespread in the rural south by the late 19th century. Urban or 'city' blues evolved in the 1920s and 1930s, and by the time Auden arrived in New York had become an important and influential musical form.[69] Perhaps it was this popular appeal of the form that Auden wanted to exploit. If so, he could hardly have chosen a less populist subject matter:

> Thought I heard the thunder rumbling in the sky;
> It was Hitler over Europe, saying: 'They must die';
> We were in his mind, my dear, we were in his mind.
>
> Saw a poodle in a jacket fastened with a pin,
> Saw a door opened and a cat let in:
> But they weren't German Jews, my dear, but they weren't
> German Jews.[70]

While blues and jazz were predominantly music of the working or unemployed poor – usually black and urban – this is not to say that they were out of touch with mainstream culture, or it with them. Eric Hobsbawm is surely right when he links the spread of the blues and jazz to technology and business. "Until the First World War," he writes, "technology, in the form of radio and the phonograph which were to be crucial to the diffusion of Negro music from the 1920s, was not yet significant".[71] Neither were they musical forms unaffected by those forces of emigration and exile under discussion here. Among other things, they are diaspora music. Their history, as Hobsbawm says, "is part of the mass migration out of the Old South, and it is, for economic as well as often psychological reasons, made by footloose people who spend a lot of time on the road".[72] Their influence was not confined to the States. Transatlantic travel took them in the opposite direction to which Auden had come, meaning that essentially jazz rhythms such as the foxtrot had first appeared in Europe from as early as 1914. As has already been noted, Stravinsky for one had been composing under the influence of Jazz since 1918.

Auden's use of the blues is in some ways similar to that of Tippett in his *A Child of Our Time*, first performed in 1941. Inspired by the story of a 17 year old Jewish boy, Herschel Grynspan, whose shooting of a German diplomat in Paris provided the immediate excuse for Kristallnacht and the terrible pogrom that followed, Tippett looked to Negro spirituals as a modern equivalent to the Lutheran chorales which Bach incorporated into his Passions. "I thought at first of using Jewish tunes," Tippett later wrote:

> but then I heard a black vocalist on the radio sing the Negro spiritual 'Steal Away to Jesus' … I was blessed with an intuition: that I was being moved by this phrase far beyond its obvious context. I sent to America for a book of American spirituals, and when it came I saw that there was one for every key situation in the oratorio.[73]

Bach was not the only point of reference for Tippet's oratorio. Just as Stravinsky was looking back to the Baroque and to early Classical models, and 'New Year Letter' was to be influenced by 17th and 18th century poetic models, so *A Child of Our Time* uses Handel to structure both its musical and dramatic ideas.

The influence of Black America is also there in Auden's 'Calypso', written in May 1939. Unlike 'Refugee Blues' the subject matter of this poem is more directly satirical in tone and the setting more specifically American:

> Dríver drive fáster and máke a good rún
> Down the Spríngfield Line únder the shíning sún.
>
> Flý like an aéroplane, dón't pull up shórt
> Till you bráke for Grand Céntral Státion, New Yórk.

Characterised technically by arbitrary shifts in the accentuation of everyday English words, calypso usually addresses the kind of topical themes clearly present in Auden's poem: "But the póor fat old bánker in his sún-parlor cár/Has nó one to lóve him excépt his cigár."

What links the two poems is that they use forms that entered American culture through the slave trade with Africa and the West Indies. What is more, both the blues and calypso became expressions of political protest as well as existential suffering. As such they managed to embody precisely those themes of social and economic exclusion which preoccupied Auden. What they also provide is a means of setting contemporary events within an historical context.

The transatlantic slave trade produced one of the largest forced migrations in history. From the early 16th to the mid-19th centuries, somewhere between 10 and 11 million Africans were forcibly taken from their homes. About six percent of the total (600,000 to 650,000 people) came to the United States. In using the blues, therefore, Auden is implicitly drawing a parallel between the 20th century experience of Europe's Jews and that of earlier generations of Africans. It is a parallel which, like his speech to the Foreign Correspondents' Dinner Forum, clearly implicates Britain and other western economies.

In many ways Auden's connecting these two events goes against the grain of modern thinking about the uniqueness of the Holocaust. It is important to remember, however, that the Holocaust as it is understood today is largely a construct of the post-war decades. To Auden and his contemporaries there was nothing unique in what was taking place. As Peter Novick writes:

> Every historical event, including the Holocaust, in some ways resembles events to which it might be compared and differs from them in some ways. These resemblances and differences are a perfectly proper subject for discussion. But to single out those aspects of the Holocaust that were distinctive (there certainly were such), and to ignore those aspects that it shares with other atrocities … is intellectual sleight of hand.[74]

Novick's argument has much in common with the sub-text of 'Refugee Blues'. Writing about the Jewish diaspora in an essentially American idiom meant that Auden was taking issue with the idea that events in Europe marked an absolute point of difference between the morality of the Old World and the New. Rather, 'Refugee Blues' and 'Calypso' were intended to bring home to the American reader a fact which Novick sees as having become purposefully blurred:

> [Talk] of uniqueness and incomparability surrounding the Holocaust in the United States performs the opposite function: it promotes evasion of moral and historical responsibility. The repeated assertion that whatever the United States has done to blacks, Native Americans, Vietnamese, or others pales in comparison to the Holocaust is true – and evasive. And whereas a serious and sustained encounter with the history of hundreds of years of enslavement and oppression of blacks might imply costly demands on Americans to redress the wrongs of the past, contemplating the Holocaust is virtually cost-free.[75]

We can only wonder how much or little of this Auden had in mind. What is apparent, however, is that the same historical forces that in the 19th century drove thousands of English, Welsh, Irish and German young men and women into exile in America continued, though under changed economic and political circumstance, well into the 20th century.

VIII

In 1935 President Roosevelt ordered the American State Department to allow consulates to give refugees from Germany "the most considerate attention and the most generous and favourable treatment possible under the laws".[76] Roosevelt's words were not always acted upon. This may in part have owed something to anti-Semitism among American officials in Europe. It was a prejudice, allied to a belief that it was the Jews who were largely responsible for the Bolshevik revolution, which meant that Jews from Eastern Europe found it almost impossible to gain a visa.[77]

Auden first published 'Refugee Blues' in the *New Yorker* in April 1939, where it appeared under the title 'Say this city has ten million souls'. Earlier that year the American government had refused to allow Jewish refugees on board the German liner *St Louis* to dock in a US port unless they had the appropriate visa. With hindsight we know that those people who were returned to Europe and given refuge in Belgium, Holland and France were, in all likelihood, to become victims of the Final Solution. As such, the incident is damning of American immigration policy. It was, however, not simply immigration law that was at issue. Though unemployment had been falling in the States since 1933, the situation worsened in 1938. By the early months of 1939 the number of people out of work stood at between eight and ten million. The economy did not reach 1937 levels until after the war had begun. The argument was a familiar one: each refugee who found a job was putting an American out of work. As far as America was concerned, Europe's refugee crisis was not simply a moral but an economic issue. Such is the immediate background to 'New Year Letter'.

When, in January 1940, Auden started work on the poem, he began by contrasting the violence in Europe with the seeming tranquillity and prosperity of America. It is the figure of the poet – "a man alone" – who, like the summer weather in 'In Memory of Ernst Toller', has a "neutral eye" and is able to view dispassionately the overall pattern and momentum of historical events. As in 'Dover' and the elegy for Yeats, Auden adopts a hawk-eyed view of things, one that enables him to see "A ship abruptly change her course,/A train make an unwonted stop,/A little crowd smash up a shop". America, however, is insulated from such a history of "visible hostilities" and "sharp crude patterns", though Europe, in the form of art, still has influence:

> The very morning that the war
> Took action on the Polish floor
> [The sun] Lit up America and on
> A cottage in Long Island shone
> Where Buxtehude as we played
> One of his *passacaglias* made
> Our minds a *civitas* of sound
> Where nothing but assent was found,
> For art had set in order sense
> And feeling and intelligence,
> And from its ideal order grew
> Our local understanding too.[78]

There remains something here of Auden's conclusion to 'Epithalamion', with its vision of the family as a microcosm of the

State. What has noticeably changed is the role designated to art in bringing about an equitable society. Whereas 'Epithalamion', written only months earlier, holds out the promise of art as "Vowing to redeem the State", with "every girl and boy/To the heaven of the Great/All their prayers and praises lift[ing]", 'New Year Letter' provides a more sober, and sombre, commentary: "Art is not life, and cannot be/A midwife to society".

Much had changed between the composition of the two poems. The outbreak of full-scale European war made any return to England, had he wanted it, if not impossible then highly dangerous. Atlantic shipping remained as vulnerable as it had been in 1915 when the *Lusitania* was sunk. And despite the salving influence of Buxtehude, Auden was becoming increasingly aware of the social realities of America outside the comfort of Elizabeth Mayer's Long Island home:

> Now in that other world I stand
> Of fully alienated land,
> An earth made common by the means
> Of hunger, money and machines,
> Where each determined nature must
> Regard that nature as a trust
> That, being chosen, he must choose,
> Determined to become of use[.][79]

In deciding how best "to become of use", Auden was again placed in a position whereby he would have to balance the competing claims of the personal and the public. The key word here is alienation. As suggested earlier, it is a word that unites Auden's preoccupation with exile as both an historical and economic fact, as well as providing access to those psychological truths which form the basis of 'September 1, 1939'. What it also provides is a crossroads between aspects of Marxist economics and Freudian psychology.

The term gained wider currency through Marxist theory. It is used with special prominence in Marx's manuscripts of 1844, written while he was a political exile in Paris. Marx derived the term from Hegel's *Entäusserung and Entfremdung*, where it is used to portray the "unhappy consciousness" of individuals in the Roman world and later during the Christian Middle Ages. Deprived of the harmonious social and political life of pagan antiquity, Hegel argues, people turned towards God as a way of satisfying their aspirations. Marx modified Hegel's terminology to portray the situation of modern individuals – specifically the labouring class – denied either communal action or ownership of their own lives or the products of their labour. Read in these terms, Auden's use of the blues and calypso can be regarded as analogous to Marx's rewriting of Hegel. The alienation of slaves from Africa and the West Indies, given voice in the often mournful rhythms and lyrics of blues or in the satirical lyrics of calypso, is thus used by Auden to give a voice to the alienation of modern European Jewry.

While 'Refugee Blues' deals with the facts of economic and political alienation, under the auspices of Freud, Auden began writing poems that looked to find the root causes of Hegel's "unhappy consciousness" elsewhere. In childhood, Auden wrote in *The Prolific and the Devourer*, he had learnt "certain attitudes, call them prejudices if you like, which I shall never lose." Among them, though he disclaimed any supernatural beliefs, was "a conviction … that life is ruled by mysterious forces".[80] It was to this apprehension of "mysterious forces" with their origins in childhood, which he turned in 'Where do They come from?'

Where "They" come from is, as Auden had written in 'The Creatures' from 1936, "our past and our future: the poles between which our desire unceasingly is discharged". It is clear, then, that "They", in Freudian terms, belong to our unconscious, to those impulses we repress and which must subsequently appear transformed and unrecognisable in our daily behaviour. Out of economic alienation, Auden is saying, comes self-estrangement, what Freud understood as the rift between the conscious and the unconscious. We have seen how in 'Refugee Blues' Auden speaks out against the culture of the Unjust City, arguing that its causes are determined by repeated patterns of historical behaviour. The hounding of Jews into exile and the denial of human rights to America's migrant populations can have only one result: "Those to whom evil is done/Do evil in return." That which is exiled, whether from the material or psychological world, returns to haunt our aspirations for a Just City. "They", the "Terrible Presences", are thus unmasked and shown to be aspects of our psyche which we either force into 'emigration' or keep locked up. However, as Freud diagnosed, that which is repressed simply returns in another form:

> We are the barren pastures to which they bring
> The resentment of outcasts; on us they work
> Out their despair; they wear our weeping
>   As the disgraceful badge of their exile.[81]

Political and emotional repression, as Auden later commented in *The Enchafèd Flood*, only create "the Trivial Unhappy Unjust City ... an image of modern civilisation in which innocence and the individual are alike destroyed."[82] While 'Where do They come from?' refers to Auden's past, it is also part of a movement forward in his work. For just as the group of poems he wrote during the winter of 1938-39 culminated in the great elegy for Yeats, so 'They' and other poems written in the spring and summer of 1939 ('Like a Vocation', 'Heavy Date' and 'Another Time') investigate the means by which we might reconcile the fragments of our social and psychological selves, re-learning how 'To say I am'. As the concerns of those poems about the role of artist are most fully articulated in 'In Memory of W.B. Yeats' (and, to a lesser extent, 'In Memory of Ernst Toller'), so this progressive development in Auden's thinking culminates in an elegy where psychoanalysis is represented as a process of voluntary exile/self-alienation.

When Auden wrote his elegy for Freud he was in a very real sense rehearsing all those acts of mourning which he foresaw the coming war as making necessary:

> When there are so many we shall have to mourn,
> when grief has been made so public, and exposed
>   to the critique of a whole epoch
>   the frailty of our conscience and anguish
>
> of whom shall we speak?

Writing about Freud, a man he never met, prepared the way for more personal losses. In doing so it returned Auden to the problem of how we are to strike a balance between our public and our private selves, and how the latter, with its griefs and sufferings, is put under increasing pressure by the need to be authentic. Less than five years later, after the full scale of the atrocities of the Nazi death camps was beginning to be known, Adorno analysed precisely this 'commodification' of personal experience:

The realm of reification and standardization is thus extended to include its ultimate contradiction, the ostensibly abnormal and chaotic. The incommensurable is made, precisely as such, commensurable, and the individual is now scarcely capable of any impulse that he could not classify as an example of this or that publicly recognized constellation. However, this outwardly assumed identification, accomplished, as it were, beyond one's own dynamic, finally abolishes not only genuine consciousness of the impulse but the impulse itself. The latter becomes the reflex of stereotyped atoms to stereotyped stimuli, switched on or off at will.[83]

The level of killing during the war led Adorno to repudiate Freud's theories of the unconscious, regarding them as a denial of the uniqueness and sanctity of individual consciousness analogous to the exploitation of human emotions under Hitler. Once mobilised, Adorno felt that these emotions could then be used to provoke and justify genocide. It is a reading of psychoanalysis clearly at odds with Auden, for whom analysis made less rather than more possible the effectiveness of what Adorno calls "stereotyped stimuli".

Adorno regarded Freud's ideas as exerting a dangerous and powerful influence, wresting responsibility for our actions away from the conscious to the unconscious self. Auden was interested in similar things, and in many ways the conclusions he drew parallel Adorno. We have seen how one aspect of Auden's poetry began to be increasingly concerned with childhood and with the repression of instinctual urges. In the Freud elegy these appear as "the fauna of the night" who "beg us/dumbly to ask them to follow". They also appear in the guise of the lost souls from Dante's *Inferno* – "the injured/lead[ing] the ugly life of the rejected". As in 'Where do They come from?', the theme remains that of exile and self-alienation. For in Dante's universe the damned are so because of a wilful rejection of God's love. If in nothing else Dante has at least this much in common with Hegel and Marx: alienation is a self-perpetuating separation from the source of one's true nature. Neither is there anything necessarily new in the way Auden personifies our unconscious desires as animals. The image of "the fauna of the night" gathering round Freud's bedside, for example, is strikingly similar to Goya's "The sleep of reason produces monsters" from *Los Caprichos*.

The rooting of such projections of the unconscious in the Enlightenment is an analysis that forms the basis of the opening chapter of Adorno and Horkheimer's *Dialectic of Enlightenment*:

> Enlightenment has always taken the basic principle of myth to be anthropomorphism, the projection onto nature of the subjective. In this view, the supernatural, spirits and demons, are mirror images of men who allow themselves to be frightened by natural phenomena. Consequently the many mythic figures can all be brought to a common denominator, and reduced to the human subject. Oedipus' answer to the Sphinx's riddle: "It is man!" is the Enlightenment stereotype repeatedly offered as information, irrespective of whether it is faced with a piece of objective intelligence ... Men pay for the increase of their power with alienation from that over which they exercise their power. Enlightenment behaves toward things as a dictator toward men. He knows them in so far as he can manipulate them.[84]

As Auden was to write in 'New Year Letter', such claims can only lead to a situation where emotion is prized above intellect, passion over reason. However seductive such views might be, it is one the poem exposes and associates with "the Accuser", "the great Denier". It is also the amplified voice of Nuremberg, colonialism, Empire, the forces of nationalism and, as the word "appreciates" suggests, Capitalism. In other words, Auden's Accuser speaks not only to, and for, our private desires, but for all those vested interests responsible for the war and for America having become "a fully alienated land".

After the annihilation of families, the mass bombing of houses and the fragmentation of social bonds, we are all, Adorno says, homeless in the world. "The house is past", he wrote, and in this new-world order the only means by which the alienated individual can show some solidarity with other people is through "inviolable isolation". For, Adorno says, "All collaboration, all the human worth of social mixing and participation, merely masks a tacit acceptance of humanity. It is the sufferings of men that should be shared: the smallest step towards their pleasures is one towards the hardening of their pains".[85] Adorno's is a hard and lonely path. What it shares with Auden and, ironically, with a particular aspect of Freud's writings, is an emphasis on the kind of vision of human relationships that only reveals itself in the lives of the unhoused, the unsettled, the *unheimlich*.

First published in English in 1925, Freud's essay on the 'uncanny', or more accurately 'unhomely', is an investigation of those phenomena which arouse fear in the individual and which, Freud argues, "lead back to what is known of old and long familiar."[86] So while *Dialectics of Enlightenment* turns to the Greek myths for an understanding of post-Enlightenment consciousness, suddenly in poems such as 'The Prophets', 'Like a Vocation' and 'New Year Letter', Auden begins constructing a sustained narrative of his childhood, one preoccupied with "the issue of identity itself [and] with a young figure's search for a personal voice."[87] What is more, in his elegy for Freud Auden clearly associates this search for self-definition with the act not of writing but of trying to remember:

> He wasn't clever at all: he merely told
> the unhappy Present to recite the Past
> like a poetry lesson till sooner
> or later it faltered at the line where

> long ago the accusations had begun[.]

In a speech in Vienna to mark Freud's eightieth birthday in 1936, Thomas Mann commented that "Infantilism – in other words, regression to childhood – what a role this genuinely psychoanalytic element plays in all our lives".[88] What is interesting in Auden's version of what Mann goes on to call the "mythical identification as survival, [the] treading in footsteps already made" is that it is not the words and lines we remember that are important but those which repression has us forget. It is from these retrieved fragments, Auden seems to be suggesting, that we then construct an identity which is faithful to our essential selves – "The one who needs you, that terrified/ Imaginative child". This construction of narrative material from fragments of repressed childhood memories is, Freud says, one of the clearest examples of the *unheimlich* as it appears in literature.

Freud's essay ends on an interesting note, one that has much in common with Adorno's assertion that "inviolable isolation" has become the moral and aesthetic responsibility of the creative artist. It is an acceptance of what, in other circumstances, Jakobson called "transcendental homelessness" and Freud, at the very close of his essay on the *unheimlich*, "the factors of silence, solitude and darkness ... from which the majority of human beings have never become quite free."[89] In other words, it is a withdrawal from the world in order to speak of and reclaim that world:

> In the main we adopt an unvarying passive attitude towards real experience and are subject to the influence of our physical environment. But the storyteller has a *peculiarly* directive power over us; by means of the moods he can put us into, he is able to guide the current of our emotions, to dam it up in one direction and make it flow in another, and he often obtains a great variety of effects from the same material.[90]

This reclamation of experience through a fragment that proves capable of independent life clearly brings us close to aspects of Walter Benjamin's writings, particularly those that came to influence Adorno while he was writing *Minima Moralia*.

For a long while suspicious of Benjamin's use of the aphorism, Adorno seems to have changed his mind in the early years of the Second World War. While previously Adorno's Hegelian theory couldn't admit the aphorism because of its fundamental isolation, its refusal to engage in a dialectical exchange, suddenly it became of primary importance to his thinking. Writing under conditions where a sustained engagement with his native culture and language was restricted, and under historical circumstances where the life of the individual was threatened, Adorno turned to the aphorism as the only available way of authenticating the world in speech. Moreover, the rise of Nazism, the spread of war and growing knowledge of the scale of the Holocaust convinced him that it was individual experience in the form of the fragment/aphorism which now needed to be relied upon rather than "the larger historical categories, after all that has meanwhile been perpetrated with their help."[91]

The fragment, Benjamin argued, is the means by which we 'brush history against the grain', therefore dissociating ourselves from any record of the past which sees history as belonging to the victors rather than their victims. "There is no document of civilisation," Benjamin famously wrote, "which is not at the same time a document of barbarism."[92] The fragment – charged with those powers of remembrance which the elegy for Freud celebrates – can be used to undermine and, in Auden's words, unsettle "the ancient cultures of conceit", thereby bringing about "the fall of princes, the collapse of/ their lucrative patterns of frustration".

Minima Moralia, the closest Adorno came to Benjamin's ideal of a book made up solely of juxtaposed fragments of text, is divided into three sections, each of which takes as its starting-point "the narrowest private sphere": that of the intellectual in exile. From this follow a dazzling series of considerations concerning anthropology, psychology, aesthetics, and science as they relate to their subject. Even in outline, it is a description that seems tailor-made for Auden's 'New Year Letter'. However, before examining what this poem has to say about Auden's developing sense of himself as an émigré poet, I want briefly to look at another aspect of the American scene that had a marked influence on him.

IX

'In Memory of Sigmund Freud' marked another stage in Auden's growing awareness of the rhythms and idioms of American poetry, and how he might adopt them to his own practice. As critics have pointed out, his use of syllabics in this and other poems acknowledges an enormous debt to Marianne Moore. Taking this further, Rosanna Warren has shown how Auden's stanzas with their syllabic patterning of 11, 11, 9 and 10 mirrors the alcaic stanza favoured by Horace in some two thirds of his odes. The significance of this to Auden's predicament in 1939 cannot be overestimated: born in 630 BC, Alcaeus was an aristocrat who fought against a tyrant and, defeated, was sentenced to exile. The conclusion Warren draws from this is that Auden's adoption of the alcaic stanza is evidence that by the time he came to write the elegy he had "outgrown the fantasy of belonging to a literal community [and] had accepted exile as the essential, not the accidental, human condition".[93] This, as we will see, is developed further in 'New Year Letter'. It is also not without significance to what, in Chapter Two, I will have to say about Joseph Brodsky. But to return to Marianne Moore.

Auden seems to have been aware of Moore's work from the mid 1930s, probably from 1935 when her *Selected Poems* was published in Britain with an introduction by T.S. Eliot. His first attempts at reading her, however, resulted in confusion. "I could not 'hear' the verse," he later wrote, stressing the difficulties for "an English ear" in trying to make sense of verse "in which accents and feet are ignored and only the number of syllables count." What attracted him, however, was a "tone of voice [and] distaste for noise and excess".[94] Auden was hardly alone in not being able to make metrical sense of Moore's verse. Writing to her in 1918, Ezra Pound expressed a curiosity about where, literally, her poetry was coming from, and what it might have to say about developments in American poetics:

> I want to know, relatively, your age, and whether you are working on Greek quantitative measures or on René Ghil or simply by ear (if so a very good ear). ... Do you see any signs of mental life about you in New York? I still retain curiosities and vestiges of early hopes, though doubt if I will ever return to America, save perhaps in a circus.
> How much of your verse *is* European? How much Paris is in it? This is, I think, legitimate curiosity on my part IF I am to be your editor, and as I am still interested in the problem of how much America can do on her own.[95]

Given Auden's adoption of the blues and calypso at various times in the 1930s, it is also not inconceivable that Moore's poetry attracted him because of something else that puzzled Pound: was she Black?

> And are you a jet black Ethiopian Othello-hued, or was that line in one of your *Egoist* poems but part of your general elaboration and allegory and designed to differentiate your colour from that of the surrounding menagerie?[96]

What Auden would instinctively have responded to in Moore's work was a poet whose interests and reading accorded so closely with his own. In *The Prolific and the Devourer* Auden had recalled the formative influence his father's library had on him as a child and later as a poet. "The study," Auden writes:

> was full of books on medicine, archaeology, the classics ... It was not the library of a literary man nor of a narrow specialist, but a heterogeneous collection of books on many subjects ...

45

> In consequence my reading has always been wide and casual rather than scholarly, and in the main non-literary.[97]

With her references to, and borrowings from, Classical history, botany, biology, geography and a whole range of non-literary sources, Moore must have seemed to Auden a poet who, like himself, was on the look out for new ways of allowing art and science to communicate with each other and to reconcile the historical divisions that had grown up between them.[98] In many ways this is the theme of 'In Memory of Sigmund Freud'.

What Auden also admired in Marianne Moore was, as he told her in a letter written while he was at work on the Freud elegy, the fact that "Like Rilke, you really do 'Praise'."[99] Here then, at a time when Auden was increasingly turning to German writers, artists and thinkers was an *American* poet from whom he could learn. What it also highlights is yet another instance of the ways in which Auden's imagination was intent on finding connections between German and American culture that he could then use to express his anxieties about the descent into war and his own personal isolation.

Auden's essay on Moore provides a further clue as to why he may have had her in mind as a model for 'In Memory of Sigmund Freud'. As with Goya's satires on the Enlightenment in *Los Caprichos* – a donkey performs the bedside role of a doctor, an ape strums a guitar, a parrot addresses what appears to be an assembly of learned professors – so Auden saw Moore's use of animals in her poetry as being a continuation of the literary tradition of 'The beast fable':

> In these, the actors have animals' bodies but human consciousness. Sometimes the intention is simply amusing entertainment, but more often it is educative. The fable may be a mythical explanation of how things came to be as they are ... What perverts man, individually and collectively, from behaving reasonably and morally is not so much ignorance as self-blindness, induced by some passion or desire. In a satirical beast fable, the beast has the desires of his kind which are different from those which govern man, so that we can view them with detachment and cannot fail to recognize what is good or bad, sensible or foolish behaviour ... If a human being is introduced into a beast fable ... he appears not as a man but as a God.[100]

It is a description which has much in common with aspects of 'In Memory of Sigmund Freud', particularly if we substitute 'self-alienation' for "self-blindness" and recognise in the costumed actors those same outlawed presences which gather round the dying Freud.

Moore's influence also played a part in what John Fuller has characterised as "a relaxed conversationalism [which] seems to have been the chief stylistic influence that America provided [for Auden]".[101] Such discursiveness certainly marks out the Freud elegy from either of those for Toller or Yeats. And though the adoption of a conversational tone was hardly new in Auden's poetry – we might think of *Letter to Lord Byron*, for example – it assumes a much greater significance in 'New Year Letter'.

X

"In writing a letter," Lucy McDiarmid says:

> Auden could exploit the genre's connotation of both 'naturalness' and 'literariness'. Insofar as a letter is 'natural', a 'substitute for direct speech', it links two actual people; it projects an image of its author at a given point in time and negotiates a relationship with a particular person.[102]

What the form also provides is a forum to comment implicitly on the relationship between the private and the public: "may .../This private minute for a friend,/Be the dispatch that I intend;/Although addressed to a Whitehall, Be under Flying Seal to all".[103] It is therefore interesting to place Auden's poem in the context of what William C. Dowling sees as the defining features of the Augustan verse epistle:

> When we speak of the Augustan verse epistle we are normally talking about a situation in which a male speaker, educated in classical values and seeking refuge, in the company of a few kindred souls, from a fallen social reality, addresses a male friend in a way meant to be exemplary for their society as a whole.[104]

Though Dowling is wrong in seeing the epistle as predominantly a man-to-man affair – Pope, for example, was not averse to addressing a number to his great friend Martha Blount – 'New Year Letter' is clearly occupied by similar concerns regarding the poet's ability to speak in an exemplary manner. Moreover, the poem's addressee and the context in which Auden expected it to be read and understood raise important questions about his changing sense of what poetry could achieve – and for whom. For while 'Refugee Blues' and 'Calypso' mark an attempt at writing in a popular style, 'New Year Letter' can be read as a retreat from such democratic and multi-cultural ideals, marking a further admission of defeat on Auden's part as he recognises the fact that poetry cannot speak for and to all people, only some 'ten persons'.

'New Year Letter' is addressed to Elizabeth Mayer, a German refugee who lived on Long Island with her psychiatrist husband. Like Ovid's *Epistulae ex Ponto*, it is also addressed "under Flying Seal" to an official audience back home. In doing so, Auden is implicitly commenting on the fact that poetry must in some essential way exist in a kind of no-man's land – or floating island – between the public and private. For while Auden's theme is historical rather than purely personal, the distinctions between the two merge in the representative figure of the exiled poet who, both a part of and apart from his home and native language, can only watch the New Year celebrations of the milling crowds.

A similar crisis of identity has been noted as a feature of English poetry from the late-17th to the mid-18th century. While Stephen Cox has described Gray's Eton ode as the very image of "the isolated self, reflecting bitterly on its inability to accomplish anything of significance in either thought or action",[105] Patricia Spacks has noted that "the grim specter of solipsism that haunts Eliot's modern wasteland ..." is the same as that haunting Pope's Augustan landscape, with the crucial difference that the "solipsism which is assumed by such later poets as Eliot to be a necessary condition of life seems to Pope a symbol of ultimate evil."[106] Dowling, meanwhile, has analysed the role the verse epistle played in both expressing and defining "a grand movement out of solitude and back toward community, [which does so] precisely by exploiting the purely formal resources of language as a system of signification unimaginable outside some collective or communal form of existence."[107]

For all the civilised comforts of his Long Island home-from-home, Auden was quite obviously haunted by a fear similar to Pope's: that the poet should become merely a voice talking to itself in the dark. And if we want to discover a connection between 'New Year Letter' and any single one of the Augustan poets, it is in the figure of Pope who comes most readily to mind. A Catholic, and therefore denied full participation in the affairs of his country, Pope lived "almost in the situation of a naturalised alien ... personally dispossessed, disinherited, and deprived [inhabiting] both the garden and the city, actively engaged in the political fisticuffs of his turbulent times and yet holding himself in reserve."[108] As with Marvell before him, Pope's "emblem of this divided life" is the garden. In actuality this meant the "five rented acres" of his grotto at Twickenham which, like Elizabeth Mayer's apartment, existed as a "a shrine to family life". Indeed, Auden could almost have had Pope's garden with its "dense array of historical and mythological references [and] geological discoveries"[109] in mind while writing 'New Year Letter'.[110]

Auden was decisively outside the vision of communal life suggested by Dowling. Or perhaps it is nearer the truth to say that the America Auden felt tempted to commit himself to was one in which no such sense of collective identity could easily be had. An exile among other exiles, émigrés and refugees, the poet is simply "A tiny object in the night" circled by an "Horizon of immediacies", speaking not of community but desperation and bewilderment. Despite this, or perhaps because of it, 'New Year Letter' is determined to make a home for itself in the Manhattan and America it describes. As such it is best understood as Auden's most coherent attempt up until then at exploring and defining those boundaries of a common world shared by poet and reader alike, however temporary a shelter the resulting structure might turn out to be.

As Edward Mendelson has pointed out, critics have generally followed Jarrell's lead in condemning 'New Year Letter' for its neo-classicisms, seeing them as a reason to lament the passing of the modernist Auden. It is a charge to which we will return. For now, however, it is worth pointing out, as Mendelson says, that such a view ignores:

> the way in which the conservative order of its syntax and metre [struggles] to restrain the anarchic whirlwind of its ideas. Rhymed octo-syllabic couplets give it the air of a patterned, rational argument, but this eighteenth-century manner ... masks

a restless idiosyncratic exploration of vast historical changes and uncertainties.[111]

The relationship between the poem's metrical form and these "changes and uncertainties" has also been commented on by John Fuller, who writes that "The octosyllabic couplet is perhaps too narrow for discursive verse ... and thus appears to be continually pushing further and further away the decisive statement".[112] Such discursive restlessness is only heightened by the fact that Auden's text is constantly referring to and spilling over into the pages of notes and additional poems included at the poem's conclusion.

Where Mendelson and Fuller go astray is in their assessment of the historical resonances of Auden's verse epistle. Fuller's comment that octosyllabics are "too narrow" for discursive verse would certainly have come as a surprise to Marvell, mention of whom serves to relocate the poem's ancestry not, as Mendelson has it, in the eighteenth but in the seventeenth century.[113] Marvell is also an instructive guide to other aspects of the poem, particularly its "idiosyncratic exploration of vast historical changes" and its efforts at striking a balance between the lyric and the satire.

Written in the early 1650s, Marvell's 'Upon Appleton House' is a meditation on the competing claims of contemplation and action. Couched in the form of an address to the Fairfax family, whose young daughter, Mary, was Marvell's pupil, like 'New Year Letter' it blurs the distinctions between public and private. But Marvell was equally at home using octosyllabics for more obviously personal and enigmatic lyrics such as the two Mower poems or 'The Picture of little T.C. in a Prospect of Flowers'. What these formal considerations demonstrate is that Marvell, like Auden, was capable of using the same form to approach and discuss a range of subjects and emotional states. It is an "interdependence of opposites" which, as George Lord comments:

> comprises Marvell's particular version of a favorite seventeenth-century theme known as *concordia discors* [and] not only led him to shun partisan and absolutist positions but to treat in an original way the conflicting claims of the active life and the contemplative life, a venerable theme which the Civil War made of compelling interest to many Englishmen.[114]

It is a theme and a form which, during another time of war, Auden clearly thought worth re-visiting.

Marvell's response to the choice of action or contemplation was, like Auden's, to choose both. Though he didn't see active service in the Civil War – the evidence suggests that he spent most of the war years abroad in Italy and France – neither was he a pacifist, as is shown by the opening lines of 'An Horation Ode upon Cromwel's Return from Ireland':

> The forward Youth that would appear
> Must now forsake his Muses dear,
> Nor in the Shadows sing
> His Numbers languishing.
> 'Tis time to leave the books in dust,
> And oyl th'unused Armour's rust[.]

Given the political circumstances and his own personal situation – he was by now Cromwell's Latin Secretary – Marvell's advice that we "both act and know" is necessarily circumspect. And though the ostensible theme of 'Upon Appleton House' is the bucolic ideal of a withdrawal from the world into a state where the pleasures of contemplation annihilate, as Marvell has it in 'The Garden', "all that's made/To a green thought in a green Shade", still he knew that it is to the world of action that we must return. Never more so than at times of civic crisis.

It is a conclusion Auden himself must have had in mind. As noted earlier, Auden distrusted all utopias yet he returned to the theme in 'New Year Letter', where he takes issue with the idea that art can ever be "A midwife to society":

> What they should do, or how or when
> Life-order comes to living men
> [Art] cannot say, for it presents
> Already lived experience
> Through a convention that creates
> Autonomous completed states.
> Though their particulars are those
> That each particular artist knows,
> Unique events that once took place
> Within a unique time and space,

In the new field they occupy,
The unique serves to typify,
Becomes, though still particular,
An algebraic formula,
An abstract model of events
Derived from dead experience,
And each life must itself decide
To what and how it be applied.[115]

As Marvell makes plain in 'The Garden', a life lived according to the sole principles of art would be possible only if we could "wander solitary" in Eden. As it is, we must return to the complex world of society if we are to avoid the dangers of solipsism and alienation.[116] As with the verse epistle, such a world is premised upon an acknowledgement both of the existence of other people and the claims they have on our time. Such, anyway, is the conclusion implicit throughout the dialectical arrangements of 'New Year Letter' and which, a decade later, in the final paragraph of *The Enchaféd Flood*, Auden was to return to and reiterate more fully:

> We live in a new age in which the artist neither can have such a unique heroic importance nor believes in the Art-God enough to desire it, an age, for instance, when the necessity of dogma is once more recognized, not as the contradiction of reason and feeling but as their ground and foundation, in which the heroic image is not the nomad wanderer through the desert or over the ocean, but the less exciting figure of the builder, who renews the ruined walls of the city.[117]

XI

Accounting for the vicissitudes in critical response to Adorno's writings, Fredric Jameson has said that "It is not, indeed, people who change, but rather situations".[118] Much the same could be said about Auden's reputation, both during his life and posthumously. We have already noted how Jarrell's review of *The Double Man* stressed the fact that Auden appeared to be back-tracking from the modernist project and that 'New Year Letter', with its borrowings from the 17th and 18th centuries, has much in common with, say, Stravinsky's ironic and playful use of earlier musical forms in his neoclassical compositions. Since Jarrell wrote his review, however, a number of critics, including Jameson, Tyrus Miller and Peter Nicholls, have seen neo-classicism not so much as a retreat as a marked development, what Jameson calls a "transition" between modernism and postmodernism. It is a transition that Jameson has defined thus:

> 'late modernism' – the last survivals of a properly modernist view of art and the world after the great political and economic break of the Depression, where, under Stalinism or the Popular Front, Hitler or the New Deal, some new conception of social realism achieves the status of momentary cultural dominance by way of collective anxiety and world war.[119]

Central to this movement, Jameson argues, were artists "who had the misfortune to span two eras and the luck to find a time capsule of isolation or exile in which to spin out unseasonable forms".[120] Likewise Miller, in developing Jameson's defence of the concept of Late Modernism, sees the experience of exile and migration as central to the phenomena and its renewed political engagement:

> late modernist literature … mark[s] the lines of flight artists took where an obstacle, the oft mentioned 'impasse' of modernism, interrupted progress on established paths. Facing an unexpected stop, late modernists took a detour into the political regions that high modernism had managed to view from the distance of a closed car, as part of a moving panorama of forms and colours.[121]

What is significant about Miller's argument is that it throws into doubt whether critics are right in ever having seen Auden as a modernist. He certainly never disengaged himself from politics in the way Eliot and Yeats did. As we have seen, Auden's preferred viewpoint was not the "closed car" but the cockpit or, in 'New Year Letter', a plate glass window overlooking Manhattan. Indeed, Miller's summary seems ever more fitted to explaining some of the reasons why 'New Year Letter' adopted the form it did, and why it received such a mixed critical reception:

> Late Modernist writing was not particularly successful in either critical or commercial terms, and each work tended toward formal singularity, as if the author had hit a dead end and had

to begin again. In content, too, these works reflected a closure of the horizon of the future: they are permeated with a foreboding of decline and fall, of radical contingency and absurd death.[122]

Though 'New Year Letter' gives in to neither closure nor death, it does lend a coherent voice to the historical despair described by Miller:

> Twelve months ago in Brussels, I
> Heard the same wishful-thinking sigh
> As round me, trembling on their beds,
> Or taut with apprehensive dreads,
> The sleepless guests of Europe lay
> Wishing the centuries away,
> And the low mutter of their vows
> Went echoing through her haunted house,
> As on the verge of happening
> There crouched the presence of The Thing.[123]

What Auden may also have meant his readers to hear in these lines is a voice and an apprehension and dread similar to that of the anonymous author of *Beowulf* when he describes how the Geats lay in their beds awaiting Grendel's attack:

> Then down the brave man lay with his bolster
> under his head and his whole company
> of sea-rovers at rest beside him.
> None of them expected he would ever see
> his homeland again or get back
> to his native place and the people who reared him.[124]

A further part of Jarrell's criticism of 'New Year Letter' was that it was too caught up in 'scientific' or 'modern' thought. "The poets of the last generation," Jarrell writes:

> were extremely erudite, but their erudition was of the rather specialized type that passed as currency of the realm in a somewhat literary realm. About Darwin, Marx, Freud and Co., about all characteristically 'scientific' or 'modern' thinkers,

most of them concluded regretfully: 'If they had not existed, it would not have been necessary to ignore them.'[125]

Auden's response to this might simply have been to quote Locke's *An Essay Concerning Human Understanding*: "Our business here is not to know all things, but those which concern our Conduct."

Jarrell's belief that these 'modern' thinkers are not fit subject matter for Modernist poetry is an argument which accepts precisely that fracture between the languages of art and science which Auden was concerned with healing. It is a legacy which Susan Buck-Morss summarises thus:

> Ever since the seventeenth century, in the wake of the Newtonian revolution in science, the realms of art and knowledge, 'mere' fiction and factual 'truth,' had been split into two opposing camps. In the context of this dualism, Enlightenment reason took the side of science. The *philosophes* were hostile to art, which, secularized and hence robbed of its aura as a theological symbol, was no longer considered a form of truth in itself but rather a pedagogic tool, a means of moral persuasion ... In protest against the Enlightenment, nineteenth-century romanticism championed art as a source of truth in its own right, but it remained within the existing paradigm by accepting without question the notion of a dichotomy between reason and art.[126]

There were exceptions. We might think of Goethe, for example, or Coleridge and Shelley. But Buck-Morss' argument about the specialisation of knowledge has much in common with what Eliot had to say about the "dissociation of sensibility" that"'set in" in the 17th century and "from which we have never recovered". The comparison Eliot famously drew between the Metaphysical poet who "possessed a mechanism of sensibility which could devour any kind of experience" and later poets (Eliot singled out Dryden[127] and Milton) who "performed certain poetic functions so magnificently well that the magnitude of the effect concealed the absence of others", is only part of a wider argument most famously attacked in Snow's *Two Cultures* (1959).

With western society becoming increasingly industrialised and automated, science, as technology, was a daily part of life. War, as Spain had proved, would only make it more so. Furthermore, Auden knew that recent developments in scientific thought meant that our understanding of the parameters of the physical universe had shifted. While Newton and the 17th century could assume a clear separation between observer and observed, no such assumption was possible after what Heisenberg had to say about quantum physics. And these new scientific discoveries and terms could be applied not only to the natural universe but to human society. It is in these terms that Auden chose to describe the poet of 'New Year Letter': "A particle, I must not yield/To particles who claim the field,/Nor trust the demagogue who raves,/A quantum speaking for the waves".[128]

What Auden is suggesting would have seemed impossible prior to 1927. Before then Newtonian physics held that the path a particle took was not only fixed but also pre-determined. With the formulation of his Uncertainty Principle, Heisenberg challenged this. Stating that it is impossible to specify simultaneously the position and momentum of a particle with either any certainty or precision, his theory further states that the small changes in a particle's trajectory are caused by the fact that the particles are being observed. In other words, just by being present human beings affect the course of nature. By drawing a parallel, then, between the individual human will and atomic determinism, Auden challenged those assumptions spelled out in the title poem of *Another Time* – "So many try to say Not Now,/So many have forgotten how/To say I am, and would be/Lost, if they could, to History" – by emphasising the moral, ethical and artistic necessity of choice. It also marks a point at which Auden was able to reconcile the seeming contradictions between science and literature. However rarely, the two could meet, as Freud acknowledged in the opening paragraph of 'Das Unheimliche': "it does occasionally happen that [the scientist] has to interest himself in some particular province of that subject [i.e. literature]; and this province usually proves to be a rather remote one."[129]

The language of quantum physics also plays a part in 'New Year Letter' because of the way in which it assumes an objectivity that, however paradoxical it might seem, implicates the subject. It therefore provides precisely that "model of 'disinterested' discourse [that] held the particular interests of participants in check and rendered their private identities irrelevant".[130] This enabled Auden to balance the competing claims of the private and the public self. We can go further and say that the reference to Heisenberg's Uncertainty Principle, which states that time and place – position and velocity – have no meaning in nature makes, in David Kennedy's words, "traditional metaphors and narratives redundant and offers the liberating challenge of writing new ones".[131]

Heisenberg was hardly the first to challenge Newton's authority (that honour goes to Newton himself!). In the past, however, the source of the challenge had come from the artist rather than the scientist. 'Outsiders' such as Blake, Rousseau, Baudelaire and Kierkegaard – exiles from, in George Steiner's words, "the spaces, relations and events that advanced mathematics deals with [and which have] no necessary correlation with sense-data"[132] – continued to shout insults, weep, mutter and go mad in defence of a "common grammar all have grounds/To study." Only now modern science had proved them right: "for their guess is proved:/It is the Mover that is moved./Whichever way we turn, we see/ Man captured by his liberty,/ The measurable taking charge/Of him who measures". Against such enlightened despotism – an analysis which pre-empts Adorno and Horkheimer by only a couple of years – Auden offers a vision of society which proposes a life of conscious choice and responsibility. And he locates it in multi-cultural America:

> More even than in Europe, here
> The choice of patterns is made clear
> Which the machine imposes, what
> Is possible and what is not,
> To what conditions we must bow
> In building the Just City now.[133]

The split – or what Steiner calls a history of "progressive untranslatability"[134] – between the languages of art and science is central to 'New Year Letter', as it was to Adorno. Indeed, part of Adorno's volte-face in relation to the use of aphorisms was his belief that after the Holocaust, philosophy, particularly the Germanic tradition of Kant, Hegel and Marx, could no longer make any claims for providing a blueprint for what might constitute the Good Life and the Just City. Such philosophies could only examine the observable facts of what our 'damaged' life is like, hoping to provide an interpretation of sufficient rigour to allow intimations of a possible undamaged life to shine through. Such was the purpose of art.[135] This isn't to say that Adorno favoured transforming philosophy from a scientific inquiry into an artwork, simply that he rejected as extremely dangerous to human well-being the view that art and science were irreconcilable. For as 'New Year Letter' explains, both simply offer differing views of understanding the world, "That one in tangents, this in chords".

Throughout 'New Year Letter' Auden imports into the text a wide range of intertextual references, so that the poem ends up resembling Eliot or Pound's High Modernism much more closely than Jarrell allowed. What the poem also provides is a dazzling array of quotes and aphorisms from Italian, Latin, French, Greek and German. This may be a part of the poem's dedication to European civilisation, or it may simply be an accurate representation of the number of migrant tongues American culture had had to assimilate. What it also does is parallel Joyce's *Ulysses*, from which it inherits a concern for verbal and linguistic dexterity, as well as a structure that manipulates time and place. Though the poem is ostensibly set during the evening and early hours of New Year's Eve and New Year's Day, like *Ulysses* it is far ranging in both its historical and intellectual references. Amongst the poem's many achievements, as Edward Mendelson has commented, is the seamless way these languages "fall neatly into metrical step at Auden's command".[136] Mendelson might have gone further and made the connection Auden no doubt intended: the debt that English owed to other languages, and how it is itself a record of centuries of migration. What the inclusion of these quotations in their original language also does, especially in a remarkable passage from Part Three of the poem, is to signal the fact that there are certain experiences and states of mind which belong specifically to a particular language and which cannot be readily translated.

XII

"Do you care what happens to England?" Auden asked rhetorically in a letter to E.R. Dodds. His reply must have been easier to write in America than it would have been in England:

Qua England, not in the least. To me England is bits of the country like the Pennine Moors and my English friends. If they were all safely out of the country, I should feel about the English as I feel about the Spanish or the Chinese or the Germans. It matters what happens to them as it matters to all members of the human race, but my concern is as a fellow human being not as a fellow countryman.[137]

Auden's response to the insular claims of nationalism is, like Melville's Bartleby, to say "I prefer not to". But in a time of war, as Auden recognised, such a position was something of a luxury: "But where to serve and when and how?/O none escape these questions now". His response, eccentric but conscious, was to accept and serve not a geographical England but the English language in all its verbal promiscuity: "England to me is my own tongue,/And what I did when I was young."[138]

But English wasn't the only language the adult Auden could speak, read or write. His learning other languages, including German, augmented his sense of himself as English. And so when he comes to "tell ... what we mean" as regards his early childhood experiences of the English landscape and his love of abandoned mining equipment, it is not English but German he turns to in order to express himself, alerting us to the fact that what he felt was something unnameable (and unknowable?) in his native tongue:

> Alone in the hot day I knelt
> Upon the edge of shafts and felt
> The deep *Urmutterfurcht* that drives
> Us into knowledge all our lives,
> The far interior of our fate
> To civilise and to create,
> *Das Weibliche* that bids us come
> To find what we're escaping from.
> There I dropped pebbles, listened, heard
> The reservoir of darkness stirred;
> 'O deine Mutter kehrt dir nicht
> Wieder. Du selbst bin ich, dein' Pflicht
> Und liebe. Brach sie nun mein Bild.'
> And I was conscious of my guilt.[139]

What *was* expressible was a pervasive sense of guilt that returns us to that complex network of historical associations that underpin 'Refugee Blues'. What is also unmistakable in this passage is Auden's portrayal of his childhood self as acting out some form of unconscious alienation or exile, figured in the reference to "The far interior of our fate", which pre-empted the sexual 'homecoming' of the time he spent in Berlin in the late 1920s.[140] What is unarguable is that the poem shows Auden responding to and empathising with the plight of German refugees to such an extent that he has now begun thinking and speaking/writing in their language. If readers back in Britain remained in any doubt as to why he left England, 'New Year Letter' is surely as clear an *apologia* as he could write. It is unthinkable that Auden could have expressed this kind of identification and solidarity for the German victims of Nazism at a time when it was not simply the Nazis but the whole German nation – and language – with which Britain was at war.[141] We can take this sense of empathy further, bearing in mind that of the defining features of the 'uncanny', Freud noted, is that the word *heimlich* has among "its different shades of meaning ... one which is identical with its opposite, '*unheimlich*' ... Thus *heimlich* is a word the meaning of which develops in the direction of ambivalence, until it finally coincides with its opposite, unheimlich".[142] And it is foreign words and phrases which, Shierry Weber Nicholsen argues, constitute "the quintessence of the Other of and within language."[143]

Weber Nicholsen is summarising that aspect of Adorno's thinking which was profoundly affected firstly by his experience of resisting German nationalism at home, and secondly by his becoming an émigré in America. "Foreign words," Adorno wrote in 'Words From Abroad', "constituted little cells of resistance to the nationalism of the First World War. The pressure to think along prescribed lines forced resistance into deviant and harmless paths, but in times of crisis gestures that are in themselves irrelevant often acquire dispro-portionate symbolic significance".[144] Adorno continues, however, by arguing that the use of foreign words in this way is not down to purely political considerations:

> Rather, since language is erotically charged in its words, at least for the kind of person who is capable of expression, love drives us into foreign words. In reality, it is that love that sets

off the indignation over their use ... At that time foreign words
made us blush, like saying the name of a secret love.[145]

Adorno's formulation might remind us of what Stravinsky said about
his own relationship to neo-classicism and the music of the past:
"Whatever interests me, whatever I love, I wish to make my own." It
also brings us to the heart of so many of Auden's concerns, allowing
us to see his writing in German as both an act of political defiance
and a coded form of sexual affirmation, with exile and homosexuality
existing in a state similar to that suggested in 'The Exiles'. It is even
possible that such a linguistic practice can transcend the privileges
of class and education – charges levelled at Adorno for incorporating
excessive foreign words into a radio broadcast entitled 'Short
Commentaries on Proust' – in that, as Weber Nicholsen says, they
can contain "the explosive force of enlightenment":

> Tact, the ability to make fine distinctions without resorting to
> rigid definitions, an essential feature of humanness, is the 'seal
> of authority' of the utopian as opposed to the oppressive use
> of foreign words.[146]

Thus language becomes the cornerstone on which the Just City is
to be erected. And in a similar way to how, in his elegy for Yeats,
Auden used images of the city to figure the relationship between
language, the poet and society, so Adorno turned to similar material
in an early unpublished essay called 'On the Use of Foreign Words':

> For the old organic words are like gas lights in a street where
> the violet light of an oxyacetylene welding apparatus suddenly
> flames out; they stare into it, inconsolably past, prehistoric
> and mythological. The power of an unknown, genuine language
> that is not open to any calculus, a language that arises in pieces
> and out of the disintegration of the existing one; this negative,
> dangerous, and yet assuredly promised power is the true
> justification of foreign words.[147]

Adorno's vision of outmoded words staring into the light of a
technological present and knowing themselves as "inconsolably past,
prehistoric and mythological" is remarkably similar to those lines in
'In Memory of Sigmund Freud' where the "fauna of the night,/and

shades that still waited to enter/the bright circle of [Freud's] recognition/turned elsewhere". Where they subsequently turn – or are turned – is, as we have seen, crucial. Rejected, they become the repressed and exiled powers described in 'Where do They come from?'; welcomed in to the Just City they are charged with those erotic, creative powers which gathered to mourn Freud's death in exile:

> One rational voice is dumb. Over his grave
> the household of Impulse mourns one dearly loved:
> > sad is Eros, builder of cities,
> > and weeping anarchic Aphrodite.

In using the form he does in 'New Year Letter', Auden exposes precisely these ambiguities. The verse epistle shared many of the attributes of the Enlightenment – common sense, moderation, reason over emotion, elegance over brevity – and its discursive confidence came from a renewed sense of the power of Empire, radical discoveries in the sciences, and an awareness of the new horizons which were being opened up by the exploration of the non-European world. All of these influences contributed to a belief in Progress. Having said this, such intellectual, artistic and spiritual developments also left many feeling threatened and isolated. What safeguards were there that the individual would not be left behind and find themselves stranded? What is more, when so much that one previously took for granted about the world and one's place in it was suddenly open to question, how was the individual to guarantee that the world as they experienced it actually existed rather than being mere "fragments of the solitary mind."[148] Such, as was proposed earlier, was the case with those Augustan poets who turned to the verse epistle as confirmation of the fact that not only themselves but a small coterie of readers existed capable of understanding and appreciating the allusions and sentiments of their poetry.

For all its urbanity, 'New Year Letter' must also be understood as Auden's renewed attempt to rid himself of those inherited cultural impulses which he characterised to Kallmann as an "O-so-genteel anti-semitism". The poem is riddled with ambivalences and is constantly moving in the direction not of rational argument but, as the prayer-like ending makes explicit, the uncertainties and doubts of faith. Once again there are interesting parallels to be drawn with the 17th century which, as James Sutherland has written, was "an age in which poetry had come more and more to deal with public concerns, it had become less easy to express the inner and private life of the spirit".[149] As with the writing of poetry, prayer is addressed *to* someone or something. It is, if nothing else, evidence of a belief that the universe exists somewhere other than as a product of one's own consciousness. And it is significant, given what has been said about the ways in which Auden used animal imagery in his memorial to Freud, that 'New Year Letter' ends on a similar note, one which unites the various themes of the poem:

> O Unicorn among the cedars,
> To whom no magic charm can lead us,
> White childhood moving like a sigh
> Through the green woods unharmed in thy
> Sophisticated innocence,
> To call thy true love to the dance,
> O dove of science and of light,
> Upon the branches of the night,
> O Ichthus playful in the deep
> Sea lodges that forever keep
> Their secret of excitement hidden,
> O sudden Wind that blows unbidden,
> Parting the quiet reeds, O Voice
> Within the labyrinth of choice ...
> Instruct us in the civil art
> Of making from the muddled heart
> A desert and a city where
> The thoughts that have labour there
> May find locality and peace[.][150]

What is invoked here is a series of primal forms symbolising various human achievements in the realms of art, science and politics. Addressed defiantly *elsewhere*, Auden uses the prayer to unite the lyric and the epistolary, providing a form capable of integrating the private – faith – and the public – science. The result is that the world is both knowable and changeable, whether through art, Freud's psychoanalysis or Marx's dialectics. Critics who had discerned the influence on Auden of German poetry, in particular Rilke, immediately seized on lines such as these. Among them, as noted earlier, was Malcolm Cowley, who, after listing those German writers referred to in 'New Year Letter', continues:

> Auden is German not only in his sources, but in his manner of writing poetry. He delights in the German abstractions of which Edmund Wilson said that they convey 'almost the impression of primitive gods. They are substantial, and yet they are a kind of pure beings; they are abstract, and yet they nourish.'[151]

It was an influence of which Auden himself was not unaware.

In late summer 1939, Auden wrote a review of a new translation of Rilke's poetry for *The New Republic*. Between the time he wrote it and its publication in September, Britain had declared war on Germany. Auden's words are as clear a definition of the moral, ethical and artistic reasons behind his voluntary exile and rejection of nationalism as we could wish:

> It is, I believe, no accident that as the international crisis becomes more and more acute, the poet to whom writers are increasingly drawn should be the one who felt that it was pride and presumption to interfere with the lives of others (for each is unique and the apparent misfortunes of each may be his very way of salvation) ... When the ship catches fire, it seems only natural to rush importantly to the pumps, but perhaps one is only adding to the general confusion and panic: to sit still and pray seems selfish and unheroic, but it may be the wisest and most helpful course.[152]

In writing a poem made up of the decontextualised or defamiliarised fragments of previous texts alongside fragments of languages other than English; in assimilating aspects of scientific discourse so as to provide poetry with a renewed means of figuring the relationship between the individual and society; in stressing the central role of the exile or refugee in contemporary European and American history, Auden wrote, for all its flaws, a poem of greater cohesion, vision and intellectual vigour than might reasonably have been expected from a man in his position. His doing so, as was discussed earlier in response to Jameson's and Miller's analysis of

Late Modernism, was part of wider developments in European and American literature.

Notes

1   W.H. Auden, 'American Poetry' in *The Dyer's Hand* (London: Faber and Faber, 1963), 356.
2   See Stan Smith, *W.H. Auden* (London: Writers and Their Work, 1997), 51.
3   Joseph Brodsky, 'On "September 1, 1939" by W.H. Auden' in *Less Than One: Selected Essays* (New York: Farrar Straus Giroux, 1986), 305-306.
4   Eamon Grennan, 'American Relations' in *Irish Poetry Since Kavanagh*, ed. Theo Dorgan (Dublin: Four Courts Press, 1996), 95.
5   Stan Smith, 'Auden's Oedipal Dialogues with W.B. Yeats' in *W.H. Auden: The Language of Learning and the Language of Love*, eds. Katherine Bucknell and Nicholas Jenkins (Oxford: Clarendon Press, 1994), 155.
6   W.H. Auden, *The English Auden: Poems, Essays and Dramatic Writings 1927-1939*, ed. Edward Mendelson, 2nd printing (with corrections) (London: Faber and Faber, 1978), 223.
7   "He was unwilling to talk about his experiences," wrote Isherwood, who saw him immediately on his return, "but they had obviously been unsatisfactory; he felt that he hadn't been allowed to be really useful." Stephen Spender recorded much the same thing: "He returned home after a very short visit of which he never spoke." Quoted in Humphrey Carpenter, *W.H. Auden: A Biography* (London: Unwin Paperbacks, 1983), 215.
8   Ibid., 206-207.
9   Quoted in Stephen Coote, *W.B. Yeats: A Life* (London: Hodder and Stoughton, 1998), 548.
10   Louis MacNeice, *The Poetry of W.B. Yeats* (1941), (London: Faber and Faber, 1967), 156.
11   W.B. Yeats, *The Poems*, ed. Daniel Albright (London: Everyman's Library, 1992), 340, 341.
12   W.H. Auden, *The English Auden*, 237.
13   Quoted in Valentine Cunningham, *Spanish Front: Writers on the Civil War* (Oxford: OUP, 1986), 220.
14   *New Verse*, nos.26-27 (1937), 10.
15   Quoted in Humphrey Carpenter, *W.H. Auden: A Biography* (London: Unwin Paperbacks, 1983), 217.
16   W.H. Auden, *The English Auden*, 212.

[17] Valentine Cunningham, *Spanish Front: Writers on the Civil War*, xxxi.
[18] W.H. Auden, *The English Auden*, 211.
[19] Valentine Cunningham, *Spanish Front: Writers on the Civil War*, xxxi.
[20] See Hugh Thomas, *The Spanish Civil War* (London: Eyre and Spottiswoode, 1964), 419.
[21] W.H. Auden, 'The Poet & The City' in *The Dyer's Hand*, 85.
[22] *The English Auden*, 396.
[23] Christopher Isherwood, *Christopher and His Kind* (London: Methuen & Co., 1977), 251.
[24] W.H. Auden, *The Dyer's Hand*, 358.
[25] Christian Meier, *Athens: A Portrait of the City in its Golden Age*, trans. Robert and Rita Kimber (London: Pimlico, 2000), 45.
[26] George Szirtes, 'Being Remade As An English Poet' in *The New Hungarian Quarterly* (30:113), 156.
[27] Richard Davenport-Hines, *Auden* (London: Minerva, 1996), 182.
[28] Auden first published 'Lay your sleeping head, my love', 'Palais [sic] des Beaux Arts', 'The Novelist', 'Refugee Blues', 'The Leaves of Life' and 'In Memory of Ernst Toller' in *New Writing*. Lehmann also published translations of Lorca's 'The Dawn' (trans. A.L. Lloyd) and 'Song' (trans. Stanley Richardson). In his anthology *Poems from New Writing: 1936-1946* (London: John Lehmann, 1946) Lehmann has this to say about poetry and the civil war in Spain:

> The Spanish War is a gloomy milestone for creative writers, marking as it does the second descent of the twentieth century into the violence of International anarchy, a descent made the more destructive for them by the warring ideologies with warring empires. Rare and lucky were the poets who could find the calm and leisure in the midst of such events for continuous poetic creation at the deepest level; and yet these events, by the passions they excited and the drama they manifested, involving the oldest beliefs and allegiances and spiritual hankerings of our civilisation, were material that most young poets would find it difficult to refuse in any age. Our age, however, has been distinguished above all ages by the tendency, in all fields of activity, to exploit whatever comes to hand as immediately and intensively as possible (5-6).

[29] Federico García Lorca, *Selected Poems*, Trans. Merryn Williams (Newcastle-upon-Tyne: Bloodaxe, 1992), 189.
[30] W.H. Auden, *The English Auden*, 243.
[31] W.B. Yeats, *The Poems*, 838.

32   Federico García Lorca, 'Play and Theory of the Duende' (1933) in *Deep Song and Other Prose*, trans. Christopher Maurer (New York: New Direction, 1980), 49-50.

33   See Ian Gibson, *Federico García Lorca* (London: Faber and Faber, 1990). In 'Theory and Function of the *Duende*' Lorca turns to the example of the bullfighter whenever he wants to clarify what he has to say about the nature of poetry. The death of Sánchez Mejías quickly assumed, therefore, the status of prophecy for Lorca: "Ignacio's death is like mine, the trial run of mine" (quoted in Gibson, 391). This extraordinary sense of empathy for his dead friend and the circumstances of his death remained with Lorca for the remaining two years of his life. A bullfighter's death, he explained, had nothing to do with sport but was "a religious mystery," "the public and solemn enactment of the victory of human virtue over the lower instincts ... the superiority of spirit over matter" (Ibid, 391). Such a "mythical view", as Gibson calls it, is not dissimilar to aspects of the final section of Auden's elegy for Yeats.

34   Joseph Brodsky, 'To Please A Shadow' in *Less Than One*, 361-362.

35   Quoted in Edward Callan, 'Disenchantment With Yeats: From Singing-Master to Ogre' in *Modern Critical Views: W.H. Auden*, ed. Harold Bloom (New York: Chelsea House Publishers, 1983), 163.

36   W.H. Auden, *The Dyer's Hand*, 81.

37   See *W.B. Yeats: A Life*, 544. Ossietsky was successfully awarded the 1935 Nobel Peace Prize. Hitler saw it as politically motivated and took offence, forbidding German citizens to thereafter accept any Nobel prizes.

38   W.H. Auden, *Collected Poems*, ed. Edward Mendelson (London: Faber and Faber, 1976), 249.

39   W.H. Auden, *The English Auden*, 455-456.

40   Ibid., 405.

41   John Berger, *Success and Failure of Picasso* (London: Penguin, 1965), 167-169.

42   Stan Smith, 'Disenchantment With Yeats: From Singing-Master to Ogre', 164.

43   Edward Mendelson, *Later Auden* (London: Faber and Faber, 1999), 63-64.

44   Quoted in Federico García Lorca, *Poet in New York*, trans. Greg Simon and Steven F. White, ed. and with an introduction by Christopher Maurer (London: Penguin, 1988), xi-xii.

45   Ibid., 202.

46   Ibid., 11.

47   Subsequently included in *The Dyer's Hand* the essay was originally given as the first of Auden's 1957 Oxford Lectures.

48 W.H. Auden, 'Robert Frost' in The *Dyer's Hand*, 348.
49 W.H. Auden, *Collected Longer Poems* (London: Faber and Faber, 1974), 255-256.
50 Klee's experience was not without its ironies. Though born near Bern, Klee's father was German and so, consequently, was he. Germany, however, was where he lived, serving in the German army during the Great War, and teaching at the Bauhaus from 1920 to 1931, before becoming a professor at the Düsseldorf Academy. In 1933 he was dismissed from his post and he returned to Switzerland. Repeated applications for citizenship were turned down, and he died a foreigner in his own country in 1940.
51 The word appears in 'New Year Letter' itself, where Auden uses it to refer to the ways in which industries in the States sought out the cheapest labour market, and in doing so undermined the social and economic fabric of a stable society:

> ... and even yet
> A *Völkerwanderung* occurs:
> Resourceful manufacturers
> Trek southward by progressive stages
> For sites with no floor under wages,
> No ceiling over hours; and by
> Artistic souls in towns that lie
> Out in the weed and pollen belt
> The need for sympathy is felt,
> And east to hard New York they come;
> And self-respect drives Negroes from
> The one-crop and race-hating delta
> To northern cities helter-skelter;
> And in jalopies there migrates
> A rootless tribe from windblown states
> To suffer further westward where
> The tolerant Pacific air
> Makes logic seem so silly, pain
> Subjective, what he seeks so vain
> The Wanderer may die[.]

52 Quoted in Donald Mitchell, *The Language of Modern Music*, with an Introduction by Edward W. Said (London: Faber and Faber, 1993), 98.
53 Theodor W. Adorno, *Minima Moralia: Reflections from Damaged Life* (1951), trans. E.F.N. Jephcott (London: Verso, 1978), 50.
54 Quoted in Paul Griffiths, *Modern Music: A Concise History* (London:

Thames and Hudson, 1994), 63.

55 John Fuller, *A Reader's Guide to W.H. Auden* (London: Thames and Hudson 1970), 176. Time, or the artist's need to assert control over it, was uppermost in Auden's mind when writing in the *New York Times* in February 1951 about collaborating with Stravinsky on his neo-classical opera, *The Rake's Progress*: "To achieve anything today, an artist has to develop a conscious strictness in respect of time which in former ages might have seemed neurotic and selfish, for he must never forget that he is living in a state of siege. His workroom has also to be a fortress; the stop-watch and the metronome are his shield and buckler. Similarly, in a howling storm, a theatrical and purple artistic style is ridiculous; only clarity and economy will work as charms against the void. Intervals, as Stravinsky says, must be treated like dollars." See Robert Craft (ed.), *Stravinsky: Selected Correspondences*, Vol. 1 (London: Faber and Faber, 1982), 302.

56 Igor Stravinsky and Robert Craft, *Conversations with Igor Stravinsky* (London: Faber and Faber, 1979), 129.

57 Robert Craft, 'Music and Words' in *Stravinsky in the Theatre*, ed. Minna Lederman (New York: Pellegrini and Cudahy, 1949), 86.

58 See *W.H. Auden: The Critical Heritage*, ed. John Haffenden (London: Routledge and Kegan Paul, 1983), 311.

59 Richard Davenport-Hines, *Auden*, 87.

60 Michael Tippett, *Those Twentieth Century Blues: An Autobiography* (London: Hutchinson, 1991), 47.

61 E.M. Forster, *Two Cheers For Democracy* (London: Edward Arnold & Co., 1951), 43.

62 Ibid., 47.

63 Ibid., 35.

64 "A nasty side of our nation's character has been scratched up – the sniggering side. People who would not ill-treat Jews themselves, or even be rude to them, enjoy tittering over their misfortune; they giggle when pogroms are instituted by someone else and synagogues defiled vicariously. 'Serve them right really, Jews!' … The grand Nordic argument 'He's a bloody Capitalist so he must be a Jew, and as he's a Jew he must be a red,' has already taken root' (Ibid., 25).

65 Jorge Luis Borges, 'Notes on Germany & the War' in *The Total Library: Non-Fiction 1922-1986*, ed. Eliot Weinberger, trans. Esther Allen, Suzanne Jill Levine and Eliot Weinberger (London: Allen Lane/Penguin Press), 201.

66 Edward Mendelson, *Later Auden*, 57.

67 Ibid., 36.

68 It was not the first time Auden had written blues-based poems. 'Blues'

and 'Roman Wall Blues' both date from 1937. 'Blues', like 'Calypso', was written for Louis MacNeice's future wife, the émigré cabaret singer Hedli Anderson; and 'Roman Wall Blues' tells of a Roman soldier on duty at Hadrian's Wall. Reviewing *Another Time* in *New Statesman and Nation*, T.C. Worsley commented that Auden "has gone as far as he can along the road to creating a popular poetry; the other necessary condition, the change in society which will remarry culture with everyday life, is another problem, and does not belong to him as a poet" (see *W.H. Auden: The Critical Heritage*, 303).

69   See *Uncommon People: Resistance, Rebellion and Jazz* (London: Weidenfield & Nicolson, 1998). Hobsbawm is particularly sharp on "the milieu in which the extraordinary art of blues and jazz was incubated", a milieu not unconnected to Auden's movements during the pre-war years:

> The most immediate impact of Roosevelt's America on jazz came through the political left, ranging from New Deal enthusiasts for a democratic people's culture to the Communist Party, which took jazz to its bosom from 1935 on. ... The contribution of the left was not only to discover talent, though nobody else took a serious interest in obscure – and, more important, non-commercial – Southern blues singers ... What the left did was – deliberately and successfully – to bring black music out of the ghetto by mobilizing that curious combination of radical Jews and well-heeled liberal Wasps, the New York establishment (275-276).

70   W.H. Auden, *Collected Poems*, 265.
71   Eric Hobsbawm, *Uncommon People*, 265.
72   Ibid., 239.
73   Michael Tippett, *Those Twentieth Century Blues*, 50.
74   Peter Novick, *The Holocaust and Collective Memory* (London: Bloomsbury, 2000), 9.
75   Ibid., 15.
76   Ibid., 49.
77   "In 1935 Roosevelt had the State Department order American consulates to give refugees 'the most considerate attention and the most generous and favourable treatment possible under the laws ...' But the new policy was not consistently implemented down the line, sometimes the result of anti-Semitism among American officials in Europe. It didn't help matters that many of the consular and visa officers had attended the Georgetown University of Foreign Service, where the dean, the Reverend

Edmund A. Walsh, emphasized in seminars that 'the Jew was ... the entrepreneur [of the Bolshevik Revolution], who recognized his main chance and seized it shrewdly and successfully'" (Ibid.).

[78] W.H. Auden, *Collected Longer Poems*, 80

[79] Ibid., 114.

[80] W.H. Auden, *The English Auden*, 397.

[81] Ibid., 243.

[82] W.H. Auden, *The Enchafèd Flood* (London: Faber and Faber, 1951), 31.

[83] Theodor W. Adorno, *Minima Moralia*, 65-66.

[84] Theodor W. Adorno & Max Horheimer, *Dialectic of Enlightenment* (1944), trans. John Cumming (London: Verso, 1997), 6-9.

[85] Theodor W. Adorno, *Minima Moralia*, 26.

[86] Sigmund Freud, 'The Uncanny' (1919) in *The Penguin Freud Library, Vol. 14* (London: Penguin, 1990), 340.

[87] Naomi B. Sokoloff, *Imagining the Child in Modern Jewish Fiction* (Baltimore and London: The John Hopkins University Press, 1992), xi.

[88] Thomas Mann, *Essays of Three Decades*, trans. H.T. Lower-Porter (London: Secker & Warbourg, n.d.), 426.

[89] Sigmund Freud, 'The Uncanny', 376.

[90] Ibid., 375.

[91] Theodor W. Adorno, *Minima Moralia*, 17.

[92] Walter Benjamin, 'Theses on the Philosophy of History' (1950) in *Illuminations*, trans. Harry Zohn (London: Fontana Press, 1992), 248.

[93] Rosanna Warren, 'Alcaics in Exile: W.H. Auden's 'In Memory of Sigmund Freud'" in *Philosophy and Literature* (20:1), 118.

[94] W.H. Auden, 'Marianne Moore' in *The Dyer's Hand*, 296-297.

[95] Bonnie Kime Scott, (ed.) *The Gender of Modernism: A Critical Anthology* (Bloomington and Indianapolis: Indiana University Press, 1990), 360.

[96] Ibid., 362.

[97] W.H. Auden, *The English Auden*, 397.

[98] This Auden spelled out in curriculum for the 'College of Bards' in 'The Poet & The City': "Courses in prosody, rhetoric and comparative philology would be required of all students, and every student would have to select three courses out of courses in mathematics, natural history, geology, meteorology, archaeology, mythology, liturgics, cooking" (*The Dyer's Hand*, 77).

[99] See Edward Mendelson, *Later Auden*, 86.

[100] W.H. Auden, *The Dyer's Hand*, 300.

[101] John Fuller, *A Reader's Guide to W.H. Auden* (London: Thames and Hudson, 1970), 166.

[102] Lucy McDiarmid, *Auden's Apologia for Poetry* (Princeton, New Jersey: Princeton University Press, 1990), 77.

[103] W.H. Auden, *Collected Longer Poems*, 88.

[104] William C. Dowling, *The Epistolary Moment: The Poetics of the C18th Verse Epistle* (Princeton, New York: Princeton University Press, 1991), 8.

[105] Ibid., 23.

[106] Ibid.

[107] Ibid., 11.

[108] Alexander Pope, *A Critical Edition of the Major Works*, ed. Pat Rogers (Oxford and New York: OUP, 1993), x.

[109] Ibid.

[110] Pope's feelings of literary isolation were expressed in a letter to Swift in March 1736:

> The climate (under our heaven of a court) is but cold and uncertain: the winds rise, and the winter comes on. I find myself but little disposed to build a new house; I have nothing left but to gather up the relics of a wreck, and look about to see what friends I have! Pray whose esteem or admiration should I desire now to procure by my writings? whose friendship or conversation to obtain by 'em? I am a man of desperate fortunes, that is a man whose friends are dead: for I never aimed at any other fortune than in friends (Ibid, 362).

[111] Edward Mendelson, *Later Auden*, 100-101.

[112] John Fuller, *A Reader's Guide to W.H. Auden,* 131.

[113] I am indebted to Professor John Lucas for bringing this point to my attention. The discussion of Marvell, here and elsewhere in this chapter, is a result of his comments.

[114] Andrew Marvell, *Complete Poetry*, ed. George deF. Lord (London: Everyman, 1984), xvii.

[115] W.H. Auden, *Collected Longer Poems*, 81-82.

[116] On 9th May 1936 Thomas Mann gave a speech in Vienna to celebrate Freud's eightieth birthday – a speech he may well have talked about with Auden – in which he discussed, in terms of psychoanalysis, precisely this relationship between the private and public, and the part played by 'contemplation', thought or the creative process. Mann began by commenting on the fact that an author rather than a scientist had been invited to lead the celebrations, drawing the conclusion that though the affinities between literature and psychoanalysis had long been known, his being invited to speak was, to the best of his knowledge, the first

time it had been officially recognised and made public. He continues:

> The relation with the outer world is decisive for the ego, it is the ego's task to represent the world to the id – for its good! For without regard for the superior power of the outer world the id, in its blind striving towards the satisfaction of its instincts, would not escape destruction. The ego takes cognizance of the outer world, it is mindful, it honourably tries to distinguish the objectively real from whatever is an accretion from its inward sources of stimulation. It is entrusted by the id with the lever of action; but between the impulse and the action it has interposed the delay of the thought process, during which it summons experience to its aid and thus possesses a certain regulative superiority over the pleasure principle which rules supreme in the unconscious, correcting it by means of the principle of reality (*Essays of Three Decades*, 417).

[117] W.H. Auden, *The Enchafèd Flood*, 126.

[118] Fredric Jameson, *Late Marxism: Adorno, or The Persistence of the Dialectic* (London: Verso, 1996), 4).

[119] Quoted in Tyrus Miller, *Late Modernism: Politics, Fiction, and the Arts Between the World Wars* (Berkeley, Los Angeles, London: University of California Press, 1999), 10.

[120] Ibid.

[121] Ibid., 13.

[122] Ibid.

[123] W.H. Auden, *Collected Longer Poems*, 79.

[124] Seamus Heaney, *Beowulf* (London: Faber and Faber, 1999), 23.

[125] See *W.H. Auden: The Critical Heritage*, 313.

[126] Susan Buck-Morss, *The Origin of Negative Dialectics: Theodor Adorno, Walter Benjamin and the Frankfurt Institute* (Hassocks, Sussex: The Harvester Press, 1977), 122.

[127] Whereas in 'New Year Letter' Auden includes Dryden – "The master of the middle style" – among the members of the self-elected 'summary tribunal' which sit in judgement of a poet's achievements.

[128] A similar image appears in *The Age of Anxiety*: "The prudent atom/ Simply insists upon its safety now,/Security at all costs; the calm plant/ Masters matter then submits to itself,/Busy but not brave" (*Collected Longer Poems*, 259).

[129] Sigmund Freud, 'The Unhomely', 339.

[130] Craig Calhoun (ed.), *Habermas and the Public Sphere* (Cambridge,

Massachusetts: The MIT Press, 1992), 36.

[131] Kennedy's comments form part of a discussion on the relationship between poetry and science published in *Poetry Review* (83:2) and prompt the following response from Paul Mills which, though it appears to deny the possibility of ever our telling each other anything meaningful, reaches a conclusion that has much in common with aspects of 'New Year Letter':

> The Uncertainty Principle ... defers the position of a reliable narrator. It has to do this because what it observes at one time, given the same set of circumstances, cannot be predicted for another ... Reliable narratives must, can only be, a narrative afterwards, which not only predicts events but somehow knows them, as though they had already happened. But [with] Heisenberg there appeared ... the acute possibility that no narrative afterwards can be found ... A lead might be found in the work of Zbigniew Herbert, whose combinations of science-perspective, philosophy, narrative, religion, ironic monologue, remove discourses from whichever institutions own them ... [This, in turn, allows perspectives no longer] confined to, [say], nationalist epic [or] the spurious build-up of sexual or racial privilege (27-28).

[132] George Steiner, *Language and Silence* (London: Faber and Faber, 1985), 33.

[133] W.H. Auden, *Collected Longer Poems*, 125.

[134] Ibid., 32.

[135] See Simon Jarvis, *Adorno: A Critical Introduction* (Cambridge: Polity Press, 1998), 9.

[136] Edward Mendelson, *Later Auden*, 101.

[137] Ibid., 116.

[138] W.H. Auden, *Collected Longer Poems*, 112.

[139] W.H. Auden, *Collected Longer Poems*, 114. "*Das Weibliche* (the feminine) [is] from *Faust*; *Urmutterfurcht* (primal maternal fear) and the voice of darkness are from *Siegfried*. The voice that speaks from the well to urge the young poet toward adulthood – *deine Mutter kehrt dir nicht/Wieder* – speaks in the language the young [Auden] learned in order to break away ... into psychological and sexual autonomy." (Edward Mendelson, *Later Auden*, 119).

[140] There is also the possibility that Auden's use of German to express some personal experience in a way that only certain people would be able to read refers back to the dedication to Isherwood, written in "dog-German

full of private jokes", which prefaced his first published collection (Christopher Isherwood, *Christopher and His Kind*, 41).

[141] An exchange that took place on a BBC broadcast to India serves to demonstrate precisely the point that, had he remained in England, Auden's poetry would have been hindered or its meaning wilfully misconstrued. On the 8th September 1942 George Orwell organised a talk on war poetry which, though Orwell insisted that the programme was purely literary in subject, had a clear ideological and pedagogic slant. The first poem to be read was Auden's 'September 1, 1941', chosen, so the panel said, because they were looking for a poem which, though unjingoistic, was broadly supportive of the war. Thus the programme, as Adam Piette writes:

> carefully defuses Auden's poem [and] in case the very mention of the word 'political' might signal insidious propaganda ... the editors make a great effort to distance themselves from the word, banishing it back into the 1930s and Social Realism:
>
> ANAND: But Auden is still a political poet. That poem has what you would describe as a direct political purpose.
>
> EMPSON: I think the younger poets who are writing now are really unpolitical. They merely feel that the only way to deal with the war is to start from their personal situation in it.
>
> Empson's intervention is cunning: it draws the Indian student listeners into line by proposing identification with these "younger poets". By identifying themselves, they are really being asked to abandon their own political purposes, which might be dangerously anti-British. Saying that these poets now "are really unpolitical" also manages to disguise the propaganda purposes behind the use of Auden's poem – it was simply a personal choice (Adam Piette, *Imagination at War: British Fiction and Poetry 1939-1945* (London: Papermac, 1995), 153.

[142] Sigmund Freud, 'The Uncanny', 345, 347.

[143] Shierry Weber Nicholsen, *Exact Imagination, Late Work: On Adorno's Aesthetics* (Cambridge, Massachusetts; London, England: The MIT Press, 1997), 84.

[144] Theodor W. Adorno, 'On the Use of Foreign Words' (1920) in *Notes to*

Literature, Vol. 2, ed. Rolf Tiedemann and trans. Shierry Weber Nicholsen (New York: Columbia University Press, 1991), 187.

[145] Ibid.

[146] Shierry Weber Nicholsen, *Exact Imagination*, 88.

[147] Theodor W. Adorno, *Notes to Literature,* Vol. 2, 291.

[148] *The Epistolary* William C. Dowling, 11.

[149] James Sutherland, *English Literature of the Late C17th* (Oxford: Clarendon Press, 1969), 177.

[150] W.H. Auden, *Collected Longer Poems*, 129-130. Compare the role of animals in Auden's invocation to the building of a Just City and that of Marvell in 'Upon Appleton House':

> Why should of all things Man unrul'd
> Such unproportion'd dwellings build?
> The Beasts are by their Denns exprest:
> And Birds contrive an equal Nest;
> The low roof'd Tortoises do dwell
> In cases fit of Tortoise-shell:
> No Creature loves an empty space;
> Their Bodies measure out their place.

[151] Quoted in *W.H. Auden: The Critical Heritage*, 311.

[152] Edward Mendelson, *Later Auden*, 70.

2

Here and There:
Exile as Homecoming in the Poetry of Joseph Brodsky

If the poem has no obvious destination, there's a chance that
we'll all be setting off on an interesting ride.

Paul Muldoon, *Harper's*, September 1999.

I

Adam had only to name the animals once. For the displaced poet it is
a creative act that needs to be revisited and revised. Used to working
within the metaphorical and symbolic connotations language grants
to the phenomenal world, exile means having to re-learn and adapt
oneself to a wholly different set of discursive registers. Or, as Proust
said, "if God the Father had created things by naming them, [the
artist] recreate[s] them by removing their names, or by giving them
another name."[1] Life thus becomes determined by syntax.

"A writer's biography," Brodsky wrote, "is in his twists of
language." With its ghostly pun on twists of fate, what this sentence
alerts us to is the fact that Brodsky denied himself an existence
separate from, or external to, his writing. In doing so he stressed the
fact that exile was less a political than a semantic act. His, therefore,
was a life necessitating the stepping across geographical boundaries
into not only different vocabularies but historical currents. As Derek
Walcott has said, "Grammar is a form of history ... concerned with
the action in a sentence."[2]

This rooting of self-identity in language appears in Brodsky's
biographical essay 'Less Than One' where he recalls, aged 10 or 11,
learning to resist the prevailing Soviet culture. While Marx asserted
that "existence conditions experience", Brodsky counters by arguing
that this is so only until we learn the "art of estrangement". The

phrase is significant, referring as it does to Victor Shklovsky's Formalist theory of *ostranenie*. It is, as Svetlana Boym explains, a provocative word:

> The theory of estrangement is often seen as an artistic declaration of independence, the declaration of art's autonomy from the everyday. Yet in Shklovsky's 'Art as a Device' (1917), estrangement appears more as a device of mediation between art and life. By making things strange, the artist does not simply displace them from an everyday context into an artistic framework; he also helps to 'return sensation' to life itself, to reinvent the world, to experience it anew … [It] harbours the romantic and avant-garde dream of a reverse mimesis: everyday life can be redeemed if it imitates art, not the other way round.[3]

The relationship between art and life is one I want to return to in relation to Osip Mandelstam's influence on Brodsky. For now, however, it should be enough to recognise that for Brodsky the art of estrangement is one which determines that "consciousness is on its own and can both condition and ignore existence."[4] It is, as it were, a process that means entering language not only as a noun but as a verb, able to operate and effect change in the past, present and future tenses. What is of further significance is that Brodsky's essay goes on to associate estrangement with his first remembered lie. For what else is lying but the ability to present a fictionalised self or set of circumstances in language. This becomes still more important when we read that the lie was to do with the complex issues of national and racial identity and access to knowledge within the USSR, and came about when Brodsky visited his school library in order to fill out a membership form. Asked to provide his nationality, he told the library attendant that he didn't know. Refused membership, he was required to go home and ask his parents:

> I never returned to that library, although I did become a member of many others which had the same application forms. I wasn't ashamed of being a Jew, nor was I scared of admitting it … I was ashamed of the word 'Jew' itself – in Russian, '*yevrei*' – regardless of its connotations.[5]

Brodsky's refusal to identify himself as '*yevrei*' has less to do with what the word means than the cultural allusions and slights associated with it and which, to his mind, denied him his individuality. Clearly there is a great deal of hindsight at work in Brodsky's re-telling of the story. Nevertheless, the insistence on seeing identity as inseparable from the structures of language is a coherent and persistent strain throughout his work. The essay continues:

> I remember that I always felt a lot easier with a Russian equivalent of 'kike' – '*zhyd*' (pronounced like André Gide): it was clearly offensive and thereby meaningless, not loaded with allusions. A one-syllable word can't do much in Russian. But when suffixes are applied, or endings, or prefixes, then feathers fly. All this is not to say that I suffered as a Jew at that tender age; it's simply to say that my first lie had to do with my identity.

In order to clarify and focus our attention on the precise nature not only of what Brodsky is saying but the allusive way in which he says it, it's worth unpacking the contents of this paragraph.

As well as providing the reader in English with an aural equivalent for the Russian '*zhyd*' in the form of a rhyme, the mention of Gide is significant in itself. A Nobel laureate in 1947, Gide's fiction and criticism were concerned with precisely those things Brodsky is himself writing about in 'Less Than One': the analysis of the individual's efforts at self-realisation, and the relationship between individual freedom and social responsibility. The reference to Gide has further significance. In 1936, in *Return from the USSR*, having previously supported the Soviet 'experiment', he began to express a profound disillusionment with what he had seen of the state system. The rhyme – '*zhyd*' and 'Gide' – is intended, therefore, to do much more than draw an equivalence in sound; for as Brodsky wrote in reference to the poetry of W.H. Auden, the purpose of rhyme is to provide a poem with "a sense of inevitability. A rhyme turns an idea into law."[6] His preference for the slang term for 'Jew' also suggests an affinity for the demotic rather than the literary or bureaucratic, for language as a fluid, unstable and anti-authoritarian force. Even the mention of prefixes and suffixes in the paragraph have connotations of a refusal to conform, biographically or syntactically. For in Russian vocabulary large families of words are derived from the same root by means of a prefix or a suffix. Thus Brodsky again signals his determination to go it alone.

If these constitute some of the forces against which the young Brodsky defined himself, we need also, if he is not simply to appear an angry young man, take note of those things that he and his generation did attach themselves to. Again, it is not surprising to find that these take the form of literary influences:

> Nobody knew literature and history better, ... nobody could write in Russian better ... nobody despised our times more profoundly. ... This was the only generation of Russians that had found itself, for whom Giotto and Mandelstam were more imperative than their own personal destinies ... [T]hey still retained their love for the non-existent (or existing only in their balding heads) thing called 'civilisation'.[7]

On one level, Brodsky refuses to identify himself with this generation. He prefaces this paragraph by saying "And now I must drop the pronoun 'we'", and throughout he refers to the individuals he is describing as 'they'.[8] And yet there in parentheses is a self-portrait of the already-balding thirty-six year old, declaring his faith in the "non-existent" like a monk in his cell.

Though no doubt necessary if Brodsky was to determine for himself an identity within the Soviet Union, such verbal and syntactic distinctions became unavoidable once he was domiciled in the west. As he goes on to say, talking about his life after being exiled in 1973, "it's been my impression that any experience coming from the Russian realm ... simply bounces off the English language, leaving no visible imprint on its surface."[9] This assertion may contain an ironic reference to Ovid, who wrote (in Homi Bhaba's words) that "like wax, migration only changes the surface of the soul, preserving identity under its protean forms."[10] Whatever the historical and textual echoes, 'We' becomes 'they' and Brodsky consigns himself to the margins of his own formative years.

Written in English, 'Less Than One' declares that experience is untranslatable because languages do not share the same histories. Exile from Russia meant exile from its language; exile from, and in, language meant an estrangement from a younger self who, like Ovid's wax, was stamped by experiences located within that language. This is not to privilege the suffering of those millions who lived and died under Stalinist rule, only to be clear that what they experienced was specific to a certain historical, and therefore linguistic, context. Hardly surprising, then, that Brodsky begins *Less Than One* by declaring "As failures go, attempting to recall the past is like trying to clutch the meaning of existence." For existence, as the essay makes clear, is a matter of vocabulary. And for Brodsky that vocabulary came to belong both to the past, another language and another continent.

It is significant that throughout his writings Brodsky refused to define himself as an exile. Perhaps the word has come to wear too much the patina of the heroic, or offer a special pleading for the individual as a victim of circumstance. What is certain is that at a time in history when, as he says in 'The Condition We Call Exile', "Displacement and misplacement are this century's commonplaces", it seemed to Brodsky that the case of the exiled writer was, when compared to Turkish *Gastarbeiters*, Vietnamese boat people or Mexican wetbacks, a privileged one:

> The truth of the matter is that from a tyranny one can be exiled only to a democracy. For good old exile ain't what it used to be. It isn't leaving civilised Rome for savage Sarmatia anymore … No, as a rule what takes place is a transition from a political and economic backwater to an industrially advanced society with the latest word on individual liberty on its lips. And it must be added that perhaps taking this route is for an exiled writer, in many ways, like going home – because he gets closer to the seat of the ideals which inspired him all along.[11]

None of this is to say that Brodsky was either unfamiliar with or unsympathetic towards the very real difficulties and sorrows that accompany the exile on his or her journey. His poems are brim-full of such things, though usually alluded to with a certain lightness of touch or irony. What we need to keep at the forefront of our minds when reading him is that Brodsky always stressed that exile was a matter of language. It is as if the ethical "going home" mentioned in the passage earlier, when allied to the loss – the profound loss – of a native language, created, in Jacobson's phrase, a "transcendental homelessness". It is his awareness of this that allows his poetry access to the tragic.

II

I want now to follow up these leads along three routes. Firstly, to do what Brodsky himself felt unable to do and to return him to the context of that generation for whom "Giotto and Mandelstam were more imperative than their own personal destinies." In doing so I hope to show how the stance adopted and adapted by Brodsky is itself a continuation and development of a long-standing tradition within Russian literature. Secondly, I want to examine the nature of Brodsky's translation – less in terms of biography than, as George Steiner says, "a theory of language itself". And thirdly, to examine those 'parts of speech' which articulate most clearly the condition of exile, translation and metamorphosis: metaphor and metonym.

"When we think about language", Steiner writes, "the object of our reflection alters in the process ... In short: so far as we experience and 'realize' them in linear progression, time and language are intimately related: they move and the arrow is never in the same place."[12] Steiner's words have much in common with aspects of Brodsky's thinking about the relationship between consciousness and identity as they are 'reflected' (a word to which we will return) in language, and the essential instability of this relationship. Language, Steiner continues, is open at every moment to "mutation". New words enter as old ones lapse from currency (as Brodsky himself demonstrates, favouring the slang *zhyd* over the officialese of *yevrei*), grammatical conventions shift, and taboos are broken while new ones are fashioned. Steiner's ideas also coincide with Brodsky's when, quoting Leonard Bloomfield, he writes that "linguistic change is far more rapid than biological change."[13]

There are moments in history when aspects of these changes are accelerated, while others slow to a crawl. A microcosm of this existed in Russia during the 20th century. Initially the 1917 Revolution heralded rapid and extreme developments in the vocabularies of art: Meyerhold in the theatre, Mayakovsky in poetry, Shostakovich in music, and Malevich in painting, to name just a few. Less welcome was the revolution that was taking place within the Russian language itself, as the jargon of 'class struggle', 'class enemy', and 'dictatorship of the proletariat' began increasingly to enter common usage and to define all social relations. And though massive advances were made in adult literacy during the early years of the Soviet regime,[14] by the time of Stalin's first five-year plan in 1928 and the forced collect-ivisation of agriculture in 1929 the language of the State and that of autonomous artistic and intellectual discourse began to be seen as mutually incompatible. World-wide revolution had been rejected for entrenchment, and the polyphony of new forms of creative expression became a threat to the idea of a homogenous Soviet identity. As Homi Bhabha says:

> To violate the system of naming is to make contingent and indeterminate what Alisdair Macintyre, in his essay on 'Tradition and translation', has described as 'naming *for*: the institutions of naming as the expression and embodiment of the shared standpoint of the community, its traditions of belief and enquiry'.[15]

The revolutionary energies of the immediate Soviet decade were curbed and ultimately crushed when, in 1934, the first All-Union Congress of Soviet Writers accepted socialist realism as the only officially sanctioned form of artistic representation.

Brodsky's description of the bald-headed writer who kept alive the "non-existent" (i.e. non-Soviet) ideal of civilisation throughout these years reminds us not only of the many photographs of Brodsky taken after his arrival in the West but of the last portrait we have of the man with whom, for Brodsky and others, the belief in the survival of Russian civilisation was most closely associated: Osip Mandelstam.

Though born in Warsaw, Mandelstam came to be identified with St Petersburg and that aspect of Russian culture which had always looked to the West for inspiration. Just as the Soviet authorities, by moving the capital from the imperial city of Petersburg to the old Russian capital, Moscow, made a clear statement about the change in cultural perspective and emphasis, so the harassment, persecution and eventual murder of Mandelstam spoke volumes for their attitude towards the kind of culture they aimed to promote. For while St Petersburg was famous for producing such masterpieces as Pushkin's 'French' elegies, Glinka's 'Italianate' opera, and Tchaikovsky's 'Germanic' symphonies – art, in other words, "that felt itself at home in Europe"[16] – the change of emphasis brought about by shifting the seat of political and cultural power to Moscow was one which aimed first at isolating, then alienating, and finally expelling this heritage from the new Empire.

For Mandelstam the influence of a wider European context on Russia was essential. "The Russian language", he wrote in 'Nature and the Word', "just like the Russian national spirit, is formed through ceaseless hybridisation, cross-breeding, grafting and external influences."[17] Mandelstam's is a vision of an organic process of free cultural exchange that could not but find itself at odds with Stalin's policy of consolidating his stranglehold over the country by cauterising this bloodline with the West. Nor can Mandelstam's horticultural imagery have gone down well at a time when the first five-year plan determined to change the Soviet economy from a base in agriculture to heavy industry. In such circumstances, hybridity becomes heresy.[18]

In Mandelstam's holistic vision the Russian language is heir to those "vital forces of Hellenic culture, [which,] having ceded the West to Latin influences and having tarried a while in childless Byzantium, rushed headlong into the bosom of Russian speech, imparting to it the self-assured mystery of the Hellenistic world view, the mystery of free incarnation."[19] It isn't difficult to see why Brodsky and his generation, concerned as they were with asserting their own cultural and biographical identity through a rejection of Soviet culture, came to see Mandelstam's invocation of the logos, the word becoming flesh, as a rallying cry. Neither is it difficult to see why this Jewish-Russian poet should be of special personal significance to Brodsky.[20] To be Jewish in the Soviet Union was, literally, to be exiled from language. As Brodsky himself says, the Russian word *yevrei* appeared in print "nearly as seldom as, say, 'mediastinum' or 'gennel' in American English." To be Jewish was, like certain four-letter words or a name for VD, a taboo, unspoken and unspeakable.[21] Therefore it is as a Jew that Mandelstam is contracted to another tradition that could only have attracted Brodsky's attention.

We have seen in what terms Brodsky recognised exile less as a biographical than a metaphysical condition, one he equated with both homecoming and homelessness; an essentially linguistic phenomenon which, in the only translation into English he made of a poem by Mandelstam, he defined as "the great craft of separation".[22] In holding such a view, he proved himself an heir to Mandelstam, who was in turn a link in that chain of Russian exiles and émigrés stretching back through Tsvetaeva and Nabokov to Pushkin. It was an inheritance that saw Russian writers joining the wider current of European exile that includes Heine, Byron, Mickiewicz, Dante, Petrarch, Ovid and all the writers of the Jewish diaspora. Such was the legacy that Mandelstam consciously exploited even before his sentence to internal exile in Voronezh in 1934 made him a literary martyr.[23] *Tristia* (1922), his second collection of poems, takes its cue from Ovid's elegy on his last night in Rome before being banished to the Black Sea; and in the essay 'Conversation about Dante', written the year before being forced to leave Petersburg, it is specifically Dante's role as an exile that excites him.

In addition to seeing Dante as part of a tradition that includes Pushkin, Byron and Victor Hugo, Mandelstam introduces a contemporary note, referring to Dante as an 'internal *raznochinets*'. As Jane Grey Harris and Constance Link explain, the Russian word is significant:

> Mandelstam's use of the word *raznochinets* begins to develop as an image in *The Noise of Time*, where it is first used in reference to his mentor and friend, V.V. Grippius, and to himself, the poet, in the last chapter. In 'Fourth Prose', 'Jew' substitutes for *raznochinets* and broadens the image of the poet as 'outsider'. *Raznochinets* and 'Jew' also have the moral power to oppose the authorities.[24]

Translated as 'intellectual upstart', *raznochinets* provocatively fuses Dante's experience with that of 20th century Russians. What it also does, as David M. Bethea has pointed out, is to turn Dante into the quintessential figure of the Wandering Jew.[25] There is clearly some overlap here between Mandelstam's own sense of alienation within Russia and his idiosyncratic reading of Dante, but time and again in the essay it is to language and poetic speech as a '"hybrid process' ... growing out of the self-perpetuating interplay of its own devices"[26] that Mandelstam returns. Dante thus becomes an image – or projection – of Mandelstam's own self, a man who is "unable to behave himself [and] does not know how to proceed, what to say, how to bow."[27] In other words, he is the kind of figure – the eternal outsider – whom we see appearing not only throughout Mandelstam's writings but also Brodsky's earliest poems in which the figure of the poet inhabits a world of shadows or, in the Homeric or Dantesque sense, shades. The past speaks to him and words, as objects, are numinous with the voices of those who have handled them before.

In many ways Brodsky's early poems deal with the traditional subject matter of lyric poetry: love, loss, and – most powerfully of all – the young poet's sense of having been called to a vocation. Such poems set their face sternly – though not a little humorously – against the world of socialist realism. The material world is animate with an ill-defined spiritual message. The setting is predominantly Petersburg in winter. Even when it is not night it is dark. Even in company the poet is alone:

> it's fine that you are free of all connections,
> it's fine that in this world there is no one
> who feels obliged to love you to distraction.[28]

Written in 1961 when Brodsky was 21, 'You're coming home again. What does that mean?' is a bravura piece, designed to echo the kind of poetic persona we can recognise from, say, Baudelaire. We might argue that in both a Marxist and Freudian sense it is 'overdetermined'. Such criticism, however, misses the point. It is precisely the poem's confidence-in-the-face-of-adversity, its facing up to individual responsibility, this very self-consciousness, that must have struck contemporary Russian readers so forcibly. Add to this the fact that the poet states a belief in God and the soul, and the poem becomes something altogether more radical than on first reading it might appear. To quote Bethea again:

> It was not that there was anything openly seditious or even political in Brodsky's early verse (although feelings of alienation and corrosive questioning were definitely present from the start) but rather that what was there could not be defined as belonging to the regnant idiom. Aesthetic discourse becomes unsettling to a tyrant when its statements move off in too many directions at once and its memory is older than the current social contract.[29]

This sense of a memory "older than the current social contract" is clearly tied to the fact, discussed earlier, that for Brodsky and his peers "Giotto and Mandelstam were more imperative than their personal destinies". Mandelstam died in December 1938, a year and a half before Brodsky was born; Giotto, some 600 years earlier in Florence in 1337. What united them was a Judaeo-Christian tradition that celebrated the word becoming flesh. For Giotto and the early Renaissance this meant a rejection of stiff formalism in favour of fluid narrative, the importance of which to Mandelstam's generation was that it supported the Acmeist rejection of Symbolism in favour of a return to the things of this world. What this meant to Mandelstam in particular was, in Seamus Heaney's words, "a sense of the poem as an animated structure, an equilibrium of forces, an architecture. All of which boiled in Mandelstam as a furious devotion to the physical word, the etymological memory bank, the word as its own form and content – the word is a bundle and meaning sticks out of it in various directions".[30]

It would be short-sighted not to recognise the fact that for Mandelstam the word as its own 'form and content' meant, in effect, a kind of metaphysical hybridity: the word becoming flesh through the poetic form of the metaphor, with its particular meaning for him of the "*freedom* to say, and of course to believe, *this is that*".[31] In a society where language, to return to Bhabha's phrase, could "make contingent and indeterminate" all forms of authoritarian control, Brodsky's poem acknowledges the fact that there are times when it is safer to go undercover: "it's fine to walk, alone, in this vast world/ …/It's fine to catch yourself, while rushing home,/mouthing a phrase that's something less than candid."[32] There is, then, a strong vein of *realpolitik* in Brodsky's outlook. And it is this freedom to doubt while assuming the tragic mask of ideological belief that is the source of the poem's vitality. This dissenting voice, operating primarily on a subtextual level, is best seen as a deliberate breaking with the immediate burden of Soviet history. Hence Bethea's claim that "'Brodsky' became 'Brodsky' only with the thorough study and assimilation into his native tradition of certain Western, especially Anglo-American sources".[33]

While 'Elegy for John Donne' (1963) and 'Verses on the Death of T.S. Eliot' (1965) are the poems which most clearly and powerfully articulate the dramatic change of gear that took place in Brodsky's writings in the 1960s, hints and allusions to his studying poetry in English appear in a number of shorter lyrics.[34] In 'Once more we're living by the Bay', for example, written in 1962, the poet imagines himself and his lover buried alive after a volcanic eruption. A thousand years later he is discovered by scientists, "cloaked with the ashes of our modern epoch,/and everlastingly within your arms."[35] The poem evokes Donne's 'The Relique', with the inference that Brodsky, like Donne before him, should become a kind of secular saint, in Donne's words, to "a time, or land,/Where mis-devotion doth command". This, however, in a State where the only relique that could be worshipped was Lenin's embalmed body in Red Square! Examine the poem a little closer and we begin to see that Brodsky is perhaps using Donne's poem and the form of the love lyric as a mask to comment upon a contemporary political crisis.[36]

In a note to his translation of the poem, George L. Kline discusses Brodsky's reference to a 'bay' or 'gulf' (in Russian, *'zaliv'*). In doing so he says that Brodsky's mention of Mount Vesuvius means that he clearly intended the Bay to be that outside Naples. If this is so, why is the reference to the volcano prefaced by *"Our own* Vesuvius?" [my emphasis]. Might Brodsky not have intended his use of the word to be more ambiguous, suggesting, as Kline admits is possible, a reference to the Gulf of Finland?[37] Furthermore, might not the poem, written while the Cuban Missile Crisis was reaching boiling point, actually be suggesting a different kind of apocalyptic end for the poet and his lover? The ambiguous use, therefore, of *'zaliv'* can be seen as a reference not just to the territorial dispute between the USSR and Finland but to the Bay of Pigs fiasco in 1961, when American attempts to overthrow the Cuban government were led by US-backed Cuban exiles. Such a reading suggests that Brodsky was using his literary sources for other than purely aesthetic reasons. Couched in the terms of a love poem and cleverly – for those few in the know – referring to Donne's 'blasphemous' poem, 'Once more we're living by the Bay' is as an acute and unsettling vision of what seemed to many to be impending nuclear war between East and West.

III

Written by an Englishman in voluntary exile in America about an Irish nationalist who wrote in English, spent a considerable part of his life in London and died in the South of France, Auden's 'In Memory of W.B. Yeats' came to influence another writer wanting to compose a 'mourning song'. Written in exile in Russia's frozen north, and subsequently translated by the American George L. Kline, Brodsky's 'Verses on the Death of T.S. Eliot' is an *in memoriam* for the work of an American poet who spent 50 years thoroughly Anglicising himself.

In imitating the structure and, in the last of its three sections, the rhythms and rhyme scheme of Auden's elegy, which in turn imitated certain developments in Yeats's poetry, 'Verses on the Death of T.S. Eliot' is an act of homage that charts a number of lines of influence between the Anglo-American and Anglo-Irish traditions, while bringing both within the compass of Mandelstam's ideas on hybridity. Indeed, so successful is the poem in its own terms that it is difficult to know whether Brodsky's aim was to turn Russian into English, or English into Russian.[38]

As David M. Bethea notes, Brodsky's involvement in a kind of literary contraband began when he first read Donne's poetry in an anthology given him by an American visitor to Leningrad.[39] The importance of this encounter with Donne, at a time when Brodsky was studying the Bible for the first time, was, says Bethea, that it allowed him a means of reclaiming:

> that intellectual ground which had been effectively lost to the intelligentsia reading public as a result of the policies of Stalinism ... This ground included in its rich topsoil the entire biblical tradition, with its issues of divine judgement and theodicy, the economy of salvation, the meaning and shape of history, death and resurrection, the relation of the soul to the body [and] the chief living expression of which was Anna Akhmatova.[40]

In regaining this lost ground, or lost time, Brodsky was able to create something entirely new within Russian literature while, by grafting it on to a body of work which reached back via Akhmatova to Tsvetaeva and Mandelstam, charging it with an authority that neatly side-stepped the stifling conformity of socialist realism.

An astonishingly sustained and bravura piece of writing, 'Elegy for John Donne' imagines Donne's death as a heavy sleep in which the whole of England joins. Over some 95 lines of muscular pentameters, the poem moves from the domestic – Donne's abandoned house – and out through a window to encompass London, Dover's 'Chalk cliffs' and, incredibly, heaven and hell:

> The angels sleep. Saints – to their saintly shame –
> have quite forgotten this our anxious world.
> Dark Hell-fires sleep, and glorious Paradise.
> No one goes forth from home at this bleak hour.
> Even God has gone to sleep. Earth is estranged.
> Eyes do not see, and ears perceive no sound.
> The Devil sleeps. Harsh enmity has fallen
> asleep with him on snowy English fields.[41]

At the beginning at least Brodsky seems to be taking his cue from Donne's 'The good-morrow' with its playful reference to the early Christian myth of the seven Christian youths who fled the persecution of the Roman Emperor Decius in AD 249 by escaping to a cave where they slept for two hundred years. We can also see how Brodsky, by implicating the whole universe in the poet's death-cum-sleep, is paralleling Donne's hyperbolic assertion that "love, all love of other sights controules,/And makes one little room, an every where". This imagining an England inseparable from Donne's vision of it in his poetry and sermons is central to the poem's meaning. There is, though, a more prosaic reason why the poem takes such a path: Brodsky's only experience of England at the time was purely a literary one. It was, however, an experience which, as he later said, took on an objective reality in which "Dickens was more real than Stalin."[42] On a deeper level, the association of word and object in the poem – the name for a thing and the thing thus named – cuts to the heart of the relationship between word, sound, and the object which, as it were, is being sounded. Unlike the Symbolists, whose writings he denounced for obscurantism, Mandelstam believed that the form and content of a word must remain an organic whole. With Symbolism, he argued, "Nothing is left but a terrifying quadrille of 'correspondences' nodding to one another. Eternal winking. Never a clear word, nothing but hints and reticent whispers."[43] What the Symbolists did, in short, was to use words in such a way as to ignore etymology.

There are similarities between Mandelstam's apologia for the word and comments made by Benjamin in 'The Task of the Translator'

(1921), written as an introduction to his translation of Baudelaire's *Tableaux Parisiens*. The essay, remarkable even by his standards, shows Benjamin's interest in translation to be as concerned with the logos – with *ur-sprache*, 'pure speech' – as was Mandelstam. We will return to this aspect of Benjaminian thought later. For now, however, it is worth supporting Mandelstam's claim that the meaning and form of a word are synonymous by noting Benjamin's concept that "life is given its due only if everything that has a history of its own, and is not merely the setting for history, is credited with life."[44] It is possible to see in this sentence a grain of the idea to which Benjamin was to return some 16 years later when he was having seriously to think about escaping Europe and going into exile in America. The belief that language must be allowed a life of its own distinct from history becomes, in 'On Some Motifs in Baudelaire' (1939), the image of an automaton as being someone who has "completely liquidated their memories."[45] In other words, at a time when the German army was preparing to march on Paris – the city which was for him the apotheosis of modern European culture – Benjamin, in an image that can only be read in terms of the advancing soldiers – "Each man is dominated by an emotion: one shows unrestrained joy; another distrust[;] a third dull despair; a fourth evinces belligerence; another is getting ready to depart from the world." – saw war as a mechanism for obliterating the past. Alienated from, and by, language, human beings thus become machines incapable of anything other than 'reflex action.'

We can understand how, subject to the Soviet insistence on a language that denied anything *other* than a specific historical and political context, Mandelstam's words must have continued to ring in the ears of the next generation of Russian poets. His belief in the Russian language as being essentially porous, necessarily open to change and influence like a border crossing between neighbouring states, was utilised by Brodsky when, in the Donne elegy and elsewhere, he imported fictional realities from abroad. And this homeland, like Mandelstam's vision of the Russian language, or like Rilke's "a makeshift hut to receive the music,/ /a shelter nailed up out of their darkest longing", provided the estranged Brodsky with a means of forging, in Salman Rushdie's phrase, an "imaginary homeland".

Between March 1964 and November 1965, however, Brodsky

found himself exiled to a very different kind of "makeshift hut". Following his trial for 'social parasitism', Brodsky received a sentence of five years hard labour – later commuted to 20 months – to be served in the small village of Norinskoya in Russia's frozen north. It was here, "in a small village lost among swamps and forests, near the polar circle"[46] that Brodsky encountered Auden's poetry. The first poem he read was 'In Memory of W.B. Yeats'. His response, recalled at a distance of almost 20 years in the essay 'To Please a Shadow', is worth noting:

> I remember sitting there in the small wooden shack, peering through the square porthole-size window at the wet, muddy, dirt road with a few stray chickens on it, half-believing what I'd just read, half-wondering whether my grasp of English wasn't playing tricks on me[.] I guess I was simply refusing to believe that way back in 1939 an English poet had said 'Time ... worships language', and yet the world around was still as it was.[47]

The precise nature of Brodsky's astonishment at Auden's words hasn't been sufficiently recognised. For what surprises him is less the belief that "Time worships language" than the fact that it is an English poet who is expressing it. The equation itself would have been far from novel to him. It was, in essence, precisely the belief which dominated Mandelstam's thinking about the relationship between individuals and the State, the State and time/history, and ultimately language. "The life of language in Russian historical reality", Mandelstam wrote:

> outweighs all other facts by the fullness of its phenomenal reality[,] by the fullness of its being, which represents only the unattainable limit for all other phenomena of Russian life ... The Russian language is historical by its very nature, inasmuch as in its totality it is an undulating sea of events, the unbroken embodiment and action of an intelligent and breathing flesh ... Such a highly organised and organic language is not merely a door to history, but is history itself.[48]

Sentenced by the Soviet state to 'do time', Auden's words can only have reminded Brodsky of Mandelstam's credo that language, in its rhythmical essence, radically restructures and reconstitutes history. Re-discovering the essence of his art in his ramshackle hut-cum-ship with its "porthole-sized windows" allowed Brodsky to explore the new horizons opened up for him by Auden's hybridisation of the Anglo-Irish and Anglo-American traditions.

Auden's vision of Yeats' stricken body as an emptying city becomes, in the opening stanza of 'Verses on the Death of T.S. Eliot', a world in which objects flinch, shrink or stiffen at the touch of Eliot's death. The physiological process of rigor mortis thus becomes characterised by metonymic details – a front door, a windowpane, a road crossing – each of which marks some kind of temporary limit or boundary between one place and another. Even the time of year, January, serves as such an intersection, admitting the dimension of time as well as space into the liminal field of the poem.[49] Named after the Roman god Janus, the god of arrivals and departures, January becomes not only the literal month of Eliot's death, but a point in time that marks the first stage in a new journey, one that sees the poet, as in the Donne elegy, withdrawing from human time – "that dry land of days where we remain" – and moving out towards the edge of land. Having travelled this far, the poet becomes translated like the human lover of a god in Ovid:

> But, as the sea, whose tide has climbed and roared,
> slamming the seawall, draws its warring waves
> down and away, so he, in haste, withdrew
> from his own high and solemn victory.[50]

What connects this image of raw creative energy to the earlier 'Elegy for John Donne', is the continuation of the idea that the poet not only inhabits a place but that his or her words give rise to a metaphysical vision of that place at once equally real, equally present, as the geographical facts of granite or limestone.

Moving from the urban to the rural, Auden's and Brodsky's poems use landscape and travel as a metaphor for the journey from life to death, thus returning us to the classical topos of elegy. The ways in which they do so, however, could not be more different. For though Yeats' poetry survives, there is a suggestion that it does so on diminished terms. Retreating to "the valley of its saying", it becomes "A way of happening, a mouth" which "makes nothing happen". For

Brodsky, Eliot's death is a triumph, with his metamorphosis into water meaning that his influence is no longer bound by "that dry land of days where we remain" but is free to flow where it will. Eliot's poetry therefore becomes "a way of happening" that connects America to Britain, Britain to the European mainland, and all three to the icy waters of Brodsky's exile. In short, Eliot's metamorphosis or translation marks, in George Steiner's words, "the leap from a local to a general force."[51]

There is in all this a suggestion that Brodsky is utilising another aspect of Mandelstam's beliefs about the Russian language: that it is essentially Hellenic rather than Latin. For in his description of the poet's soul moving from the city to the harbour, from whence it joins the sea, Brodsky is echoing what Christian Meier defines as a distinguishing factor of the differences between Greek and Roman culture:

> Rome fortified what it had won by establishing colonies and regarding the area it dominated as a strategic unit over which it sought to maintain control. The Greek cities, by contrast, merely wanted their place in the world. They sat around the sea, as Plato put it, like frogs around a pond. *The sea both separated and united them, a common free element* that could be dominated only in a city's immediate vicinity. It is above all this position that determined the attitude of the Greeks, and all that followed from that [my emphasis].[52]

The two poems are accented differently in other ways. While Auden's lament for the role of the poet within a modern capitalist economy is couched in quasi-allegorical terms – "the valley of its saying", "the parish of rich women" – the middle-panel of Brodsky's triptych uses the imagery of Russian Orthodox icons:

> Two grieving figures gaze upon the ground.
> They sing. How very similar their songs! …
>
> America, where he was born and raised,
> and England, where he died – they both incline
> their somber faces as they stand, bereft,
> on either side of his enormous grave.

However conservative this imagery might seem to a reader from the West, we shouldn't underestimate the importance of Brodsky's use of this material.[53] Such images – a 'Deposition' or 'Lamentation over the Dead Christ' – along with the use he was making of Donne and the Bible in his poetry, locates the poet's authority in a higher court of law than that of the judge who, at his trial, questioned Brodsky's right to call himself a poet. Likewise, the presence of the Magi, called for in the opening line of this middle section, suggests a link between life and death that is rooted in Eliot's 'Journey of the Magi':

> ... this birth was
> Hard and bitter agony for us, like Death, our death.
> We returned to our places, these Kingdoms,
> But no longer at ease here, in the old dispensation.

"No longer at ease here, in the old dispensation." The line must have sounded like a rallying cry for an estranged generation of Russian writers.

These references to earlier forms of Russian artistic and religious practice once again made possible certain forms of emotional and intellectual expression driven underground by the Soviet authorities. In other words, the occasion of mourning the death of a foreign poet whose influence at the time was uniquely powerful in Eastern Europe, became an opportunity to write about matters closer to home. It is an appeal – one which is, admittedly, oblique – that has much in common with Mandelstam's 'Nature and the Word', calling as it does on Russian writers to reject Symbolism and Futurism and to use the material that lay closest to hand. This material – the Russian language – is described by Mandelstam in terms that might serve as a perfect example of Shklovsky's *ostranenie*[54]:

> We have no acropolis. Even today [Russian] culture is still wandering and finding its walls. Nevertheless, each word in [the] dictionary is a kernel of the Acropolis, a small Kremlin, a winged fortress ... rigged out in the Hellenic spirit.[55]

Mandelstam's phrases are themselves dazzling examples of the "ceaseless hybridisation, cross-breeding, grafting". They also provide an example of his own highly allusive, metaphorical style. Concrete but highly associative, such ludic energies can be found in the shift that now takes place between the second and third stanzas of 'Verses on the Death of T.S. Eliot'.

While the middle section is dominated by explicit references to Christian iconography and the image of the grave, the third encompasses a Classical vision of a pastoral idyll in which the reader's gaze is directed from the ground up towards the sky.

The poem's horizons suddenly widen. The flinching, shrinking, stiffening city and the hieratic mourning at the graveside give way to dynamic movement: Apollo 'flings' the garland down, and invisible feet 'rush' across the forest floor. Like a cross between Prospero's masque and Stravinsky's *Le Sacre du Printemps*, the poem is filled with Dionysian energy. And just as a choreographer will beat time for the dancers – or, as was the case at the premier of *Le Sacre du Printemps,* shout it from the wings – so the heavy accentuated regular stresses of each quatrain return us to the well-springs of poetry :

> Forest here will not forget
> voice of lyre and rush of feet.
> Only what remains alive
> will deserve their memories.

"It should be remembered," Brodsky wrote, "that verse meters in themselves are kinds of spiritual magnitude for which nothing can be substituted."[56] In adopting the trochaic tetrameter which Auden borrowed from Yeats, Yeats from Blake's 'The Tyger', and Blake from the closing speech of Milton's 'Comus'; by his references to Classical culture – both Greek and Roman – and in his fusion of the Christian and the pagan, Brodsky makes his elegy a palimpsest through whose layers we can read, like a cross section of a hillside, how the moral, ethical and aesthetic contours of the present have been shaped by the creative rhythms of the past.

Etymologically, all poetic structures come from the earth – a verse being the point at which a plough turns at the end of a field. Mandelstam alludes to this in 'The Word and Culture', when he says that poetry "is the plough that turns up time in such a way that the abyssal strata of time, its black earth, appears on the surface."[57] Exiled to Russia's frozen north, intellectually and artistically isolated, scratching away with the nib of a pen, breaking open the blank ground of the page, turning his verses, Brodsky's immediate precedent for seeing the poet's occupation as one of cultivating language lay before him in Auden's elegy for Yeats: "With the farming of a verse/Make a vineyard of the curse,/Sing of human unsuccess/In a rapture of distress".

Ironically, given the conditions in which the two poems were written, it is Brodsky's elegy that moves with the greater conviction from darkness to light, death to re-birth. This may be because in writing about Eliot, Brodsky suffered none of the "anxiety of influence" which affected Auden when writing about Yeats. As a result, 'Verses on the Death of T.S. Eliot' can be read as being as much a matter of Brodsky having discovered a new master – Auden – as it is his mourning the loss of an old one – Mandelstam. For while there is a clear sense in which 'In Memory of W.B. Yeats' is about sloughing the past, 'Verses on the Death of T.S. Eliot' is much more a celebration of the potential of that past grafted on to the modern. Brodsky knows he has achieved something entirely new in Russian literature, and we sense that he is taking delight in sounding the differences between his Russian variations on an original theme of Auden's. We also suspect that there is a clear sense of collusion at work in Brodsky's poem: that the experience of reading Auden and Eliot, with their differing relationships to both the Anglo-Irish and Anglo-American traditions, handed him a passport with which he could revisit and make fresh use of his own Russian heritage.

IV

Brodsky's arrival at Vienna airport in June 1972 made him an immediate celebrity in the West. His reading alongside Auden at the Poetry International in London later that year only highlighted the sense that here was an important figure. But as with Solzhenitsyn in 1974 or Nureyev in 1961, there is no doubt that the reception Brodsky received was based in part at least on political rather than artistic considerations. There seems to be every evidence that the Soviet authorities had anticipated this, but also that they expected it to be a short-lived phenomena and that interest in the poet would soon quiet.

As discussed earlier, Brodsky was always to play down the severity of his sentence, commenting that unlike in the past today's exiled writer "isn't leaving Rome for savage Samartia". Nevertheless his situation and the calculated response of the Soviet authorities did, despite these protestations, have much in common with the poet whose fate he refers to.[58]

Though the reasons for Ovid's banishment to Tomis remain tantalisingly unknown, the myths surrounding the exiled poet came to assume an extra dimension in the 20th century. As Peter Green observes:

> The notion of an authoritarian regime, sniped at by literary intellectuals who wrap up their message in myth and symbol, has a contemporary, and all too familiar, quality about it. Looked at in this way, Ovid at once becomes an acceptable figure in the anti-totalitarian resistance movement.[59]

So while Brodsky's exile to the West brought none of the physical suffering and dangers recounted by Ovid, the aim of the Soviet authorities was clearly to silence him. What Peter Green says about Ovid on this point is therefore equally applicable to Brodsky:

> To execute this social butterfly, who was, after all, the most famous living poet in Rome, would have been far from easy, and might well have provoked a serious outcry at a time when Augustus had other still more serious problems on his hands. *Relegatio* was a far better answer: it gave a spurious appearance of clemency and – a crucial point – let Augustus and his advisers dictate Ovid's place of residence. Tomis, from their viewpoint, was a psychological masterstroke. It robbed Ovid not only of Rome, but of that whole cultured milieu on which he depended for his inspiration. It showed him, the hard way, how the empire he so despised was run, exposing him daily … to barbarian mores[.] It struck at his instrument of expression, the Latin language, by marooning him in a linguistic wilderness of debased Greek, 'Sarmation' and Getic: 'Composing a poem you can read to nobody,' he complained bitterly, 'is like dancing in the dark.' To the Getae, *he* was the barbarian.[60]

If Moscow thought exile would keep Brodsky silent, it was to be disappointed. And when news of Brodsky being awarded the Nobel Prize for Literature in 1987 reached Russia, the KGB called the event a political provocation on the part of reactionary circles in the West.[61]

Though the exile of an important Russian writer was an exceptional event, it was hardly unprecedented. Throughout the 19th and 20th centuries Russian and Soviet literature had been determined to a large degree by émigré writers. What is more, important works by some authors found a publisher in the West before they could be published in Russia. Nevertheless, most of this literature was, through various means, eventually made available to the Russian public. With the Revolution, however, the lines of communication between émigré writer and domestic audience became stretched to breaking point. The roll-call of writers who left Russia within a few years of 1917 is extensive, and includes such major figures as Bely, Bunin, Gorky, Ivanov, Khodasevich and Tsvetaeva. Also forced to leave were critics and scholars such as Victor Shklovsky and Roman Jakobson. Some writers chose to return. Tsvetaeva, for example, had left Moscow in 1922 to live first in Prague and then Paris, before returning to the USSR in 1939. But Tsvetaeva's experience was an extreme one. While abroad she wrote what is acknowledged to be her best work but, because her poetry was becoming more unconventional (Tsvetaeva was, said Brodsky, "an extremely candid poet, quite possibly the most candid in the history of Russian poetry. She makes no secret of anything, least of all her aesthetic and philosophical credos"[62]) she found it increasingly difficult to find a publisher. Furthermore, her political sympathies were not unequivocally anti-Soviet, and her husband, Sergei Efron, was rumoured to be a Soviet agent. In every respect, therefore, Tsvetaeva fell between the fixed and narrow divisions to which an émigré writer was expected to conform.[63]

The situation for Brodsky was equally taxing. Prior to the collapse of the Berlin Wall and the relaxation of censorship rules within the Soviet Union many non-Soviet writers remained unpublished in Russia. And while émigrés such as Nabokov saw much of what was written back in the USSR as barely worthy of the name Literature, there persisted in the Soviet Union itself the belief that nothing good could come of a writer who lived and wrote abroad. The latter belief must certainly have troubled Brodsky, as one of its fiercest advocates was no less a figure than Anna Akhmatova. And it is in relation to Akhmatova's remaining in Russia to bear witness to the terrors of the 1930s and 1940s that Brodsky, perhaps acknowledging something of his own situation, wrote:

The Russian writer never really detaches himself from the people. There's really all kinds of riffraff in a literary milieu, but if we're talking about Akhmatova, what do you do with her experience of the 1930s and much later[?] And what about all those people who used to visit her? These were by no means poets necessarily, and it was by no means engineers who collected her poems, or scientists. Typists, nurses, all those old ladies – what other kinds of people do you need? No this is a fictitious category. The writer is himself the people. Take Tsvetaeva: her poverty, her trips lugging her own bags during the Civil War ... No. No matter where you point, no poet in our beloved homeland has ever been able to break away from the common people.[64]

This phrase – "The writer is himself the people" – returns us to the central proposition of 'Less Than One': that the poet's biography is determined by language. I have already noted how Brodsky's early poems, with the isolated, fugitive – even haunted – figure of the poet can be seen as preparing the way for his actual exile. Likewise, the assumption of various exilic personae – St Simeon in 'Nunc Dimittis', Byron in 'New Stanzas to Augusta', and Odysseus in 'Odysseus to Telemachus'[65] – show Brodsky, in Solomon Volkov's words, "betting on the individual's ability to imagine himself not as an independent entity but as a unique link in a great cultural train."[66] The irony of the situation is that in the darkest years of the Soviet blackout it was left to émigré writers and artists to preserve those aspects of Russian culture – particularly Petersburgian – which were being systematically persecuted. It therefore becomes possible – perhaps necessary – to say of Brodsky what John Burt Foster, Jr. has written about Nabokov: that drawing a clear distinction between the 'European' and 'American' Nabokov is a futile occupation:

The label is not essentially chronological: it does not refer to a self-contained period ... Instead, it designates a persistent trait in his cultural identity, one that interacts with others to generate ... cosmopolitan diversity.[67]

The parallels with Nabokov (whom Brodsky persisted in regarding as a failed poet rather than a successful novelist!) become still clearer if we consider the history of Nabokov's own writings. Fleeing Russia for Berlin in 1919, Nabokov left his family in Germany while he attended Cambridge University. Although he spoke fluent English, and though the early 1920s saw the high point in English Modernism, he chose to write in Russian. It was a decision that clearly marked him and his readership as being émigrés, scattered across both Europe and America. During the 1930s, however, Nabokov began writing for a wider audience – first in French and then English – a process which eventually led in the latter half of the decade to him translating his own Russian novels into English. Only then did he begin his first major work in a language other than Russian, *The Real Life of Sebastian Knight*.[68]

The history of Brodsky's own writing, his "twists of language", is equally complex, as is the relationship between his work and its Russian-speaking audience. His was not an isolated example. Throughout the 1960s a number of Russian writers found themselves part of a so-called 'third wave' of exiles that gravitated to centres of Russian émigré culture in New York, Paris and Israel. As in the 1920s, these writers saw their work published, acclaimed and translated in the West long before it reached a wider audience in the Soviet Union. Hence the importance of samizdat or tamizdat literature, disseminated in typescript and the only means by which a small readership in the USSR could remain in touch with Russian writers abroad.[69]

For whom, then, does the émigré writer write? Nabokov's decision to continue writing in Russian was made possible by the fact that he knew there existed a large émigré readership. Some twenty years after the civil war in Russia no less than half of all Russian émigrés remained abroad. This simply wasn't an option for Brodsky. When he arrived in the West his command of English, though sufficient to allow him to read, was not up to the task of original composition. And as I touched on earlier, there was a further complication: how to write in one language about experiences that are rooted in another? So when, in 'Footnote to a Poem', his 1981 essay on Tsvetaeva's 'New Year's Greeting', Brodsky addresses the question of for whom a poet writes – "For myself and for a hypothetical alter ego." – the fact that the answer takes the form of a quotation from another Russian émigré, Stravinsky, powerfully suggests an inability to speak for and on behalf of himself. In other words, Stravinsky's words have in themselves become this 'alter ego'.

In 'Lithuanian Nocturne' (1974), first written in Russian and subsequently translated into English by himself, Brodsky addresses a number of these questions, particularly the writer's search for a signifying other who will speak on his behalf. Dedicated to the Lithuanian poet Tomas Venclova, himself later forced to leave the USSR for the States, the poem imagines what Brodsky was never able to do: return to the Soviet Union. As in 'Elegy for John Donne', this is accomplished through the intercession of sleep: the poet's spirit or soul (the word Brodsky initially uses is "specter") "abandons its frame in a fleabag somewhere/overseas" and wings homeward.[70]

Despite their geographic isolation, the Russian language with its unique alphabet and its grammatical structures links Brodsky and Venclova. Yet, ironically, it is this shared medium that also defines the differences between them: "Our cuneiform, Tomas! With my margin-prone/predicates! with your subjects, hearthbound and luckless!"[71] The tragedy of Brodsky's position, remote in both time and space, is that his evocation of Lithuania is necessarily reliant on a mixture of memory and imagination. The result is that the reader's experience of the poem, mediated through the poet's memories, becomes one of discontinuous fragments out of which we must distil a unified experience.

What is remarkable about the constellation of metaphors which determines our reading of the relationship between alienation as an existential experience and estrangement as a willed literary form, is the way in which they manage to speak so eloquently of a condition which, in Adorno's words, "is the reverse side of the world of things, is the sign of distortion – but precisely as such [is] a motif of transcendence, namely of the removal of the boundary and reconciliation of the organic and the inorganic, or the *Aufhebung* [aura] of death."[72] Written in response to Benjamin's essay on Kafka, Adorno's comments alert us not only to that aspect of Benjamin's thinking which is concerned with how an individual goes about forming an image of themselves, and in doing so assumes control over his or her own subjective experience, but also Benjamin's concept of the *aura*, the means by which subjective experience converges with, or finds an alter ego in, objective material. "The person we look at," Benjamin writes, "or who feels he is looked at, looks at us in turn. To perceive the aura of an object we look at means to invest it with the ability to look at us in turn."[73] Such is the situation imagined by Brodsky in 'Lithuanian Nocturne' when Venclova is asked to recognise Brodsky's spectre peering in through a window:

> Tomas, we are alike;
> we are, frankly, a double:
> your breath
> dims the same windowpane that my features befuddle.
> We're each other's remote
> amalgam underneath,
> in a lackluster puddle
> a simultaneous nod.
> Twist your lips – I'll reply with the similar grimace of dread.
> I'll respond to your yawn with my mouth's gaping mollusc.[74]

"To say, 'Here I see such and such an object' does not establish an equation between me and the object." Such, Benjamin argued, is the price we pay for the merging of the subjective and the objective, the blending of "the nearest and the most remote" in the aura, and which constitutes the "unique manifestation of a distance". Moving from the material to the ontological, Brodsky continues his 'double portrait' with a series of images of things attempting to return to and become unified with their origins:

> we're a stalemate, no-score,
> draw, long-shadows' distress
> brought to walls by a match that will die in a minute,
> echoes tracing in vain the original cry
> as small change does its note.

The "condition we call exile" can therefore be seen as one in which two processes occur concurrently: memory, the means by which we integrate ourselves into both a personal and cultural past, becomes broken into discontinuous episodes and events. In so doing, identity becomes synonymous with distortion ("the same windowpane that my features befuddle"), disguise ("Twist your lips – I'll reply with the similar grimace of dread"), and ultimately disappearance ("a match that will die in a minute").

In many ways 'Lithuanian Nocturne' dramatises aspects of Homi

Bhabha's definition of the "production of transcultural narratives in the colonial world."[75] Responding to Fredric Jameson's assertion that "the so-called death of the subject ... the fragmented and schizophrenic decentring [of the Self], ... the crisis of socialist internationalism, and the enormous tactical difficulties of co-ordinating local ... political actions with national or international ones ... are all immediately functions of the new international space", Bhabha writes:

> the dilemma of projecting an international space on the trace of a decentred, fragmented subject [is] figured in the *in-between* spaces of double-frames: its historical originality marked by a cognitive obscurity; its decentred 'subject' signified in the nervous temporality of the transitional, or the emergent provisionality of the 'present'.

Speaking from one colonised and colonising Empire to another, Brodsky's spectre can therefore be seen as inhabiting precisely those liminal spaces which Bhabha and Jameson map out for the migrant. Only through "splitting and displacement," Bhabha says, can "the architecture of the new historical subject emerge at the limits of representation itself". It is here, at the point where "discontinuous historical realities" are dramatised in and by speech, that Brodsky's poem is situated. Brodsky's exile thus becomes acted-out within the Russian language itself, in which his ability to make assertions about himself or to affirm his own experiences have become literally marginalised. For a different poet, or sensibility, this would become the subject of self-mourning or tragedy. But Brodsky, perhaps because the situation was one he had been imagining and preparing for since youth, never admits this possibility. Indeed, his position is remarkably close to Mandelstam's affirmation of poetry at the opening of 'Conversation About Dante':

> poetry is not a part of nature ... let alone a reflection of it – this would make a mockery of the axioms of identity; rather, poetry establishes itself with astonishing independence in a new extra-spatial field of action, not so much narrating as acting out in nature by means of its arsenal of devices, commonly known as tropes.[76]

In asserting the means by which identity survives in language not by narrating the given but by re-imagining it through the invention of metaphors which, like genes, are passed down from generation to generation, Brodsky challenges and defies the accepted destiny of those who are excluded or marginalised from language. It is poetry, as in Auden's elegy for Yeats or Mandelstam's apologia for the outcast writer, that is the epitome of this, becoming "A way of happening, a mouth" which breaks with silence and exclusion:

> like some old squinting Mongol beyond our spiked earthly fence,
> poised to put his finger in-
> to his mouth – that old wound of your namesake! – to find its
> tongue and alter, like seraphs and silence
> do, his verbs or their tense.

It is important that Brodsky sees language as able to mediate between historical and metaphysical exile and colonisation: the image of the "old squinting Mongol"[77] fusing with that of the Old Testament, post-lapsarian Adam. Furthermore, this figure then becomes one with that of the New Testament apostle, Thomas, for whom doubt and silence gave way to faith and praise. Language as metaphor thus becomes an alter ego through which we are able to assert our individual identity. It is a common medium that is both a part of and apart from ourselves. In other words, language becomes both the locus of the poet's exile and the means by which he is able to reintegrate and re-assimilate himself with his homeland.

V

In his essay 'Footnote to a Poem', written in 1984, Brodsky has this to say about language:

> Language propels the poet into spheres he would not otherwise be able to approach, irrespective of the degree of psychic or mental concentration of which he might be capable beyond the writing of verse. And this propulsion takes place with unusual swiftness: with the speed of sound – greater than what is afforded by imagination or experience.[78]

There is no ignoring the fact that Brodsky sees the relationship between exile and language, and the spheres into which the latter is capable of propelling the former, in terms which, far from being limited to individual biographies or the experience of different racial and ethnic groups at specific times in their history, can be seen as providing a metaphor for the relationship between God and the material world. As well as likening individual words to genes, human speech in 'Lithuanian Nocturne' also becomes "a chorus of highly pitched vocal/atoms, alias souls". In other words, language is uniquely capable of uniting the material and the spiritual, thereby returning us to the argument with which this chapter began: that Brodsky's work must be seen as investigating exile as an essentially metaphysical condition. Throughout 'Lithuanian Nocturne', then, it is not only the émigré poet who is estranged in, and from, language; rather, language memorialises the myth or houses the faith of a human reconciliation with God, or the Divine Logos:

> Late Lithuanian dusk.
> Folk are scuffling from churches protecting the commas
> of their candle flames in trembling brackets of hands.[79]

As such the poem can be seen as participating in a belief system which George Steiner analyses in *After Babel*.

> Language is assuredly material in that it requires the play of muscle and vocal cords; but it is also impalpable and, by virtue of inscription and remembrance, free of time, though moving in temporal flow. These antinomies or dialectical relations confirm the dual mode of human existence, the interactions of physical with spiritual agencies. The occult tradition holds that a single primal language, an *Ur-Sprache* lies behind our present discord ... This Adamic vernacular not only enabled all men to understand one another, to communicate with perfect ease. It bodied forth, to a greater or lesser degree, the original Logos, the act of immediate calling into being whereby God had literally 'spoken the world'. The vulgate of Eden contained, though perhaps in a muted key, a divine syntax ... in which the mere naming of a thing was the necessary and sufficient cause of its leap into reality. Each time man spoke he re-enacted, he mimed, the nominalist mechanism of creation ... Hence also the ability of all men to understand God's language and to give it intelligible answer.[80]

There is much here that we recognise as being central to those ideas which Brodsky inherited from Mandelstam, particularly the belief that the Logos is where the material and the spiritual, form and content meet and, in Donne's lovely word, "intertouch". Indeed, we might say that 'Lithuanian Nocturne' is pitched toward that point where, entering language, the material world is translated into metaphor, becoming both uniquely itself and the wider connotations of that self as text. Images of this process as it refers to exile litter 'Lithuanian Dusk': "Like a stone that avenges a well/with its multiple rings,/I buzz over the Baltic"; "A star, shining in a backwater,/does so all the more brightly"; and "Spurning loudspeakers, a man/here declares to the world that he lives/by unwittingly crushing an ant,/ by faint Morse's/dots of pulse, by the screech of his pen".[81] Instead of being fixed and determined, moulded into certain pre-ordained 'narratives', the trope is a hybrid which, in Mandelstam's words, "crosses two sound modes: the first of these is the modulation we hear and sense in the prosodic instruments of poetic discourse in its spontaneous flow; the second is the discourse itself."[82] It is a form of cultural hybridity, a quixotic alter ego, to which Brodsky makes specific reference in the poem:

> Take this apparition for, let's
> say, an early return of the quote back to its Manifesto's
> text: a notch more, say, slurred, and a pitch more alluring
> for being away.[83]

If this appears to be an "early return" on Brodsky's part to pre-modern theories of language and, as it were, to the idea of the Book of the World, then we can, as suggested earlier, trace this to the influence of Mandelstam. It also parallels aspects of Walter Benjamin's speculations on language, specifically his belief in "writing as such ... as magical, that is as un-mediated."[84] Another way – Mandelstam's way – of putting this is to say that poetry is that which cannot be paraphrased: "For where there is amenability to paraphrase, there the sheets have never been rumpled, there poetry, so to speak, has never spent the night."[85] It is an image which is alluded to in 'Lithuanian Nocturne': "Our imprints! In damp twisted sheets".

Essentially, the act of speech or writing for Benjamin is one of translating:

> the language of things into that of man ... The objectivity of
> this translation is, however, guaranteed by God. For God
> created things: the creating word in them is the germ of the
> cognizing name, just as God, too, finally named each thing
> after it was born.[86]

Hermetic as it may seem – and Benjamin has been taken to task by, among others, Wittgenstein for dissociating the human faculty of naming from the everyday practise of language[87] – it is a theory of language that Brodsky showed every evidence of not only being familiar with but wanting to embody in his poetry.

There are any number of instances in Brodsky's poetry where an object coincides with either its name or an aspect of language. As we have seen, 'Lithuanian Nocturne' shows the poet's exile to be a literal marginalisation within language. In 'The Fly', the insect is described in terms of its "six-legged betters,/your printed betters,//your splayed Cyrillic echoes", which Brodsky's notes clarify as: "The Cyrillic letter Ж indicates the *zh* sound". In 'New Life', chairs become the letters 'b' or 'h'; and in 'Vertumnus' trees are translated into "the mixture/of Cyrillic and Latin in naked branches: /Ж, Ч, Ш, Щ, plus X, Y, Z". In 'Lullaby of Cape Cod' even neon signs become evidence of a kind of *écriture divine*: "like the fiery warning at Belshazzar's Feast,/the inscription Coca-Cola hums in red."

Arguably the most significant example of this figurative process is 'December in Florence', Brodsky's homage to Dante, in which he alludes to "the medieval notion that facial features represent letters in the phrase OMO DEI"[90]:

> A man gets reduced to pen's rustle on paper, to
> wedges, ringlets of letters, and also, due
> to the slippery surface, to commas and full stops. True,
> often, in some common word, the unwitting pen
> strays into drawing – while tackling an
> 'M' – some eyebrows: ink is more honest than
> blood. And a face, with moist words inside
> out to dry what has just been said,
> smirks like the crumpled paper absorbed by shade.[91]

Commenting on the poem, one he sees as central to understanding the significance of the 'triangular' relationship between Brodsky, Mandelstam and Dante, David M. Bethea says that we:

> should not lose sight of the fact that, for Dante and Mandelstam, poetry and life are mystically intertwined and the peregrinations of the pilgrim become emplotted in the progress of the poet ... Their poetry is testimony to the belief that not only could the word become flesh but that, in their cases, it had. ... Exile has taken everything from him ... and left him with his writing, his letters, his punctuation marks, his 'parts of speech.[92]

While Benjamin's philosophy and Mandelstam's Acmeist poetics both involve a certain hermeticism in their approach to language, one which relies on faith as much as empiricism, it is possible to approach their concerns in such a way as to both clarify the distinctions they draw between different forms of language – namely the functional and the poetic – and in doing so throw further light on this aspect of Brodsky's writings.

In arguably his most influential essay, 'Two Aspects of Language and Two Types of Aphasic Disturbance', Roman Jakobson discusses the relationship between object language and metalanguage:

> On these two different levels of language the same linguistic stock may be used; thus we may speak in English (as metalanguage) about English (as object language) and interpret English words and sentences by means of English synonyms, circumlocutions, and paraphrases.[93]

We will return to Jakobson later. For now it is important to recognise a parallel between Benjamin's definition of the act of speech or writing as one of translation – the translation of "the language of things into that of man" – and Jakobson's model of the aphasic. Approaching Benjamin through Jakobson, we might re-read his equation thus: the translation of object language into metalanguage. Without this ability, as it were, to talk about what it is we are doing when we speak, the individual is unable either to acquire language or use it normally. The example Jakobson cites of the importance of metalanguage – "talk about language" – is that of pre-school children, but the same analysis might be applied to the émigré who is forced to adopt another language. In Jakobson's terms it thus becomes possible to read Brodsky's use of metalanguage as a way of defining and adjusting himself to the experience of living in a society that speaks a foreign language, and of learning to use that language.

VI

The exile, Adorno wrote, is a "blank space for a name that cannot be found. [It] has lost its verb the way [a] family's memory loses the emigrant who goes to ruin and dies".[94]

Until he was awarded the Nobel Prize in 1987, Brodsky did not officially exist as a poet in the Soviet Union. Many of the linguistic similes and metaphors discussed earlier are therefore specifically to do with his fate as an exile. In 'Strophes', for example, he likens himself to the thirty-third letter of the Cyrillic alphabet, 'Я' which, as Valentina Polukhina has commented, "looks like a man moving from right to left, while Russian writing moves in the opposite direction. Therefore, this image hints at Brodsky's position in relation to Russian letters."[95] Such images abound in Brodsky's verse, but as with the example I have just cited the English reader is reliant either on Brodsky's own notes or critics such as Bethea or Polukhina who are able to read Russian. Other examples are more general: "man's figure is ugly and stiff as a frightening hieroglyph,/as any illegible scripture"; "what gets left of a man amounts/to a part. To his spoken part. To a part of speech"; "Now I can state with confidence:/here I'll live out my days, losing gradually/hair, teeth, consonants, verbs, and suffixes".[96] Paradoxically, these images of physical decay and absence ultimately testify to Brodsky's very survival. It is a poetic trope with which we are familiar – that of the poet, or his subject, immortalised in words – but with the added fact that for the exile this takes on another level of significance and poignancy. As Polukhina says, "Severed from his linguistic milieu, Brodsky seems to survive thanks to language alone."[97]

Turning once more to Brodsky's 'Lithuanian Nocturne', we can understand the return of the poet's spectre to the Soviet Union in precisely these terms: not as the fidelity of a subject for a particular political state, but as the return of the subject to language. However, this locating and identifying of the self in, and with, language, is not quite what it seems.

Brodsky's revenant survives in ways similar to the concluding statement of Adorno's essay 'On the Final Scene of *Faust*': "Hope is not memory held fast but the return of what has been forgotten."[98] Adorno's argument, formulated after his own experience of exile in America, is in many ways analogous to Mandelstam's definition of poetry as "something intelligible, grasped, wrested from obscurity in a language voluntarily and willingly forgotten immediately after the act of intellection and realization is completed."[99] The "damaged life", the life of the émigré that is the subject of Adorno's *Minima Moralia*, becomes one of remembrance and reflection, the defining feature of which is a distancing from, and a diffusing of identity. Language, as it must, is the arena in which this takes place:

> That's whence, Thomas, the pen's
> troth to letters. That's what must explain gravitation,
>   don't you think?
>   With the roosters' 'Time's up,'
>   that light-entity rends
> its light self from its verbs and their tense,
>   from its hair-shirted nation,
>   from – let's loosen the trap –
> you: from letters, from pages, from sound's
> love for sense, from incorporeality's passion
>   toward mass, and from freedom's, alas,
>   love for slavery's haunts –
>   for the bone, for the flesh, and
>   for the heart – having thus
> liberated itself, that light-entity soars up to ink-
>   like dark heavenly reaches,
>   past blind cherubs in niches,
>   past the bats that won't wink.[100]

This returns us to that passage of Mandelstam's 'Conversation About Dante' quoted earlier, in which Mandelstam asserts that "poetry is not a part of nature ... let alone a reflection of it ... rather, poetry establishes itself with astonishing independence in a new extra-spatial field of action." This "extra-spatial field" is, in Brodsky's strophe, equated with "ink-/like dark heavenly reaches" presided over by Urania, the tutelary spirit of the conclusion of 'Lithuanian Nocturne'. It is significant that of all the Classical muses he might have chosen to address, Brodsky, following Milton's example in *Paradise Lost*, chooses that of Astronomy. Throughout the poem, Urania is associated with a cluster of ideas and associations that are to do with ways of communicating across vast distances: with Morse code, or with those constellations that provided the earliest reliable means of navigation. What Urania also provides is a perspective on human affairs strikingly similar to that of the night sky – "The heaventree of stars hung with humid nightblue fruit" – which dominates the penultimate chapter of *Ulysses*, and about which Joyce wrote:

> All events are resolved into their cosmic physical, psychical, etc. equivalents ... so that not only will the reader know everything and know it in the baldest coldest way, but Bloom and Stephen thereby become heavenly bodies, wanderers like the stars at which they gaze.[101]

Brodsky's muse of "dots lost in space" becomes, then, one of the objectifications of human language from the "viewpoint/of air,/of pure air", which is ultimately "That town/which all syllables long/to return to." Thus it is through language itself, and the structures created by it and peculiar to it, that the exile discovers his or her identity. As with Benjamin's convergence of subjective experience and objective material, or Mandelstam's "something intelligible, grasped, wrested from obscurity", language in 'Lithuanian Nocturne' is the means by which Brodsky's spectre, its "slurring voice – /a sound more like houseflies/bravely clicking a tin", re-enacts that movement by which, in Adorno's words, "the human becomes language, the flesh becomes word, incorporat[ing] the expression of nature into language and transfigur[ing] the movement of language so that it becomes life again."[102] It is a movement in which the subject extinguishes itself in the service of speech – a process which Brodsky personifies as the "Muse of subtraction/... without remainders" – only to be 'reborn' not as hypertrophied meaning but as a return to a "single primal language, an *Ur-Sprache*". It is to this absolute homecoming that Brodsky looks forward:

> ... Muse, may I set
> out homeward? [...]
> to your grammar without

punctuation, to your Paradise of our alphabets [...]
to your blackboard in white.[103]

Thus language becomes an alter ego about which we might say that it has 'no fixed abode', not only because it moves and flows but also because 'it is always not something else'.[104] It is a vision of poetic language as, in Benjamin's words, an origin "which emerges out of the process of becoming and disappearing."[105]

Ultimately, 'Lithuanian Nocturne' is Brodsky's attempt at 'loosening the trap' around the damaged life. It engages with, and gives metaphorical form to, profound and disquieting truths about exile, both biographical and metaphysical. But to paraphrase Adorno, it is "compounded of negation and indeterminacy and for that very reason ... signifies reconciliation and transcendence."[106] In conclusion, then, we can say that Urania becomes the muse, in Homeric terms, of *nostos* – the journey towards, and arrival at, home. It is a journey in which time and human consciousness, history and myth fuse in language to "propel the poet ... with the speed of sound", a sound which, as a "measure of the soul" denies any form of finiteness or stasis and is defined by the "physical (metaphysical) duration and distance of its wandering in time."[107]

VII

"We know," John Hollander writes, "that words are used without regard for their origins save by pedants and sometimes poets."[108] 'Lithuanian Nocturne' ends by alerting us to the cluster of meanings and associations surrounding the word 'home' in English. Indeed, we might suggest that the word has its own history of *nostos*. For as Hollander shows, the patterns of dispersed meaning run long and deep. At its simplest this involves the truism unspoken in the concluding line of Brodsky's poem: "Home is where the heart is." Derived from the Old English 'ham', home has come to involve the apparently contradictory notions of both source and destination: a place of origin returned to and, ultimately, death, the "long home" of Ecclesiastes. The essential hybridity of English, its protean ability to assimilate words from other languages, has, as Hollander goes on to say, played a part in this:

Our resonant Germanic word *home* (*Heim, ham, heem*, etc.) seems to derive from an original Indo-European *kei*, implying lying down, a bed or couch, and sometimes dear or beloved, which also yields *haunt* and even *cemetery* (from Greek *koiman*, 'to put to sleep'). The metaphorical implication of the semantic change is that home is a place to lay your head... And as is frequently the case with the poetic texture of the King James Version, an inadvertent ghost metaphor arises from the modern reader's misconstruing of the earlier English. *Long* thus becomes dimensional rather than durational, and *long home* the final, horizontal dwelling of the grave, the place of dust returned to, the place that really was our home all along.[109]

The text as a haunted house is an idea that can also be distilled from Brodsky's essay on Tsvetaeva's 'New Year's Greeting'. Commenting on the presence of Rilke in the poem, Brodsky writes: "Apart from the concrete, deceased Rilke, there appears in the poem an image (or idea) of an 'absolute Rilke', who has ceased being a body in space and has become a soul – in eternity." This "absolute, maximum removal" of the poet creates, Brodsky says, a vacuum in which Tsvetaeva can express "maximum selflessness and maximum candor".[110]

Brodsky's introductory remarks in the essay are highly revealing about his own work, especially its relationship to traditions other than an indigenous Russian one. Having argued that every 'on the death of' poem tells us as much, if not more, about the author as it does the deceased (an equation which is even truer if the person being elegised is another writer "with whom the author was linked by bonds – real or imaginary – too strong for the author to avoid the temptation of identifying with the poem's subject") Brodsky goes on to say that:

> self-mourning, at times bordering on self-admiration, can and even must be explained by the fact that the addressees were always, specifically, fellow writers; that the tragedy was occurring within native Russian literature, and self-pity was the reverse of presumptuousness and an outgrowth of the sense of loneliness that increases with the passing of any poet and is, in any case, intrinsic to a writer. If, however, the subject was the demise of a preeminent figure belonging to another

culture (the death of Byron or Goethe, for example), its very 'foreignness' seemed to give added stimulus to the most general, abstract kind of discussion, viz.: of the role of the 'bard' in the life of society, of art in general, of, as Akhmatova puts it, 'ages and peoples.' Emotional distance in these cases engendered a didactic diffuseness [...] The element of self-portraiture in these instances naturally disappeared; for, paradoxical as it might seem, death, in spite of all its properties as a common denominator, did not lessen the distance between the author and the mourned 'bard', but, on the contrary, increased it, as though an elegist's ignorance regarding the circumstances of the life of a particular 'Byron' extended as well to the essence of that 'Byron's' death. In other words, death, in its turn, was perceived as something foreign, alien – which may be perfectly justified as circumstantial evidence of its – death's – inscrutability.[111]

It is difficult to believe that Brodsky isn't also commenting here on his own elegy for T.S. Eliot. We might certainly recognise a certain "didactic diffuseness" in the elegy, though the element of self-portraiture that Brodsky sees as defining elegies for a known poet is missing. This becomes clearer if we compare 'Verses on the Death of T.S. Eliot' to the later 'Elegy: for Robert Lowell'.

Brodsky and Lowell first met at the 1972 Poetry International, where the American offered to read Brodsky's poems in English. They continued to be friends until Lowell's death in 1977. Whereas 'Verses on the Death of T.S. Eliot' is as much an elegy for Mandelstam and a eulogy to Auden as it is a memorial for Eliot, 'Elegy: for Robert Lowell', written directly in English, is a much clearer homage to Lowell's individual achievement:

> In the autumnal blue
> of your church-hooded New
> England, the porcupine
> sharpens its golden needles
> against Bostonian bricks
>
> to a point of needless
> blinding shine.[112]

The formal patterning of the first section of the poem imitates –

in a very loose and Lowell-like manner – the stanzaic form and free-floating rhymes of Lowell's 'Skunk Hour' which was itself a response to Elizabeth Bishop's 'Armadillo', a poem which she dedicated to him. It also owes a formal debt to W.D. Snodgrass' 'Heart's Needle'.[113]

In October 1957 Lowell sent Randall Jarrell a copy of 'Skunk Hour' and, hearing that he liked it, sent him more poems and a letter in which he recommended two young poets, Philip Larkin and Snodgrass, the latter of whom had been a student of Lowell's in Iowa. Lowell was later to praise Snodgrass for, in Ian Hamilton's words, "the way in which … 'Heart's Needle' managed to treat with a kind of wry nobility a subject that in other hands might not have avoided sweetness and self-pity: the separation, by divorce, of the poet from his baby daughter."[114] It is a textual history that Brodsky refers to in his elegy by introducing a porcupine into the poem instead of an armadillo or skunk and, as a nod towards Snodgrass, draws attention to its "golden needles". But it is also likely that Brodsky intends further connections, both textual and biographical.

The first section of the poem refers to Lowell, and through Lowell to Bishop; the second section riffs on Dante's *terza rima*; and the concluding two sections return us to the trochaic tetrameter of 'Verses on the Death of T.S. Eliot' and 'In Memory of W.B. Yeats'. Clearly, then, the elegy has become an occasion for Brodsky not only to mourn an individual poet but to celebrate, in a manner recognisable from his elegy for Eliot, the essential hybridity of Russian, European and now American culture.

While there does not appear to be, in Brodsky's words, any "self-mourning" within his 'Elegy', it is impossible not to see in the relationship between Snodgrass' poem – an elegy for a family – and his own, some reference to the fact that in leaving Russia he left behind him a wife and son. The first section of the poem thus becomes a self-portrait of the artist as exile. Furthermore, the armadillo in Bishop's poem – "Hastily, all alone,/a glistening armadillo left the scene,/rose-flecked, head down, tail down" – is, like the poet in Brodsky's sonnet "Once more we're living off the Bay", fleeing death by fire, wanting to avoid becoming, in an image that echoes both Eliot and Donne, "a handful of intangible ash/with fixed, ignited eyes". In Lowell's *homage* to Bishop, the skunk with its "'moonstruck eyes' red fire/under the chalk-dry and spar spire/of the Trinitarian

Church" becomes an image of all that is lacking from the ill, isolated, abandoned poet's life. Brodsky's porcupine fuses the two. The porcupine, as with Lowell's skunk, is harbouring in the shade of a church. But whereas the skunk is a Trinitarian, the porcupine is, given the Boston location, more likely to prove a free-thinking Emersonian Unitarian. It is an independence of mind that is also figured in the fact that, literally and metaphorically, the porcupine is a prickly customer, a loner who, in popular belief at least, is able to loose its quills like arrows or darts. In other words, in the same way that for Lowell the skunk represented, in Jonathan Raban's words, "a self-contained, instinctual grace"[115] so the porcupine for Brodsky becomes a self-portrait of the émigré poet.

Returning to Brodsky's essay on Tsvetaeva, we find him commenting on the relationship between poet and reader. This follows a passage where he quotes from his own translation of Tsvetaeva's poem 'Homesickness':

> Nor shall I crave my native speech,
> Its milky call that comes in handy.
> It makes no difference in which
> tongue passers-by won't comprehend me.[116]

In relation to Tsvetaeva's writing, it's easy to read this as a comment on her status as an émigré poet. Living in France and writing in Russian, she was neither understood by the people around her, who could not speak the language of her poetry, nor could people in Russia read her because her poetry remained unpublished there. Brodsky, however, sees Tsvetaeva's predicament not as an individual case study but as being in some essential way the position of all writers: "the greater – unintentionally – his demands on an audience ... the narrower that audience is." "In these instances," he continues:

> the poet directly addresses either the angels, as Rilke does in the *Duino Elegies*, or another poet – especially one who is dead ... In both instances what takes place is a monologue, and in both instances it assumes an absolute quality, for the author addresses his words to nonexistence, to Chronos.[117]

We have already seen how, in the guise of Urania, Brodsky

addresses an angel of his own making. Returning to 'Elegy: for Robert Lowell', we can now see, in light of these comments on Tsvetaeva, that the poem becomes not simply an occasion for mourning the death of a poet and a friend but, given his relationship to the language in which he is writing, a commentary on Brodsky's own émigré status. This is clearest in the second section where Brodsky switches from a stanzaic and metrical pattern based loosely on Lowell's 'Skunk Hour' to one, equally loose, based on Dante's *terza rima*.[118] And it is not just the form that is meant to put us in mind of Dante.

At its simplest, this section of the poem re-imagines Lowell's funeral as a constellation of images and scenes from Dante's *Inferno*. Brodsky, as Dante, finds himself on the banks of the Acheron, where the souls of the dead congregate before crossing over into Hell. The image of the child, "commalike, loiter[ing]/among dresses and pants/ of vowels and consonants/that don't make a word", as well as reminding us of the "Folk ... scuffling from Churches protecting the commas/of their candle flames" in 'Lithuanian Nocturne', is also Brodsky's version of Dante's vision of those souls that were neither committed to nor turned against God but who, as Virgil says, "to self alone were true". Speech has been taken away from them and they have returned to the chaos that reigned after the collapse of the tower at Babel:

> The sighs, groans and laments at first were so loud
>   Resounding through starless air, I began to weep:
>   Strange languages, horrible screams, words imbued
>
> With rage or despair, cries as of troubled sleep
>   Or of a tortured shrillness – they rose in a coil
>   Of tumult, along with noises like the slap
>
> Of beating hands, all fused in a ceaseless flail
>   That churns and frenzies that dark and timeless air
>   Like sand in a whirlwind[.][119]

The dominant image in these lines is of language struggling and failing to articulate itself because of the fact that the damned souls led a life alienated from God, their fellow human beings and themselves. Hell, in Dante's book, is the ultimate destination of every kind of spiritual exile. In one sense, this returns us to 'Elegy for

John Donne', with its central belief that when a poet dies "there are no more sounds in all the world." It may also represent Brodsky's own experience of alienation living in a country whose language, five years after his arrival in the West, he must still have been struggling to master. Without wishing to limit the meaning of these lines to Brodsky's biography, there is some evidence that this sense of being displaced as a writer among "vowels and consonants/that don't make a word" was an important factor at the time of Lowell's death.

Though 'Elegy: for Robert Lowell' was not the first poem Brodsky wrote directly in English (this was an elegy for Auden written in 1973, included in an anthology of tributes edited by Stephen Spender and later disowned by Brodsky[120]) it is the earliest poem included in any of his published collections in English. The poem therefore takes on a significance in relation to Brodsky's position that can hardly be overstated. It sees him both looking to widen his circle of readers and, as he movingly admits in his essay for Auden, 'To Please a Shadow', to engage not just with English as a language but as a code of conscience. It is, in short, Brodsky's conscious decision to leave those uncommitted souls who stand on the banks of Acheron and, in a phrase redolent of Dante's own journey, "set out to write" with Auden as his Virgil.

'Elegy: for Robert Lowell', then, can be read, in part at least, as returning to the elegy that aspect of self-portraiture which Brodsky, in his essay on Tsvetaeva, saw as missing from any poem in memory of "a preeminent figure belonging to another culture" and whose "very 'foreignness' seemed to give added stimulus to the most general, abstract kind of discussion." This is not to say that the element of self-portraiture in the poem is not hidden or disguised. What has changed, of course, is that unlike 'Verses on the Death of T.S. Eliot', Brodsky is in one essential way no longer writing about a foreign poet. In choosing to memorialise Lowell directly in English, Brodsky actively sought to lessen the distance between himself and the dead, "the sense of loneliness that increases with the passing of any poet". What is more, just as the earlier elegy for Eliot can be read as an acknowledgement of the importance of Mandelstam's influence, so the elegy for Lowell leads us to the influence of Auden in that it looks to engage with "whatever it is in the English language that made [his] code of conscience possible."

With its references to Dante, 'Elegy: for Robert Lowell' can also be seen as blurring the distinctions between the epic and the lyric. The significance of this in relation to what has just been said becomes further apparent when we read the poem in the context of Jakobson's essay 'Marginal Notes On the Prose of the Poet Pasternak':

> Whatever subject matter the lyric narrative may have, it is never more than an appendage and accessory, a mere background to the first person; and if the past is involved, then the lyric past always presupposes a reminiscing first-person subject. In the epic, on the contrary, the present refers expressly back to the past, and if the 'I' of the narrator does find expression, it is solely as one of the characters in the action. This objectified 'I' thus appears as variant on the third person; the poet is, as it were, looking at himself from outside.[121]

In a number of ways, then, Brodsky's elegy takes precisely the viewpoint Jakobson defines as belonging to the epic, while placing it within the context of what is essentially a lyric subject matter. In the first two sections of the poem – those corresponding to Lowell's 'Skunk Hour' and Dante's *Commedia* – the poet is present as a character in the action surrounding Lowell's funeral. What is interesting is how Brodsky integrates "the lyric past" into the poem through a series of inter-textual references, thus removing the past from the sphere of biography and re-locating it within the "twists of language". Furthermore, the impersonal processes of death and metamorphosis, which appear in the elegies for Donne and Eliot, are figured in the poem for Lowell by a similar displacement onto metonymic detail. What is subtly different about this technique here, however, is that it is the mourners and not the world of material objects who are thus changed: "People's/eyes glitter inside/the church like pebbles/splashed by the tide" and "When man dies/The wardrobe gapes instead./We acquire the idle state/of your jackets and ties." Again following Jakobson, the poem objectifies the experience of grief. Both grammatically, with the third person plural standing in for the first person singular, and metonymically, "the poet is, as it were, looking at himself from outside."

This is taken a step further in the poem's second section where, in the image of "A child, commalike, loiter[ing]/among dresses and pants/of vowels and consonants", there are clear parallels between that aspect of Brodsky's writing which not only sees the Word as object, but the world as text. This is a point to which it is worth returning, especially in light of Jakobson's Pasternak essay, because it helps further define what is meant when we say that Brodsky's writing is characterised by its use of metalanguage.

Quoting Pasternak's belief that "Each detail [in a poem] can be replaced by another ... Any one of them, chosen at random, will serve to bear witness to the transposed condition by which the whole of reality is seized"[122] Jakobson makes the point that Pasternak's art is one of "the mutual interchangeability of images". In its own way, this definition comes close to that aspect of Brodsky's poetry which critics have regarded as a major flaw, one Eduard Limonov calls his "catalogue of objects":

> Things are his weakness. Almost all his poems are written using one and the same method: a motionless philosophising author surveys a panorama of things around himself. Let's say that it's as if Brodsky wakes up in a room in a Venice hotel and with a sad dutifulness (there's nothing to be done, they are there) enumerates for us the things he finds in his room ... Then, (almost the only moment in the poem) the poet moves across to the window and communicates to us what he sees outside: ships, boats, launches.[123]

Jakobson clearly sees something of the same 'weakness for things' in Pasternak's writings, though here it is translated into a strength. What needs to be determined is what is signified by "the absolute commitment of the poet to metonymy". Jakobson's answer returns us to the aspect of self-portraiture discussed earlier:

> The hero is as if concealed in a picture puzzle; he is broken down into a series of constituent and subsidiary parts; he is replaced by a chain of concretized situations and surrounding objects, both animate and inanimate ... Show us your environment and I will tell you who you are. We learn what he lives on, this lyric hero outlined by metonymies, split up by synecdoches into individual attributes, reactions and situations

… But the truly heroic element, the hero's activity, eludes our perception; action is replaced by topography. ... [T]he world is a mirror to the world.[124]

Substituting 'word' for "world", it can be seen how the phrase "the word is a mirror to the world" /"the world is a mirror to the word" captures perfectly the self-reflexive aspect of Brodsky's poetry. Furthermore, Jakobson's 'lyric hero', like Brodsky, is recognised in relation to his 'parts of speech'. Language and biography fuse once more, the subject being defined by his verbal environment.

Turning to 'Venetian Stanzas II', one of the poems which Liminov might well have had in mind when he described Brodsky's "motionless philosophising author survey[ing] a panorama of things around himself", we see how the succession of individual details, far from simply recording the objects among which the poet finds himself 'marooned', provide surfaces against which he can verify his own personal and emotional reality. For example:

> Motorboats, rowboats, gondolas, dinghies, barges –
> like odd scattered shoes, unmatched, God-size –
> zealously trample pilasters, sharp spires, bridges'
> arcs, the look in one's eyes.
> Everything's doubled, save destiny, save the very
> H_2O. Yet the idle turquoise on high
> renders – like any 'pro' vote – this world a merry
> minority in one's eye.[125]

It is fitting that Venice should provide the topography for Brodsky's reflections on exile. Founded and built by refugees from other Italian states, it was here that Brodsky travelled after finishing his first semester's teaching in Ann Arbor in 1972. Whatever the personal associations the city held for Brodsky it came to assume a metaphysical dimension in his thinking:

> Yet, what is most stunning about Venice is the water. Water, if you like, is a condensed form of time. If we're going to follow the Book with a capital B, then let us recall what it says there: 'And the Spirit of God moved upon the face of the waters.' If He did move upon the face of the waters, that means he was reflected in them. He, of course, being time, right?[126]

Venice thus becomes the focus for two of Brodsky's recurrent themes: the relationship between the Logos and the material world; and the way in which language in its highest form, poetry, restructures time. In essence, it is associated in Brodsky's mind with "the possibility of change ... The changing year, the changing time; time rising up out of water."[127] Returning to Jakobson, it is striking to note how for Brodsky, as much as for Pasternak, "action is replaced by topography", and that the idea of the author as motionless philosopher is replaced by that of a dynamic interchange between environment and consciousness. Rather than simply recording the world around him, the poet actively looks to construct an identity for himself – a doubled identity – through language. The poet, like God, is only able to know himself by seeing his own reflection in the waters of creation.

Whatever its ambiguities, Louis MacNeice's celebration of what he famously called "the drunkenness of things being various" is made possible because the poet recognises around him objects that find their correlative in language. In other words, environment *and* language confirm the poet's identity. The world may be "crazier and more of it than we think", but at least the poet is able to communicate this brimming plurality to others.

The poet of 'Venetian Stanzas II', however, is one for whom the variousness of his environment – its essential doubleness – only confirms in him a sense of verbal isolation and physical obsolescence. Writing in Russian (the poem was later translated into English by Brodsky and Jane Anne Miller), a gulf opens between poet and world. Trying to arrest time in a faltering language will not work. Subsumed in his actions – writing and speaking – he has become an island, a little Russia in a sea of English; or, as he later wrote in 'Infinitive', "at the very least an island within an island." In other words, activity – language – has become metamorphosed into topography in a process recognisable from, say, 'Verses on the Death of T.S. Eliot'.

Here as elsewhere in Brodsky's work, language and writing function as metonyms for the poet himself. Metonym rather than metaphor because, as Jakobson says, metaphor works by establishing "a network of correspondences, and masterful assimilations",[128] whereas for Brodsky no such assimilation is either possible or necessarily desirable. For the young man whose tactics of estrangement were a deliberate response to the pressures of religious, racial and political assimilation, difference was a hard won distinction. For the mature poet it became both an existential fact of life and a metaphysical condition of language. Furthermore, while Jakobson sees metaphor as associated primarily in poetry with the lyrical impulse (i.e. with the subjective), metonym is the basic imagistic unit of the realist text or the epic in which, as suggested earlier, the first person is relegated to the background. While metaphor "works through creative association by similarity and contrast", metonymy functions by substituting one word for another with which it is contiguous. Both are acts of translation, the difference being that the harmonisation of experience associated with the metaphor becomes, in the metonym, one in which each object is "awakened to individual life."[129] In short, metonymy results in a world in which, like exile, "spatial distribution and temporal distribution" are transformed and dislocated. In doing so it becomes another process of estrangement,

Such an impulse can be seen at work in Brodsky's poetry right from the beginning, though it took on an added impetus and significance following his exile to Norenskaya. In 'Autumn in Norenskaya', for example, written in 1965 and included in *A Part of Speech*, literary estrangement becomes the means by which the poem portrays the experience of physical and geographical displacement. As with Venice, it is a landscape where nothing is what it seems. Having entered language each material thing becomes refracted, like a finger dipped into a glass of water. It is a landscape in violent motion. As with the fog in the opening pages of Dickens's *Bleak House*, the wind transforms everything: buckets become bells, horses are reduced to the ribs of a wooden cask. Objects are given human characteristics – the willow has a "fringe", the cart a "profile" – while humans, as we might expect in a labour camp, are reduced to the status of objects: the women are first cabbages, then blunted scissors. Only the women's ultimate destination, the sense-solid "wooden beds", remains fixed, reminding us of the line quoted earlier from 'Venetian Stanzas II': "Everything's doubled, save destiny". But even here the phrase is ominous, containing as it does intimations of mortality: coffins as "wooden overcoats" and suggestive of the "long home" of *Ecclesiastes*.

Thus made strange, such images function in a way similar to the 'catalogue of things' in a poem such as 'Venetian Stanzas II'. There the metonym is used to stress the surface of things, denying a depth of field. They are, as it were, connections across space rather than time. It is interesting, therefore, to note how the description of the women "scissor[ing] their way home" operates as both metonym and metaphor. Metonymically, it reduces the women to Bosch-like figures inhabiting a frozen Hell; metaphorically, as Polukhina has suggested, 'scissors' signifies death.[130] Thus space and time are contained in the same image.

'Autumn in Norenskaya' is also a poem that sees the poet withdrawing into the background. Indeed, he is to all intents and purposes absent. He appears in the poem's opening line – "*We* return from the field" – only for his presence to become one of observation rather than participation. In other words, his identity becomes one with the landscape described. Only in the fourth stanza is he present in even the most etiolated form:

> These visions are the final sign
> of an inner life that seizes on
> any specter to which it feels kin
> till the specter scares off for good
> at the church bell of a creaking axle,
> at the metal rattle of the world as it
> lies reversed in a rut of water,
> at a starling soaring into cloud.

These are remarkable lines to find in a poem that has so far concentrated on surfaces, on a kind of spiritual desiccation. Like a prelude to the various flights of fancy contained in 'Lithuanian Nocturne', and written just two years after 'Elegy for John Donne', we can see Brodsky creating a self-portrait of himself as a ghost, as a "specter". As was discussed earlier, in 'Lithuanian Nocturne' the spectre is associated with the survival of "highly pitched vocal/atoms, alias souls"; in the Donne elegy, the soul is "like a bird/.../which soars above the starlings' empty homes". Furthermore, we understand from 'Venetian Stanzas II' and from other comments, the significance Brodsky attached to the experience of seeing the world reflected and reversed in water.

Rather than writing, the poet's role or activity in this landscape is one of simply keeping alive the visionary, of witnessing the 'final sign' of a spiritual life ticking over within a world that is both actually and metaphorically frozen. Moreover, in merging his biographical identity with that of a collective 'we', Brodsky repositions the poet within another dimension. As at his trial for social parasitism, when he defended himself by arguing that the poet derives his authority from God, and not the Soviet authorities, so in 'Autumn in Norenskaya', written as a direct result of that stance, he declares reality to consist essentially of a verbal depth. There is nothing escapist or solipsistic about this. For while the starling may soar into cloud, the poet – in a phrase which evokes Augustine's "my love is my weight" – is held in place by "stubborn clods of the native earth".

VIII

In 'Autumn in Norenskaya' we find an example of what Polukhina calls "the figurative means by which the lyrical 'I' is constituted".[131] Here, as has already been said, it merges into a collective 'we'. In the sonnet 'Once more we're living off the Bay', however, it is part of a threatened 'us'; while in other poems it is disguised as various personae – St Simeon, Byron, Odysseus and Ovid, for example. Polukhina lists a number more, each of which "establish an equivalence between the 'I' and major historical figures [and] always carry an ironical nuance."[132] Brodsky is clearly a poet for whom consciousness of his own personality and biography is at least as important as the ways in which he sees and conceptualises the world. Underpinning both is the nature of language.

So Forth (1996), his last published collection of poems, opens with 'Infinitive'. In it we are introduced to another exilic persona:

> ... I write this with my index finger
> on the wet, glassy sand at sunset, being inspired perhaps
> by the view of the palm-tree tops splayed against the
> platinum sky like some
> Chinese characters. Though I've never studied the language.
> Besides, the breeze
> tousles them all too fast for one to make out the message.[133]

Metalanguage, as a way of talking about the self, becomes, as metonymy, a way of seeing the self objectified in space. Though we might recognise in 'Infinitive' the voice of Ovid exiled in Tomis, the fictional Crusoe on his desert island, or even Bishop's Crusoe – whom experience taught that "Pity should begin at home. So the more/pity I felt, the more I felt at home" – there is a sense by this stage in his life that Brodsky had invented his own persona, one as immediately recognisable as any of his previous models.

All the familiar elements are here: the delineation of self in terms of landscape; the interdependence of time and speech; the survival of the past in fragments; and a Logocentric vision of the material world. Reading the poem, we might also think that for all his protestations to the contrary Brodsky is beginning to feel at ease in, and with, the English language. It is as though he has decided to settle into one of those chairs shaped like the letters 'b' or 'h'. Suddenly the language fits. But does this mean that Brodsky was simply going over familiar ground? Is the persona of the exile one he simply chooses to put on like a favourite, worn overcoat? Consideration of this question brings us full circle.

In 'Constancy', exile is characterised as "an evolution of one's living quarters into/a thought: a continuation .../by means .../of the voice".[134] While this returns us to a number of central issues in Brodsky's writings – the survival of 'vocal atoms', for example – it also touches on two ways of apprehending the world: the scientific and the metaphysical. Later in the poem Brodsky goes on to develop further this idea of evolution:

> Evolution is not a species'
> adjustment to a new environment but one's memories'
> triumph over reality, the ichthyosaurus pining
> for the amoeba, the slack vertebrae of a train
> thundering in the darkness, past
> the mussel shells, tightly shut for the night, with their
> spineless, soggy, pearl-shrouding contents.

"By making things strange," as Svetlana Boyd says, "the artist does not simply displace them from an everyday context into an artistic framework; he also helps to 'return sensation' to life itself, to reinvent the world, to experience it anew". At the conclusion of 'Constancy' this means a literal return to the depths of human consciousness, to the waters from which life began. While Marx argued that "existence conditions experience", Brodsky shows how memory re-members or re-imagines the world, allowing a very different set of *associative* conditions to prevail.

In *Proust and the Sense of Time*, Julia Kristeva writes of how "perception is always in a state of being stretched between the *world of the present* and the *historical past*: that is why it is bound to be 'subjective and incommunicable'.[135] In a sense, this is precisely the situation in which both the exile and the invalid find themselves caught. It is one where the material world of objects is unstable; experience fluctuates between the objective and subjective, past and present: "a bedside table with/little medicine bottles left standing there like/a kremlin or, better yet, Manhattan."[136] Earlier we saw that such estrangement was a deliberate act on Brodsky's part. It allowed him a degree of independence. If in the beginning this was an aesthetic counter to socialist realism, all that time and geography did was to make it less a state of mind than a condition of life:

> To die, to abandon a family, to go away for good,
> to change hemispheres, to let new ovals
> be painted into the square – the more
> volubly will the gray cell insist
> on its actual measurements, demanding
> daily sacrifice from the new locale,
> from the furniture, from the silhouette in a yellow
> dress; in the end – from your very self.

Perhaps if the KGB had read this 'confession' they would have judged the decision to exile Brodsky a success. The prisoner of conscience has become a prisoner of his own consciousness. Demanding "daily sacrifices", he becomes both the god and the savages described in 'Infinitive'.

What provides the means of escape from this solipsistic universe, as Kristeva says, is the fact that the "subject of feeling turns himself into a thinker[.] In his double role as one who senses and one who meditates, he will think through his work, aiming 'to draw forth from the shadow – what [Proust] had merely felt, by trying to convert it into its spiritual equivalent'".[137] A prisoner of surfaces and of space, the poet escapes through speech: the limitations of "a parallelogram or a rectangle" are transformed – become boundless – through "the voice and, ultimately, the gray matter".

'Constancy' ends with a yearning for first causes, showing us the poet wanting to return to the sea so as to see God's face reflected in the waters of the first day. The truth, however, is that the mystery of creation – "the mussel shells, tightly shut for the night, with their/ spineless, soggy, pearl-shrouding contents" – must remain a secret. The nearest we can come to it is through language, which, as Kristeva says, "establishes imaginative connections and discloses ... unsuspected depths".[138] It is a transformation and an evolution which, in 'Lullaby of Cape Cod', is seen as the essential condition of human existence:

> ... man survives like a fish,
> stranded, beached, but intent
> on adapting itself to some deep, cellular wish,
> wriggling toward bushes, forming hinged leg struts, then
> to depart (leaving a track like the scrawl of a pen)
> for the interior, the heart of the continent.[139]

The medium for this survival instinct is memory, which, as Brodsky says in 'Less Than One', "is a substitute for the tail we lost for good in the happy process of evolution. It directs our movements, including migration ... Also, the more one remembers, the closer perhaps one is to dying".[140] There is a sense, then, in which Brodsky always saw his exile as a kind of posthumous existence – witness the returning "specter" of 'Lithuanian Nocturne'. In addition to this, there is that strain in his writings that regards all human existence as in some essential way a separation. "The perspective of years straightens things to the point of complete obliteration. Nothing brings them back, not even handwritten words ... But if the printed word were only a mark of forgetfulness, that would be fine. The sad truth is that words fail reality as well."[141]

As we have seen, the image of the exile runs throughout Brodsky's writings, before and after he himself experienced the physical, emotional and political reality. Allied to this is the literary technique of estrangement, the aim of which is to bring forth from alienation "surprise at the world, intensified perception."[142] Writing, then, for Brodsky, is always both a new departure and homecoming. Metaphysical exile is constantly exchanged for transcendental homelessness. The only point of rest in time or space is that of the pen on the page: "But now the giddy pen/points out resemblances, for after all//the device in your hand is the same old pen and ink/as before".[143] Inevitably, it is to language – in all its "twists" and "spiral splendour" – that Brodsky returns. It is language – the Logos – which brought the world into being; and it is as language – "Give me another life, and I'll be singing"[144] – that he imagined his own destination.

Notes

[1] Marcel Proust, *In Search of Lost Time*, 6 vols, General Editor: Christopher Prendergast (London: Penguin/Allen Lane, 2002), Vol. 2: 415.

[2] Derek Walcott, 'Magic Industry: Joseph Brodsky' in *What the Twilight Says: Essays* (London: Faber and Faber, 1998), 139.

[3] Svetlana Boym, 'Estrangement as a Lifestyle: Shklovsky and Brodsky' in *Exile and Creativity*, ed. Susan Rubin Sulieman (Durham and London: Duke University Press, 1996), 245.

[4] This and the previous quotations from Brodsky appear in 'Less Than One' in *Less Than One: Selected Essays* (New York: Farrar Straus Giroux, 1987), 3.

[5] Ibid., 7-8.

[6] Joseph Brodsky, 'On September 1, 1939' by W.H. Auden' in *Less Than One*, 305.

[7] Joseph Brodsky, 'Less Than One', 29.

[8] In *Hope Abandoned*, the second part of her memoirs about the life and death of her husband, Nadezhda Mandelstam comments on precisely the moral, ethical and artistic importance of the word 'we' and its relationship with 'I' in the context of the USSR:

> We witnessed the disintegration of a society which was as imperfect as any other, but which concealed and curbed its wickedness and harboured small groups of people who were truly entitled to refer to themselves as 'we'. I am quite convinced that without such a 'we', there can be no proper fulfilment of even the most ordinary 'I', that is, of the personality. To find its fulfilment, the 'I' needs at least two complementary dimensions: 'we' and – if it is fortunate – 'you'. I think M. [Osip Mandelstam] was lucky to have a moment in his life when he was linked by the pronoun 'we' with a group of others. His brief friendship with certain 'companions, co-seekers, co-discoverers' – to quote a phrase from 'Conversation About Dante' – affected him for the rest of his life, helping to

mould his personality. In 'Conversation About Dante' he also says that time is the stuff of history and that, conversely, 'the stuff of history is the joint tenure of time' by people bound together as 'we' (*Hope Abandoned*, trans. Max Hayward (London: Collins Harvill, 1989), 25.

[9] Joseph Brodsky, 'Less Than One', 30.

[10] See Homi K. Bhabha, *The Location of Culture* (London and New York: Routledge, 1994), 224.

[11] Joseph Brodsky, 'The Condition We Call Exile' in *On Grief and Reason: Essays* (New York: Farrar Strauss Giroux, 1995), 24.

[12] George Steiner, *After Babel: Aspects of Language and Translation* (London: Faber and Faber, 1975), 18.

[13] Ibid., 19.

[14] See Victor Terras, *A History of Russian Literature* (New Haven: Yale University Press, 1991), 503-509.

[15] Homi K. Bhabha , *The Location of Culture*, 225.

[16] Solomon Volkov, *Conversations With Joseph Brodsky: A Poet's Journey Through the Twentieth Century*, trans. Marian Schwartz (New York: The Free Press, 1998), 7. As with his *Testimony: The Memoirs of Dmitri Shostakovich*, Volkov's conversations with Brodsky have aroused a certain degree of controversy. The following letter from Ann Kjellberg appeared in the *TLS* on 2/10/98:

> Sir, – The Free Press have recently published in the UK a book entitled *Conversations with Joseph Brodsky* by Solomon Volkov. Your readers may wish to know that this book was prepared without the participation or approval of Mr Brodsky or his estate, and questions we have raised about the sources of the text and its compilation have not been answered to our satisfaction. Until they are, readers may prefer to approach this book with some scepticism as to its language and contents.

To the best of the author's knowledge these doubts have not yet been cleared up and so Volkov's reporting of Brodsky has, as suggested, been approached with a certain scepticism.

[17] Osip Mandelstam, 'On the Nature of the Word' (1922) in *The Collected Critical Prose and Letters*, trans. Jane Grey Harris and Constamce Link (London: Collins Harvill, 1991), 120.

[18] See Homi K. Bhabha, *Location of Culture*, 225.

[19] Osip Mandelstam, 'On the Nature of the Word', 120.

[20] Ostensibly a series of autobiographical sketches about the poet's St.

Petersburg childhood, *The Noise of Time*, like Benjamin's 'A Berlin Chronicle' or Nabokov's *Speak, Memory,* is about the complex origins of both personal, historical and verbal identity. Throughout the work, the subtext is that of Mandelstam's consciousness of, as he calls it, the symbolic chaos of Jewish history and the rational order of the Christian. His position in relation to both was one whose ambiguity troubled him. As with many of his generation, the pressures to assimilate were enormous. Added to this, Mandelstam's disgust with Judaic culture and language – "[H]ow offensive was the crude speech of the Rabbi ... how utterly vulgar all that he said" – is clearly associated with his father, with whom he had a difficult relationship. It is therefore with his mother, and with the Russian language, that he sides, though in terms that remind us of what he has to say elsewhere about the essential hybridity of Russian. It also smacks of the insecurity he always felt about his own relationship as a poet to the great tradition of Russian literature:

> The speech of the father and the speech of the mother – does not our language feed throughout all its long life on the confluence of these two, do they not compose its character? The speech of my mother was clear sonorous without the least foreign admixture ... Mother loved to speak and took joy in the roots and sounds of her Great Russian speech ... Was she not the first of her whole family to achieve pure and clear Russian sounds. My father had absolutely no language; his speech was tongue-tie and languagelessness ... A completely abstract, counterfeit language, the ornate and twisted speech of an autodidact, where normal words are intertwined with the ancient philosophical terms of Herder, Leibniz, and Spinoza, the capricious syntax of the Talmud, the article, not always finished sentence: it was anything in the world, but not a language, neither Russian nor German (*The Noise of Time*, trans. and with an introduction by Clarence Brown [London: Quartet Books, 1988], 84-85).

21 See Joseph Brodsky, 'Less Than One', 8.
22 'Tristia' in *Joseph Brodsky: Collected Poems in English* (Manchester: Carcanet, 2001), 499.
23 The phrase used by Stalin when sentencing him was "isolate but preserve".
24 Osip Mandelstam, 'Conversation About Dante' in *The Collected Prose and Letters*, 404.
25 See David M. Bethea, *Joseph Brodsky and the Creation of Exile*, (New

Jersey: Princeton University Press, 1994), 57.

26 Osip Mandelstam, 'Conversation About Dante', 404.

27 Ibid., 405.

28 Joseph Brodsky, *Selected Poems*, trans. and introduced by George L. Kline (London: Penguin, 1975), 33.

29 David M. Bethea, *Joseph Brodsky and the Creation of Exile*, 37-38.

30 Seamus Heaney, 'Osip and Nadezhda Mandelstam' in *The Government of the Tongue: The 1986 T.S. Eliot Memorial Lectures and other Critical Writings* (London: Faber and Faber, 1989), 77.

31 Ibid., 62.

32 Joseph Brodsky, *Selected Poems*, 33.

33 David M. Bethea, *Joseph Brodsky and the Creation of Exile* , 28.

34 Aleksander Wat associates Brodsky's discovery of Donne with a rejection not only of Stalinism but with the growth of institutionalised anti-semitism in post-war Communist Europe:

> [I]n 1942 the word *zhid* (Russian for 'kike') was under a rigorous taboo, but two years later, the Polish Jews deported to Ili [in Kazakhstan] were showered with that insult – and from time to time with stones as well – by children and the teenagers from the local high school. Today, in 1965, those Young Pioneers from Ili are young engineers, literary critics, apparatchiks. People in the West who are not aware of that mental 'iron barrier' will fail to understand much of the relationship between mentality and ideology, or much of the young people's rebellion in the USSR.
>
> In order to liberate themselves from Stalin's heritage in their souls, they must first 'detach themselves from the enemy' … they must throw off not only any concern with Stalinism, communism, revisionism, but those ugly words themselves. In that sense, the free people are not Andrei Voznesensky, Yevtushenko, or Tarsis but people like Joseph Brodsky … Political thinking has become so distorted and corrupted during this long, half century that one has to begin by tearing it out, roots and all, from one's soul … How delighted Joseph Brodsky was as an adolescent to discover John Donne, and what beautiful fruit that discovery bore! … Enlightened young people in the Soviet Union know the miseries and monstrosities of communism … but every word of authentic religion, idealistic thought, disinterested beauty in poetry or ethics falls on fertile ground there (*My Century: The Odyssey of a Polish*

Intellectual, ed. and trans. Richard Lourie (New York and London: W.W. Norton & Company, 1990), 199-200.

[35] Joseph Brodsky, *Selected Poems*, 46.

[36] I temper this reading with "perhaps", because it is difficult to know exactly how much the Russian population knew about the missile crisis. It is true that events – and, what is more, people's impression of those events – do not appear to have had the same marked impact in the USSR as in Europe and America. However, if news was available we can assume that Brodsky, moving in the circles he did, would at least have got a whiff of it.

[37] The historical enmity between Russia and Finland, and Peter the Great's decision to build Petersburg plays a role in Pushkin's 'The Bronze Horseman':

> [T]he shores of moss and swamp let show
> black huts in which the wretched Finn
> huddles himself against the snow ...
> and here a city shall arise
> to spite our neighbour's hautiness:
> for we by nature are decreed
> to hack out through the wooden wall
> a window upon Europe and
> firm-footed stand beside the sea[.]
> (Trans. Charles Tomlinson)

Read in the context of Pushkin's poem, the volcanic eruption of Brodsky's 'Sonnet' can be seen as mirroring the destructive flood that wrecked Petersburg in 1820 and provides the centrepiece to 'The Bronze Horseman'.

[38] It is interesting to compare Brodsky's re-working of Auden's elegy for Yeats to what Bhabha, utilising aspects of Benjamin's theory of language, says about the presence of "foreignness" within a text and "the performativity of translation":

> The foreign element 'destroys the original's structures of reference ...' not simply by negating it but by negotiating the disjunction in which successive cultural temporalities are 'preserved in the work of history and at the same time cancelled ... The nourishing fruit of the historically understood contains time as a precious but tasteless seed.' And though this dialectic of cultural negation-as-negotiation, this splitting of skin and

fruit through the agency of foreignness, the purpose is, Rudolf Pannwitz says, not 'to turn Hindi, Greek, English into German [but] instead to turn German into Hindi, Greek, English, (*Location of Culture*, 227-228).

[39] Bethea dates this as happening sometime in 1963, though on the evidence of 'Once more we're living by the Bay' we can assume that Brodsky had at least read Donne in a Russian translation some time earlier.

[40] David M. Bethea, *Joseph Brodsky and the Creation of Exile*, 84-85.

[41] Joseph Brodsky, *Selected Poems*, Ibid. 40-41.

[42] See 'Less Than One', 28. The full paragraph reads:

If we made ethical choices, they were based not so much on immediate reality as on moral standards derived from fiction. We were avid readers and fell into a dependence on what we read. Books, perhaps because of their formal element of finality, held us in their absolute power. Dickens was more real than Stalin or Beria [Lavrenty Pavlovich Beria was, under Stalin, head of the Soviet secret police and labour camps. In December 1954 he was tried and executed for high treason]. More than anything else, novels would affect our modes of behaviour and conversations, and 90 percent of our conversations were about novels.

The reference to Dickens might also be an oblique reference to Mandelstam's poem 'Dombey And Son' which appeared in *Stone*.

[43] Osip Mandelstam, 'On the Nature of the Word' in *The Collected Critical Prose and Letters*, 128.

[44] Walter Benjamin, 'The Task of the Translator' (1923) in *Illuminations*, trans. Harry Zohn (London: Fontana Press, 1992), 72.

[45] Walter Benjamin, 'On Some Motifs in Baudelaire' in *Illuminations*, 174.

[46] Joseph Brodsky, 'To Please a Shadow' in *Less Than One*, 361.

[47] Ibid., 363.

[48] David M. Bethea, *Joseph Brodsky and the Creation of Exile*, 265.

[49] January and its place within the Orthodox religion was important to Brodsky for other reasons. In the sonnet 'The month of January has flown past', written in 1962, he portrays himself, like Leonore in Beethoven's *Fidelio*, listening to 'the singing/of convicts in their labyrinth of cells'. It is likely that the "prison windows" the poet is walking past are those of the same "psychiatric hospital" on the outskirts of Leningrad which is the setting for 'Gorbunov and Gorchakov'. The month had other resonances. In 'Nunc Dimittis', written on 16th February 1972,

just prior to Brodsky's exile to the West, he uses the Biblical account of Christ's Presentation in the Temple and the figure of Simeon, traditionally seen as a bridge between Old and New Testament, to write about his own predicament: "As though driven on by the force of their looks,/he strode through the cold empty space of the temple/and moved toward the whitening blur of the doorway." The poem is also a homage to the then greatest living Russian poet, Anna Akhmatova, whose Name Day was 16th February, the Feast Day of Saints Simeon and Anna.

50 Joseph Brodsky, *Selected Poems*, 100.

51 George Steiner, *After Babel*, 270.

52 Christian Meier, *Athens: A Portrait of the City in its Golden Age*, trans. Robert and Rita Kimber (London: Pimlico, 2000), 45.

53 Brodsky's incorporating these elements of traditional Russian art into an elegy for one of the 'high priests' of Modernism has its part within a wider debate:

> The contradictory character of Russian modernism – as much anti-modern as modern ... associated the West with novelty and Russia with backwardness, and (as a result) the beginning of a tradition according to which the voicing of opposition to 'newfangled Western ways' became an important way of laying claim to a 'true Russian' identity. [C]onsciousness of international trends was as important among nationalist modernists as among their self consciously Westernizing colleagues. (Catriona Kelly (ed.) *Utopias: Russian Modernist Texts 1905-1940* (London: Penguin, 1999), xxii.

Another element in Russia's being influenced by, or incorporating aspects of, Western art into its own traditions was the time-lag between a movement peaking in the West and its gradual assimilation eastwards. What in Western literature had been autonomous phases in the modernist movement, appeared simultaneously in Russia. The situation can be seen as analogous to Russian factories having the latest machinery, only for them to be operated by "workers fresh from the village in foot-rags and bast shoes who used crosses to sign their name" (Ibid., xxiii). Clarence Brown has also pointed out that:

> For a modernist movement in verse, Acmeism was curiously conservative in both theme and technique. Mandelstam lived at a time innovation in the prosodic elements of poetry was highly esteemed, but his rhymes and meters might, with few exceptions, seem familiar to the contemporaries of Pushkin.

The diction of his slow, deliberately impeded lines occasionally recalled an earlier age ... But the imagery, the life's blood of his poetry, was wholly of his time, and of ours (*The Noise of Time*, 24).

[54] Mandelstam and Shklovsky were good friends, though the exact nature of their relationship was evidently complex. After returning from Berlin in 1923, Shklovsky lived in Moscow. Not only did he help secure Mandelstam work as a translator but encouraged him to write film scenarios:

> [Shklovsky] took refuge in a film studio, rather as a Jew in occupied Hungary might have hidden in a Catholic monastery. He strongly recommended M. to seek salvation in the same way, and urged him to write something for films. There was of course no hope, he explained, that their scripts would be passed for publication, but the point was that film studios always paid for everything they commissioned, even if it was only a few pages long ... Shklvosky gave the same advice to everyone he thought well of, suggesting they write a script together. Coming from him, a proposal of this kind was tantamount to a declaration of love or friendship (*Hope Abandoned*, 339-340).

Further information about their relationship can be found in *The Collected Critical Prose and Letters*, particularly 'I Write a Scenario' and letters 27, 28 and 47.

[55] Osip Mandelstam, 'On the Nature of the Word', 126.

[56] Brodsky wrote this in relation to translations of Mandelstam's poetry into English. The passage continues: "[Verse meters] cannot be replaced even by each other, let alone free verse. Differences in meters are differences in breath and heartbeat. Differences in rhyming are those of brain pattern. The cavalier treatment of either is at best a sacrilege, at worst a mutilation or murder" ('The Child of Civilisation' in *Less Than One*, 141).

[57] Osip Mandelstam, 'The Word and Culture' in *The Collected Critical Prose and Letters*, 113.

[58] It was an insouciance which he translated into a number of poems. As Derek Walcott has said, "The first poem in *To Urania*, 'May 24, 1980', has gone out of the range of such fury as it might arouse from the center of the empire. The nomadic Jew is out there alone on his desert, and what infuriates both the professional Jew and the professional Jew-baiter is that the expelled should enjoy the desert. 'May 24, 1980' is ... a

jeremiad with jokes ... Irreverence such as this is an irritation to any state or race" ('Magic Industry', 147). Brodsky's self-assurance may also owe something to a phenomenon commented on by Eric Hobsbawm:

> I recently read an article on Russian Jews in Israel which claimed that, unlike the other [European] Jews, they arrived in Israel without any sense of inferiority, unaffected by the Holocaust syndrome. Their general attitude was expressed in these terms: 'We fought Hitler and we defeated him.' This was in spite of the anti-Semitism they suffered in Russia (*The New Century* [London: Little, Brown and Company, 2000], 40).

59 Ovid, *The Erotic Poems*, trans. Peter Green (London: Penguin 1982), 68.

60 Ibid., 47.

61 See Solomon Volkov, *Conversations With Joseph Brodsky*, 5.

62 Ibid., 4.

63 A further problem that Tsvetaeva faced were the divisions within Russian Modernism itself. As a Moscow-born writer, her sympathies with the Soviet avant-garde meant that even in exile she was out of kilter with a Petersburg movement dominated by émigré circles in Paris and in Berlin.

64 Solomon Volkov, *Conversations With Joseph Brodsky*, 219.

65 Joseph Brodsky, *Selected Poems*, 165-167, 57-62, 168.

66 Solomon Volkov, *Conversations With Joseph Brodsky,* 9.

67 John Burt Foster Jr. *Nabokov's Art of Memory and European Modernism*, (Princeton: Princeton University Press, 1993), 10.

68 Ibid., 4-9.

69 Victor Terras, *A History of Russian Literature*, 607-609.

70 Joseph Brodsky, *Collected Poems in English*, 215.

71 Ibid., 217.

72 Shierry Weber Nicholsen, *Exact Imagination, Late Work: On Adorno's Aesthetics* (Cambridge, Massachusetts; London, England: The MIT Press, 1997), 234.

73 Walter Benjamin, 'On Some Motifs in Baudelaire', 184.

74 Joseph Brodsky, *Collected Poems in English*, 218. There are parallels to this experience of the 'other', the 'double' and what Freud writes in 'Das Unheimliche':

> The theme of the 'double' has been very thoroughly treated by Otto Rank ... He has gone into the connections which the 'double' has with reflections in mirrors, with shadows, with

guardian spirits, with the belief in the soul ... For the 'double' was originally an insurance against the destruction of the ego, an 'energetic denial of the power of death' ('The Uncanny' (1919) in *The Penguin Freud Library*, Vol. 14 (London: Penguin 1990), 356.

[75] Homi K. Bhaba, *The Location of Culture*, 215-216.

[76] Osip Mandelstam, 'Conversation About Dante', 397.

[77] It seems fair to assume that Mongolia stands as a representative of the experience of any number of states colonised by the USSR.

[78] Joseph Brodsky, 'Footnote to a Poem' in *Less Than One*, 203.

[79] Joseph Brodsky, *Collected Poems in English*, 215.

[80] George Steiner, *After Babel*, 58.

[81] Joseph Brodsky, *Collected Poems in English*, 216, 217.

[82] Osip Mandelstam, 'Conversation About Dante', 397.

[83] Joseph Brodsky, *Collected Poems in English*, 216.

[84] Rainer Roschlitz, *The Disenchantment of Art: The Philosophy of Walter Benjamin* (London: The Guildford Press, 1996), 14.

[85] Osip Mandelstam, 'Conversation About Dante', 397.

[86] Walter Benjamin, *Reflections: Essays, Aphorisms, Autobiographical Writings*, trans. Edmund Jephcott (New York: Harcourt Brace Jovanovich, 1978), 325-326.

[87] See Rainer Roschlitz, *The Disenchantment of Art*, 17.

[88] Joseph Brodsky, *Collected Poems in English*, 322, 352, 381.

[89] Ibid., 118.

[90] Ibid., 514. Examining the differences between Benjamin's and Wittgenstein's philosophies of language, we can say that while both sought to put an end to the "myth of interiority" and "the elimination of the inexpressible in language" (see Rainer Roschlitz, *The Disenchantment of Art*, 3), for Benjamin this meant concentrating on the poetic and essentially 'theological' function of naming, while for Wittgenstein such an approach limited language to an occult process in which "Naming appears as a *queer* connexion of a word with an object" (ibid., 17). What is interesting is to bring both philosophies within the orbit of this medieval notion of the words 'Man' and 'God' being inscribed on the human face. "The human word is the name of things," Benjamin wrote. "Hence it is no longer conceivable, as the bourgeois view of language maintains, that the word has an accidental relation to its object, that it is a sign for things (or knowledge of them) agreed by some conviction. Language never gives *mere* signs" (*Reflections*, 324). Equally suspicious of a priori claims to knowledge rather than the methods by which we seek and construct understanding, Wittgenstein's notion of perspicuous

representation is to do with bringing awareness of "the way we breed problems in our misuse and misunderstanding of language. In a conflict we must find the liberating word, because only when we hit upon the 'physiognomy' of the situation exactly can we move on" (see John M. Heaton, *Wittgenstein and Psychoanalysis* (Cambridge: Icon Books, 2000), 25). The telling word here, of course, is "physiognomy". Understanding comes, Wittgenstein says, from observing human actions and behaviour and then finding the exact words for understanding these: "The physiognomy is a matter of taking the pulse of a situation, rather than taking blood, analysing it, and giving an explanation. *The right human word has a physiognomy. It is 'whatever' like a face* – not a universalisation nor an individuation ... We cannot get outside the interweave of life and language [my emphasis]" (ibid., 25-26).

91 Joseph Brodsky, *Collected Poems in English*, 131,
92 David M. Bethea, *Joseph Brodsky and the Creation of Exile*, 71-72.
93 Roman Jakobson, 'Two Aspects of Language and Two Types of Aphasic Disturbance' (1956) in *Language in Literature*, ed. Krystyna Pomorska and Stephen Rudy (Cambridge, Massachusetts: Harvard University Press, 1996), 103.
94 Quoted in Shierry Weber Nicholsen, *Exact Imagination*, 56.
95 Valentina Polukhina, *Joseph Brodsky: A Poet For Our Time* (Cambridge: Cambridge University Press, 1989), 170.
96 Joseph Brodsky, *Collected Poems in English*, 143, 114, 69.
97 David M. Bethea, *Joseph Brodsky: A Poet For Our Time,* 170.
98 Theodor W. Adorno, 'On the Final Scene of *Faust*' (1959) in *Notes to Literature,* vol. 1 ed. Rolf Tiedemann, trans. Shierry Weber Nicholsen (New York: Columbia University Press, 1991), 120.
99 Osip Mandelstam, 'Conversation About Dante', 398.
100 Joseph Brodsky, *Collected Poems in English*, 222.
101 Richard Ellmann, *Ulysses On The Liffey*, 3rd Printing (with corrections), (London: Faber and Faber, 1984), 156.
102 Theodor W. Adorno, 'In Memory of Eichendorff' in *Notes to Literature,* vol. 1, 69.
103 Joseph Brodsky, *Collected Poems in English*, 224.
104 Shierry Weber Nicholsen, *Exact Imagination*, 66.
105 Susan Buck-Morss, *The Dialectics of Seeing: Walter Benjamin and the Arcades Project* (Cambridge, Massachusetts; London, England: The MIT Press, 1991), 9.
106 Shierry Weber Nicholsen, *Exact Imagination*, 59.
107 Joseph Brodsky, 'Footnote to a Poem', 203-204.
108 John Hollander, *The Work of Poetry* (New York: Columbia University Press, 1997), 72.

[109] Ibid., 73.

[110] Joseph Brodsky, 'Footnote to a Poem', 202.

[111] Ibid., 196-197.

[112] Joseph Brodsky, *Collected Poems in English*, 147.

[113] For pointing this out, I'm grateful to Professor John Lucas.

[114] Ian Hamilton, *Robert Lowell: A Biography* (London: Faber and Faber, 1982), 235.

[115] Robert Lowell, *Poems: A Selection*, ed. with an Introduction and notes by Jonathan Raban (London: Faber and Faber, 1974), 171.

[116] Joseph Brodsky, 'Footnote to a Poem', 200.

[117] Ibid.

[118] Whatever the literary connotations of this reference, it may also serve as a homage to Lowell's passion for Dante's poetry and which Brodsky later recalled: "We talked about this and that, and finally we settled on Dante ... He knew Dante inside out, I think, in an absolute obsessive way" (see David M. Bethea, *Joseph Brodsky: A Poet For Our Time*, 35).

[119] Dante, *The Inferno of Dante*, trans. Robert Pinsky (London: J.M. Dent, 1996) 25.

[120] See David M. Bethea, *Joseph Brodsky and the Creation of Exile*, 235.

[121] Roman Jakobson, 'Marginal Notes on the Prose of the Poet Pasternak' in *Language in Literature*, 304.

[122] Ibid., 312.

[123] See Valentina Polukhina, *A Poet For Our Time*, 148-149.

[124] Roman Jakobson, 'Marginal Notes on the Prose of the Poet Pasternak', 313.

[125] Joseph Brodsky, *Collected Poems in English*, 307.

[126] Solomon Volkov, *Conversations With Joseph Brodsky*, 191-192.

[127] Ibid., 193.

[128] Roman Jakobson, 'Marginal Notes on the Prose of the Poet Pasternak', 306.

[129] Ibid., 308.

[130] See Valentina Polukhina, *A Poet For Our Time*, 26.

[131] Ibid., 108.

[132] Ibid.

[133] Joseph Brodsky, *Collected Poems in English*, 345-346.

[134] Ibid., 363.

[135] Julia Kristeva, *Proust and the Sense of Time*, trans. and with an introduction by Stephen Ban (London: Faber and Faber, 1993), 54.

[136] Joseph Brodsky, *Collected Poems in English*, 363.

[137] Julia Kristeva, *Proust and the Sense of Time,* 54-55.

[138] Ibid., 67.

[139] Joseph Brodsky, *Collected Poems in English*, 124.

[140] Joseph Brodsky, 'Less than One', 30.

[141] Ibid.

[142] Valentina Polukhina, *A Poet For Our Time*, 238.

[143] Joseph Brodsky, *Collected Poems in English*, 120.

[144] Ibid., 452.

3

A Brightness to Cast Shadows:
Photographic Memory and the
Poetry of George Szirtes

The deeper and more permanent the effect of a momentous event, the harder it is to imagine that event not having taken place (or having had a different outcome). From there it is a small step to the belief not just that the event happened but also that it had to happen. Thus, in retrospect, history loses its unpredictability.

Christian Meier,
Athens: A Portrait of the City in Its Golden Age.

I

Noted for the witness his poetry bears to events that engulfed Central Europe in the middle years of the 20th century, George Szirtes has consistently written about how the objective events of history become intermingled with the private material of memory. Balanced between description and reflection, his poetry enacts the dramatic tension between the stories we are told and subsequently re-tell ourselves to explain our presence in the world, and the significant objects and places that govern the provinces of the imagination. Thus his poems are, as Szirtes describes them, "intimate spaces arising from the no-man's-land of childhood memory".[1] The phrase is telling. Born in Budapest in 1948, Szirtes arrived in England as a refugee in 1956 following the Soviet military crackdown in November of that year. Along with an estimated 200,000 other Hungarians who fled the country in the aftermath of the Soviet invasion, Szirtes' family had to pack hurriedly, taking just two suitcases and a small case of photographs. By the time they arrived in England in December, they had with them only the latter. It was photographs, therefore, that formed their only tangible link to home and to the past. Given Szirtes' subsequent fascination with the medium, the story seems too good to be true. But in a century of mass migrations the photograph has become a potent image. Defined memorably by Susan Sontag as a "featherweight portable museum", in Szirtes' particular case photographs can be seen as providing a link between the experience of being the child of refugees and what we might call the portmanteau of memories and objects that constitutes the exile's life.[2] More specifically the significance of the photograph for Szirtes, as he has commented, is that it allows him a degree of objectivity over personal experience. Acting as an intermediary between history and memory, photographs and photography have provided Szirtes with the means and subject matter of his poetry.

"Memory," Timothy Garton Ash writes, "is ... the great adversary for anyone who tries to establish what really happened, whether as historian, journalist or writer".[3] It is a subject matter that Szirtes has consistently mined. In 'The Lost Scouts' for example, he describes how the aged members of his father's scout troop – "Old men from Canada, Spain, the States, Australia/with wives and children" – gather every three years round a camp fire in Budapest to sing and tell stories of their childhood. It is a homecoming with special significance for these men. All Jews, they are survivors of what the poem calls the "places/the century saved for them/ ... /behind a fence or a high wall,/fifty-five years ago".[4] What complicates Szirtes' writings about historical events is the fact that his poems, like the grown-up scouts, occupy a territory between two shifting worlds: childhood memory and adult reminiscence. This is not to say that his version, or vision, of history is any the less valid. On the contrary. "The past," as Maurice Halbwachs wrote, "is not preserved but is reconstructed on the basis of the present".[5] What is often most significant in Szirtes' work, then, is the way he examines how we experience a necessarily fragmented past and then use the pieces to construct and integrate an identity for ourselves in the present.

Szirtes studied Fine Art in Leeds and in London, and his first published poems appeared at the same time as he began exhibiting his paintings. It is hardly surprising, then, that his poetry should bring with it an acute sense of the visual world, with painting and paintings remaining a part of Szirtes' subject matter from his first collection,

The Slant Door (1979), through to *An English Apocalypse* (2001). Writing in 1983 about the future development of his poetry, however, Szirtes said that he wanted it to become "more personal", that there were "too many poems about pictures in *The Slant Door* and I [want] the next book to be more concerned with things I like and things I am afraid of."[6] The distinction Szirtes is here drawing between art and 'things' is hinted at in 'Group Portrait With Pets' from *The Slant Door*:

> The little group seems perfectly at ease
> Though drapes and scattered toys confirm the truth,
> It was the clever painter's artifice
> That fixed the glimmer on each eye and tooth.

Designed to show a family at home with themselves and with each other, the portrait, with its display of mannered ease, shows only a painterly convention. It testifies to the skill of the painter's art rather than to a truthful likeness of the sitters as they actually are. While the purpose of the painting is to suggest that time can be frozen and life captured in a moment of idealised calm, such a vision is fatally circumscribed: "The bright, transparent skins will fold and crack/ Before the painter leaves by the back door." Inner details also militate against the fable:

> That satin, crinoline, so much like blood
> Splashed across the canvas, find an echo
> In the bird's breast, the cat has understood
> Who simply bides his time while others go,
> Who has seen terror written on a face
> Just as the limb is torn and the claw sinks.

Despite the artist's best endeavours, time cannot be stopped. The harmonious image will begin to fall apart and fragment even before the paint has dried; while beneath the veneer of civility violence lies. It is this juxtaposition of familiar objects and rituals with the violence, threatened or actual, of the world at large, which has remained a pervasive aspect of Szirtes' work.

In 'A Dual Heritage', published in *Poetry Review* in February 1986 to accompany three poems from the sequence 'The

Photographer in Winter', Szirtes wrote that:

> my second book [was dominated] by two conflicting themes:
> an interior world animated by horrors and hauntings, and an
> external one full of beauty. The first was often to be found in
> a room with one or two figures, my own home for instance,
> where the apparent composure of the people involved suddenly
> faced a larger, more impersonal, quite violent force. The second
> looked for natural fragments ... and tried to find some new
> appropriate richness of expression.

The challenge, as he goes on to describe it, was to discover formal
poetic structures within which to contain such experiences:

> When my mother died ... I wanted very much now to write
> something in her memory. It took a long time and a complete
> reordering of my language and perceptions. ... I had to exercise
> the greatest objectivity, and to allow the power or pathos of
> the facts to develop out of the diffidence which I instinctively
> identified in [English] literature and manners.
>   In the case of the poem for my mother it meant finding
> some key incident which would speak for me, and from which
> I could remove myself almost entirely. It meant bringing down
> the temperature of the writing to near freezing point so that
> the poem could begin to melt from the centre outwards, that is
> to say from the life of the incident itself. ... Often this [key]
> could be found in pictures, either paintings or photographs,
> anything that held life still enough for me to transfuse it into
> my own experience.

The punning reference to 'still life' or *nature morte* in the last sentence
is of central importance to 'The Photographer in Winter', as it is
elsewhere. In 'Golden Bream', for example, Szirtes writes how
painting is "a kind of sanctification/of the sensible world". The poem,
however, breaks the frame of the painting and allows in to its calm
and rarefied air all that is either excluded or, as memento mori, only
symbolically present: "a child in a fever,/the soldier in his trench,
the burning villagers trapped/in a hut by the military".

Unlike a painting, where it is the surface of the object to which
we pay attention, thus implicating ourselves in the fundamental
deception of the art work, and where a gap is opened up between

what is represented and *how*, the photograph, Barthes says in *Camera Lucida*, "is never distinguished from its referent ... [A] pipe, here, is always and intractably a pipe".[7] And a photograph, he continues, "is always invisible: it is not it that we see". This is not to say that a photograph is any the less charged an image. The difference, as John Berger has argued, is between a medium that is self-referential, whose tensions are contained within its own frame and written across its surface, and one that refers the viewer back to the world outside its co-ordinates:

> The power of a painting depends upon its internal references. Its reference to the natural world beyond the limits of the painted surface is never direct; it deals in equivalents. Or, to put it another way: painting interprets the world, translating it into its own language. But photography has no language of its own. One learns to read photographs as one learns to read footprints or cardiograms. The language in which photography deals is the language of events. All its references are external to itself.[8]

Berger's associating the photograph with the body (or more accurately, the record of an absent body) is particularly interesting when placed in the context of 'The Photographer in Winter', written in memory of Szirtes' mother, Magdalena, who died as a result of an overdose in 1974.

II

The Photographer in Winter (1986) was Szirtes' fourth full-length collection and is dominated by his experience of returning to Hungary in 1984 for the first time since 1956. There is a sequence called 'Budapest Postcards' and a number of poems about his Hungarian relatives and his earliest childhood memories. Also included are translations of four major twentieth-century Hungarian poets: Attila József, Miklos Rodnóti, Dezsö Kosztolányi and Ottó Orbán. The collection is therefore permeated by an acute sense of the familiar; a familiar, however, that has undergone significant change. It is a return that both invites and deters, offering the tantalising possibility of reclaiming something while simultaneously refusing access: "The key won't fit the lock./The key won't turn. The key is firmly stuck/

inside the door" ('The Courtyards'[9]).

Nowhere is this more apparent than in the title poem – a sequence of eight poems juxtaposing the day-to-day life of a female photographer, now dead and referred to only as "Dear woman", with reminiscences and/or observations of her by, in Szirtes' words, "someone who identifies with her and is at the same time betraying her."[10] In three of the poems the woman speaks for herself. This unidentified narrator speaks the remaining five.[11] The sequence provides few concrete biographical facts, and there are no explicit references to historical events. There are, however, a number of cultural references – the music of Johann Strauss, the Radetzsky March – but all the reader knows for sure is that we are present, at least some of the time, in a city with a river in winter.

The poem begins with a physical gesture. It follows this with a verbalised thought or commentary, before presenting an imagistic description of a snow-bound city:

> You touch your skin. Still young. The wind blows waves
> Of silence down the street. The traffic grows
> A hood of piled snow. The city glows.
> The bridges march across a frozen river
> Which seems to have been stuck like that for ever.

Using a technique analogous to montage, the poem moves in a series of rapid snapshots from an isolated individual to a panoramic shot of the whole city, from the particular to the general. As with montage it is the juxtaposition of images rather than any single image in isolation that creates meaning. Furthermore, as in the use of a zoom lens, which makes it impossible to distinguish any exact relationship between the distance separating an object and the person observing it, the poem immediately begins by establishing a dialectic between near and far that can be read as evoking the temporal as well as the spatial.

The effect of the opening lines is to blur those claims to a single unmediated truth with which photography – especially documentary photography – became associated in the early decades of its development. These claims were attacked by, among others, Walter Benjamin, who advocated a shift away from such deceptive claims to truth telling towards a photography that put the emphasis on how meaning is itself ideologically constructed. The techniques best equipped for doing so were montage or close-up which, Benjamin explains, "by focusing on hidden details of familiar objects, by exploring commonplace milieus [extend] our comprehension of the necessities which rule our lives".[12]

The effect of Szirtes' montage-like opening is to invest each 'frame', each close-up, with a detail suggesting that the city's apparent calm is poised on the brink of some more violent action or event. Implicit in each of these 'shots' is the threat of aggression. The "hoods" of snow, the glowing skyline and the marching bridges all suggest a military presence in the city. This is developed in the third stanza, though to different effect:

> ... Pagodas, ziggurats;
> The follies of the snow. Geometries
> In miniature, the larger symmetries
> Of cars, the onion domes of bollards, spires
> On humble kiosks, stalactites on wires[.]

Compared to the barely-disguised menace of the first stanza, this description of the disorientating effect snow has in making the familiar seem strange and exotic appears merely playful. But, as the Photographer says, "What seems and is has never been less certain – /The room is fine, but there beyond the curtain/The world can alter shape." The effect is to juxtapose an apparent composure with "larger, more impersonal, quite violent force". With their Baroque *trompe l'oeil*, the "follies of the snow" trick the spectator into believing in the surface appearance of things rather than the hidden internal structures, identified in the poem as "the larger symmetries".

In 'A Small History of Photography', Benjamin developed further his ideas about the particular effect photography can have in altering our perception and understanding of even the most mundane activities and objects:

> No matter how artful the photographer, no matter how carefully posed his subject, the beholder feels an irresistible urge to search [the] picture for the tiny spark of contingency, of the Here and Now, with which reality has so to speak seared the subject, to find the inconspicuous spot where in the immediacy of that long-forgotten moment the future subsists so eloquently

that we, looking back, may rediscover it. For it is another nature that speaks to the camera than to the eye: other in the sense that a space informed by human consciousness gives way to a space informed by the unconscious.[13]

Benjamin goes on to describe the work of the photographer Karl Blossfeldt (1865-1932) in terms which anticipate Szirtes' transformation of the snow-bound city in the opening poem of 'The Photographer in Winter':

> Photography, with its devices of slow motion and enlargement, reveals ... the existence of [the] optical unconscious, just as we discover the instinctual unconscious through psychoanalysis. Details of structure, cellular tissue ... photography reveals in this material the physiognomic aspects of visual worlds which dwell in the smallest things, meaningful yet covert enough to find a hiding place in waking dreams, but which, enlarged and capable of formulation, make the difference between technology and magic visible as a thoroughly historical variable.[14]

It is interesting to compare Szirtes' oblique presentation of a nominal Budapest with Ivan V. Lalic's sequence 'Belgrade from Old Photographs'. Born in Belgrade in 1931 Lalic never defined himself as a Serbian or even a Yugoslav poet, but as a Mediterranean poet. As such, he saw his poetry as laying claim to the rich cultural heritage of the area, with its roots in both Greece and Rome, Byzantine and Catholic Christianity and, as regards Yugoslavia, the melting-pot of ethnic and cultural diversity that defined the country until the events of the 1950s. Lalic's poetry, as his English translator Francis R. Jones writes, "follows [these] cultural threads further back towards their sources [and is] concerned with what survives ... and why".[15] As will be examined later, these aims have much in common with Szirtes' own, though the means of resuscitation are significantly different.

'Belgrade From Old Photographs' is prompted by the poet's flicking through a book of 19th-century photographs of the city. This leads to a meditation on the survival of cultures, with the book of photographs becoming a metaphor for the interdependence of history and memory:

> ... this is how history
> Merges with memory, as the Danube with the Sava;
> Now try to turn the pages
> Back –
>   ash is left on your fingers[.]

The image is similar to that in the closing poem of 'The Photographer in Winter', where the poet looks through an album of family photographs. But whereas Lalic's poem, as the mention of the Danube and Sava demonstrates, gives specific dates and place names, Szirtes, is much more reticent. This is partly because in Lalic's sequence these rivers function as metaphors for the fact that Belgrade has served as a locus for the often troubled relationship between Eastern and Western Europe.[16] It also alerts us to another fundamental difference between Lalic's and Szirtes' approach. For while Lalic remains an impersonal recorder of events – he appears only as the hand which turns the page – we sense that he nevertheless still feels himself to be part of an essential continuity of cultural experience. In Szirtes' case, no such continuity is possible.

Commenting on this lack of 'hard facts' in 'The Photographer in Winter', Szirtes has written that most of the poem is simply "imagination working over-time". To therefore read the poem in the light of biographical information about Szirtes and his mother is in some ways to undermine the ambiguities on which the poem is founded. Having said this, by replacing the sequence within its biographical and historical context – much of which is provided in 'A Dual Heritage' – we can begin to judge the nature of Szirtes' departure from the kind of poem he might have written. Furthermore, by recognising the precise nature of Szirtes' refusal to write a straight-forward biography of his mother, we are better able to understand the significance of what it is he means when he says: "To many Central Europeans, Surrealism isn't a glorious game of life and death; it's just life until death comes along."

This is not to say that Szirtes is in any accepted definition of the word a Surrealist, though we do need to be careful in too narrowly limiting our understanding of the nature of European Surrealism in the first few decades of the last century. In Hungarian literature at least there does exist a model of an avowedly Surrealist poet who, as Szirtes does, made use of regular metres, rhyme and traditional stanzaic forms – Attila József.[17] Furthermore, if, as David Macey says, Surrealism "is, among other things, an exploration of and meditation upon the production of signification" – the focus of this being the image – we can see how the city, which Benjamin defined as a clash between imagination and reality, became the Surrealist image par excellence.

Benjamin saw the city as record of the fragmented and seemingly disconnected events of human history. And just as seemingly insignificant details in photographs 'step out' and make themselves visible to the optical unconscious, so the secret histories of cities lie not in the main boulevards and squares but in the hidden life of the backstreets and alleyways. As Szirtes sees the snow transforming bollards into onion-domed palaces and kiosks into cathedrals, so Benjamin describes the "ancient columns [and] gothic tracery" of plants, previously invisible but now revealed courtesy of the camera's mechanical eye. In both, the modern, the Here and Now is, as it were, X-rayed by Benjamin's "optical unconscious" and shown to contain otherwise buried fragments of past histories. Looked at in this way, photography can function to "blast a specific era out of the homogenous course of history" or blast "a specific life out of the era or a specific work out of the lifework".[18] In doing so, the spectator is offered the possibility of re-writing his or her conception of that past in a radically redefined relationship to the present. And this is done, literally, through illumination: "This winter is not metaphorical./The sun has broken into tiny pieces/And goes on fracturing as it releases/ More and more light".

What emerges from 'The Photographer in Winter', in Benjamin's terms, is less a fixed version *of* the past than a unique experience *with* it. Such an experience is central to Benjamin's concept of "profane illumination", defined by Helga Geyer-Ryan as "the flash-like identity of subject and object, or the capacity of personal memory to interrelate the biographical past and present".[19] Though such moments are rare, they provide a 'dialectical image' – a fragment or relic of a scattered totality – the significance of which is that it allows "the deconstruction of questionable totalities and the remounting of the fragments into artefacts, the meaning of which has no resemblance to their former function".[20] The medium for this process of re-reading and re-writing history is the image.

It would be difficult to imagine a more vulnerable series of images than those created by the snow in the opening section of 'The Photographer in Winter'. The poem contains numerous others which, however fragile, contain those explosive energies needed to blast open the continuum of history: there are "unexploded tears" and children throwing "White bombs at one another which explode/ Splattering their clothes". Frozen within each, like the speck of dirt at the centre of a hailstone, is some unspoken history of violence.

What unites Benjamin and those surrealists who took an interest in photography is the idea of the modern city as a stage for the projection of desire and memory in the spectator. The urban photography favoured by the surrealists tended to show scenes of city life emptied of human participation. Of the twelve photographs included in the text of Breton's *Nadja* (1928) showing Parisian street scenes, seven are absent of any human physical presence. The aim was to draw the spectator's eye to those objects which, once separated from their relationship to the human, became evidence of the 'marvellous' in daily life. Szirtes' poem obviously shares similar concerns. The shots of the city he presents are likewise emptied of human figures, and the implicit threat of past or future violence hints at some sort of crime.

A further significance of the inclusion of Boiffard's photographs within the text of *Nadja* is that although they give every appearance of reportage, they also allow, in their juxtaposition with Breton's text, a reading of reality that exposes the relationship between what 'seems' and what 'is'. For while these photographs appear as documentary or archival evidence that the story and the places Breton writes about exist, thus convincing us of the objective truth of Breton's narrative, as with montage the sudden illumination of details within the frame of a photograph, like the sighting of a familiar building viewed from an unexpected angle, allows us a momentary experience of reality as plural.

At the conclusion of 'A Small History of Photography', Benjamin examines those directions photography might possibly take in the future, and those it should avoid. He mentions in this respect an aspect of photography that both its critics and supporters had thus far failed to recognise: its claims to 'authenticity'. Benjamin's concept of the authentic is not about maintaining the status quo but salvaging something otherwise in danger of being lost. The ecstatic moment of perception he called "profane illumination" is all about an experience of the authentic that destabilises political and ethical hegemony. Advocating a sensuous language of images rather than a second-hand repertoire of theoretical poses and visual clichés, Benjamin argued that for as long as photography relied on imitating painting without developing a visual language of its own, its development as a creative art would be still-born. What follows is one of those remarkable passages in Benjamin's writing when, like Alice disappearing down the rabbit hole, he side-steps conventional logic and enters the world of his own imaginative thought:

> But is not every square inch of our cities the scene of a crime? Every passer-by a culprit? Is it not the task of the photographer – descendant of the augurs and haruspices – to reveal guilt and to point out the guilty in his pictures? [21]

Why does Benjamin mention "crime" and "guilt"? The passage about photographs as records of the scenes of a crime continues:

> 'The illiteracy of the future,' someone has said, 'will be ignorance not of reading or writing, but of photography.' But must not a photographer who cannot read his own pictures be no less accounted an illiterate? Will not the caption become the most important part of the photograph?

If the photographer cannot read his or her own work they will remain ignorant of that detail, revealed to the optical unconscious, where, Benjamin says, "the future subsists so eloquently that we, looking back, may rediscover it." The caption, however, by reducing life to a single point of authorial intent, commands us, as does the speaker in the second of Szirtes' poems, to "Hold it right there. Freeze." The past will therefore remain unrecognised, its crimes unsolved and beyond redemption.

In an early unpublished version of 'The Photographer in Winter' each section is provided with a title, or caption: 'Wintering', 'The Pursuer to the Pursued', 'The Retoucher', 'Gracious Living', 'The Art of the Hand Colourist', 'Sun on Snow', 'The Photographer's Monologue' and 'Doppelgänger'. The second of these is a monologue in the voice of a civilian informer or a member of the secret police:

"Where are you going? To work? I'm watching you./You cannot get away. I have been trained/To notice things". This same version of the sequence is headed by an epigraph taken from *Hamlet*: "Nay/it is. I know not 'seems'." We can only assume that Szirtes decided that Hamlet's words, especially when read in full – "'Seems', madame? Nay, it is. I know not 'seems'" – might encourage the reader to view the sequence in too autobiographical a light. Certainly, the epigraph to the published version radically alters our perception of the poem:

> He was hurrying along with frozen hands and watering eyes
> when he saw her not ten metres away from him. It struck him
> at once that she had changed in some ill-defined way.

Taken from Orwell's *1984*, the focus shifts away from the domestic (while remembering that Hamlet and Gertrude's argument takes place in a very public arena) towards the political, specifically the relationship between the individual and the state.

Given the political situation in post-war Hungary, where the balance of power swung to the Moscow loyalists, led by Mátyás Rákosi, and where the political culture encouraged and supported a proliferation of civilian informers and secret police, the banning of certain classic works of Hungarian literature, the imprisoning of church leaders, and a cult of personality that saw Rákosi's face dominate the country like a towering and omnipresent Big Brother, Orwell's novel can be seen as only an extreme version of day-to-day reality rather than a parable or a prophecy of the future. As such, the epigraph suggests that 'The Photographer in Winter' can be read as reportage.

To return, however, to Benjamin's comments about captions serving to reduce and limit meaning by deflecting attention away from the complexity of the image towards a single authorial voice, so Szirtes' original titles suggest that meaning exists outside of the 'dialogue' between the photographer and the poet. In Benjaminian terms, these then reduce the living complexity of that dialogue to 'mere literature'. By cutting them, Szirtes re-focused attention on the arresting details contained in each 'frame'. Furthermore, the effect of taking those sentences from Orwell's *1984* and blasting them out of context, is to turn them into a fragment, one which we are then free to read in the Benjaminian sense of it being a trace of some hidden and silenced history. A dialogue is thus established between the original text and its new context.

The concluding poem of the 'The Photographer in Winter', as stated earlier, begins with the poet flicking through an album and looking at a series of photographs of the "Dear woman". These photographs clearly describe events from Magdalena Szirtes' life: her childhood, and later internment in Ravensbrück. The final image, however, of the woman "sitting in a chair/And wasting away under a fall of snow" is different from those preceding it because it represents a period of time when Szirtes and his family were living in England. As he writes in 'A Dual Heritage': "The most melancholy image I can conjure of my mother in her last days is a photograph of her sitting, proud yet vaguely lost in her kitchen." Why, then, does Szirtes choose to 'reproduce' these particular images of his mother? Following Benjamin's argument, one answer is that, mediated through the camera's lens, they have become capable of providing precisely that "profane illumination" – or, in the words of 'Golden Bream', "a kind of sanctification/of the sensible world" – that 'blasts' his mother's personal suffering out of an historical continuum. Functioning less as a representation of a specific woman sitting "lost" in her own home, the photograph is shown to be capable of encapsulating a sense of displacement derived directly from exile.

Each of these images therefore becomes a dialectical image, capable of revealing a past that would otherwise remain hidden and unspoken. The purpose of this goes beyond a modernist poetics of montage or the avant-garde use of found materials in constructing artefacts and is to do with Benjamin's belief that the past can be redeemed through a recognition and reconstruction of a counterfactual history, one that stresses the experience not of the victors but their victims. It is a process summed up in one of Benjamin's most famous aphorisms: "There is no document of civilisation which is not at the same time a document of barbarism".[22] Furthermore, the "successive sheets of ice" and "fall of snow" – together with the numerous other references to snow and ice in the poem – locate the sequence not only in a naturalistic landscape but an allegorical one. And it is this presence of allegorical meaning within the poem that again brings it within the compass of Benjamin's writings.

Benjamin saw allegory as functioning in ways similar to montage. In contrast to the organic symbol, allegory takes a detail and, by removing it from its context, deprives it of its original meaning, and therefore stresses – as montage can – the ideological construction of meaning and signification. What is particularly relevant here, both in relation to Szirtes' presentation of his mother "lost in her own home" and his own continuing refugee status, is that Benjamin associates allegory with melancholy and the disruption of a coherent social identity. As Helga Geyer-Ryan comments, this leads in turn to a further stage in the significance of an allegorical representation of reality: "Allegory represents history as decay. It exposes the image of a fragmented, paralysed history in the form of a frozen primal landscape".[23] This reminds us of Benjamin's famous image of the angel of history who, face turned towards the past, wings caught in the blast, is unable to do anything to redeem the catastrophe of history. Where the angel fails, however, we can succeed:

> But for the dialectical historian and those who are interested with him in the reconstruction of an alternative world, it is precisely the wreckage, the debris out of which the new foundations can be constructed.[24]

Throughout 'The Photographer in Winter' Szirtes performs a discrete ventriloquist act, one that allows the past to speak through the imagined voice of his mother. Without this voice the photographs in the family album/archive remain mute witnesses to a static past. The danger is that if these images depict the brutalisation of human beings, as the image of Magdalena Szirtes as a prisoner in Ravensbrück does, then the language they speak will of necessity be that of brutalisation and defeat. The alternative, as advocated by Benjamin's writings and John Berger's collaborations with the photographer Jean Mohr, is to construct an archive whose task it is to incorporate photography into social and political memory instead of using it as a substitute which encourages the atrophy of such a process. John Roberts has called Berger and Mohr's technique a "process of narrative redemption" that challenges the loss of historical memory.[25] It is a phrase equally applicable to Szirtes' concerns in 'The Photographer in Winter'.

Poem three of the sequence is in the voice of the photographer and immediately re-states the connection between memory and redemption:

> You can't remember and you can't redeem
> The faces loaded with a loaded brush,
> Faces who drift before you as you wash
> The prints in faint red light[.]

As in the opening description of the city, where the snow-muffled streets harbour the echoes of past violence, so this realistic description of the processes involved in developing a photographic negative contains some imminent physical danger. The darkroom's red light, like the concluding words of the previous poem – "Hold it right there. Freeze" – is an order to stop that is also a thinly-disguised threat. Likewise with the "loaded brush", which suggests the presence of a gun. But all of these things are implicit rather than explicit. It is as though the inability to give a coherent name to what has happened in the past means that the present remains in thrall to an unnamed threat. The naturalistic details of the narrative contain hidden clues to this past, except that the photographer is unable to read them. History thus becomes, as for Joyce's Stephen Dedalus, a nightmare from which we must try and wake.

Seemingly objective, the photograph can also deceive. It blurs the distinctions between past and present, life and death, absence and presence, leaving us in a position where we are perhaps unable to validate our own memories and experiences. As such, the treatment of memory, identity and the reconstruction of the biographical and historical past in 'The Photographer in Winter' has much in common with the work of the French artist Christian Boltanski.

The relationship between memory and the memorial is central to Boltanski who, since the mid-1980s, has produced a number of installations dealing with the very real problems of commemorating the Holocaust. The medium to which Boltanski has repeatedly turned in these works is that of photography, a medium which, as Andrew Benjamin has commented, allows him to explore "the multiple determinations of memory ... the relationship between experience and historical time [and] the conditions that work to construct memory".[26]

Boltanski has long been interested in working with fragments. In the early 1970s he produced works such as *Essais de reconstitution d'objets ayant appertenu à Christian Boltanski entre 1948 et 1954* which attempted to reconstruct the artist's biography through the use of otherwise unconnected objects, and which he exhibited in glass vitrines as though they were museum artefacts recording an extinct civilisation. Boltanski has also used photographs in order to reconstruct family histories. In *Album de photos de la famille D., 1939-1964* he borrowed boxes of photographs from a friend and attempted to build the family's history by arranging the photographs in chronological order. That the order Boltanski determined for the photographs meant that the family's history became distorted and fictionalised only served to underline the fact that what Boltanski was interested in, like the Berger/Mohr collaborations, was the establishment of alternative archival histories. The reasons for this can perhaps be found in Boltanski's own experiences during the war, when his family's Jewish identity had to be suppressed for fear of betrayal and capture.

By the mid-1980s, however, Boltanski's interest in reconstruction, memorial and photography had begun to engage with the Holocaust. His gradual coming to terms with his Jewishness is discussed by Lynn Gumpert in her monograph on the artist, but what is interesting to note in relation to Szirtes' work is the part played by photographs in this recovery and re-examination of a past that had fallen victim to silence and invisibility. In a work such as *Monument: Odessa* Boltanski confronted this past by using photographs in such a way as to suggest the necessity of personal memories being allowed their place within the wider concerns of history. Implicit in this process of remembrance, Andrew Benjamin says, are acts of memorialisation:

> [F]rom the monument that commemorates the dead, allowing them to be remembered, to the passing on of familial stories of the activities of relatives now gone, the latter mediated by the photographic album [...] memory and the work of memory seems to endure [and] to provide and sustain that group's history and to that extent, therefore, its identity.[27]

The particular challenge that the Holocaust offers to these processes of commemoration and identification, however, is the scale on which the murder took place. Quoting Emil Fackenheim, who has argued that the Shoah is unredeemable because the deaths of so many millions broke with the very traditions which constitute the means by which we remember and memorialise, Andrew Benjamin argues that it is this very unredeemability that makes the Shoah "*ever present* and *ever past*, where both occur at the same time" and provides a unique challenge in finding not only the means of commemorating but representing the act of remembering.

Talking about his work in 1997, Boltanski was asked to define the relationship between his art, with its reliance on found objects and fragments, and the kinds of art found displayed in glass cases in a museum. His response is pertinent not only to the post-Holocaust crisis in representation that Benjamin regards as central to his work, but offers an interesting and coherent way of re-approaching Szirtes' use of family history and photographs in 'The Photographer in Winter' and elsewhere:

> The objects I display come from my own mythology; most of these things are now dead and impossible to understand. They might be insignificant things, or just simple or fragile, but people looking at them can imagine that they were once used for something.

Boltanski is then asked if the materials he uses are meant to invoke the lives of people who are now lost:

> Yes, there is something contradictory in my work, in that it is about relics but at the same time it's very much against relics. Part of my work has been about what I call 'small memory'. Large memory is recorded in books and small memory is all about little things: trivia, jokes. Part of my work then has been about trying to preserve 'small memory', because often when someone dies, that memory disappears. Yet that 'small memory' is what makes people different from one another, unique. These memories are very fragile; I wanted to save them. [28]

Boltanski's creation of a personal mythology based on the lost, abandoned or stolen detritus of the latter half of the 20th century seems to pull him close to the orbit of Walter Benjamin's proposal in 'Theses On The Philosophy Of History' that "A chronicler who recites events without distinguishing between major and minor ones acts in accordance with the following truth: nothing that has ever happened should be regarded as lost for history."[29]

Walter Benjamin's argument that history should be read not in the exact, scrupulous and perfect records left by the victor but in the fragmented details that constitute both the debris of warfare and the material of our unconscious selves has obvious relevance to Boltanski's definition of "small memory", and what has already been stated about the role played by the "optical unconscious" in Szirtes' poetry. The similarities between Szirtes and Boltanski, and their shared roots in Benjamin, can be taken further.

When it was put to him that an artist doesn't have "to work directly about the Holocaust, because the Holocaust works through us ... shap[ing] the consciousness of most Europeans living in its aftermath", Boltanski tentatively agrees: "Yes but there have been holocausts after the Holocaust. I'm not working on the issue of being guilty or not guilty. My work is about the fact of dying".[30] By similarly refusing to ground his poem in hard biographical facts, Szirtes allows his mother's experience to break clear of its specific historical associations and, like Benjamin's allegorical process, reconstitute its own meaning and significance. Central to this process is the fragment.

In 'Losing', Szirtes deals with precisely this relationship between objects and memory. With its litany of the mundane and the throwaway, the poem not only describes the manner in which human life is destroyed with the same casual disregard as worn-out objects, but portrays the way in which human beings can become literally objectified:

> The pavements' litter, burning flakes
> of bonfires, tickets and franked stamps,
> the fragile image drops and breaks,
> the fugitive awakes, decamps.
>
> The carriages uncouple, trucks
> return unladen, suits appear
> on vacant charitable racks,
> the shelves of darkened stockrooms clear,
>
> skin lifts and peels. A cake of soap.
> The human lamp, the nails, the hair,

the scrapbooks' chronicles of hope
that lose each other everywhere.[31]

And these facts are expressed with the matter-of-fact immediacy of a news report in 'The Lost Scouts':

So history came and blew them apart. Their arms
and legs and heads flew off, their bodies aged
in camps. They froze in forests. Fires raged
in ovens at the heart of unbearable farms.

"If you lie about these things," Szirtes has written, "they fade away completely, and you will find even your interior architecture nothing but air and tantalising smells." He continues:

To look into a courtyard, walk through the gateway and suddenly recognise that warm wash of domestic sound, is not to know anything about history, but it is a form of communion with the lively dead. Every cherubic head, every caryatid, every florid bas-relief is the spirit of some unknown inhabitant. The buildings themselves are bodies in shabby clothes.[32]

As with Boltanski's use of certain symbolically-charged materials, Szirtes demonstrates how even dumb objects can become, like the photograph album in the final poem of 'The Photographer in Winter', "chronicles of hope" that implicate history, memory and art in the possibility of redemption.

III

An intermediary between absence and presence, life and death, biography and history, identity and anonymity, silence and speech, photography bears a heavy metaphorical weight. Arguably the most insightful and moving response to this complex network of relationships is *Camera Lucida,* Roland Barthes' last completed book. It is a work that Szirtes paid explicit homage to in his seventh collection, *Blind Field* (1994), which takes both its title and its epigraph from a passage in *Camera Lucida* where Barthes describes his response to James Van Der Zee's *Family Portrait* of 1926. The photograph shows a Black-American family, with a father and daughter grouped around the seated figure of the mother. The part of

Barthes' commentary that Szirtes quotes is his definition of how a previously unacknowledged detail in a photograph, a *punctum*, creates "a blind field" which gives that detail "a whole life external to [the] portrait".

Blind Field is in three sections, the first and third of which Szirtes has summarised as: "'Blind Field' (people as photographs, dispersal, disintegration) [and] 'Blindfold' (people as memory and affection)."[33] As in 'The Photographer in Winter', the collection examines the relationship between the fragmentation of history and the possible redemptive qualities of memory, implicit in photography. And central to these concerns in the opening third of the book are two sequences of poems: 'For André Kertész' and 'For Diane Arbus'.

Increasingly written about by critics such as Hal Foster, Rosalind Krauss and John Roberts, the relationship between photography and Surrealism is one where, as Roberts says, the photograph has taken on a defining role in attacking representation and "the idea of transparency of meaning in the image".[34] Furthermore, "Surrealism," as David Macey has written, "is, amongst other things, an exploration of and meditation upon the production of signification".[35] Reviewers of his work have repeatedly commented on the influence of Surrealism on Szirtes' work, and he has himself written of the early influence of French surrealists like Robert Desnos and Max Jacob.[36] In this context we might say that Szirtes' refusal in 'The Photographer in Winter' to present a straightforward narrative of his mother's post-war experiences is evidence that he has taken note of Breton's warning:

> The poetic imagination has a mortal enemy in prosaic thought; and today more than ever it is necessary to recall that it has two others, historical narration and rhetoric. For it to remain free is, in effect, for it to be by definition released from fidelity to circumstances, and especially from the *dizzying* circumstances of history.[37]

In 'For André Kertész' we recognise a similar interest in those aspects of surrealist practice and experiment that focussed on the miniature, and had such an important influence on Walter Benjamin. For though each of the four poems in the sequence refers the reader to a specific photograph by Kertész, it is clearly not Szirtes' aim simply to describe the photograph. Rather, his approach is to interrogate the means by which photographs construct an image of reality. This brings him close to Barthes, when he writes that "I may know better a photograph I remember than a photograph I am looking at, as if direct vision oriented its language wrongly, engaging it in an effort of description which will always miss its point of effect, the *punctum*".[38] It is also an approach similar to what Robert Musil had in mind when he wrote that "the law of narrative sequence [is] the most time-honoured perspective for curtailing understanding ... this age-old trick of epic narration, which nannies use to calm their charges".[39]

Each of Szirtes' poems re-orientates, or blasts out if its historical context, Kertész's original, thus allowing for the intervention of memory and the *punctum*. What remains is a significant detail, one that sparks the telling of some obscure or secret history. In other words, they are a purposeful looking for something that would otherwise remain invisible. Each poem functions like a series of enlargements designed to 'blow up' a designated area of a photograph, focussing the reader's attention on a small detail of the original.

In 'Accordionist', based on Kertész's photograph of the same name, Szirtes begins with what might be regarded as purely factual biographical information about the subject of the photograph: "The accordionist is a blind intellectual". However, with the photograph in front of us we can see that even in this opening description Szirtes departs from observable reality. In the photograph the musician is wearing clear glasses, arguing against his blindness. The radical nature of Szirtes' departure from Kertész's original is further highlighted by the sequence of rapid metamorphoses which both the musician and his instrument undergo in the opening stanza:

> The accordionist is a blind intellectual
> carrying an enormous typewriter whose keys
> grow wings as the instrument expands into a tall
> horizontal hat that collapses with a tubercular wheeze.[40]

Photography is thus shown as capable of *transforming* reality, not merely reproducing it. A further significance and layer of transformation is added when the world recorded in the photograph enters language. For as Francis R. Jones has said in connection with Lalic's poetry, "a world recorded in words is more real than a world that is merely recorded."[41]

The blindness attributed to the accordionist not only suggests a personal history that is literally absent from the photograph, but also locates him within the deeper reaches of human experience where myth and history intermingle: Kertész's accordionist becomes Homer or Tiresias or Oedipus, whose physical blindness was compensated for by poetic or prophetic insight. The accordionist's blindness also serves as a coded reference to Barthes' argument, in *Camera Lucida* (which may in turn owe something to Breton's Surrealist manifesto), that 'direct vision' orientates language wrongly by engaging it in the effort of description:

> Ultimately – or at the limit – in order to see a photograph well, it is best to look away or close your eyes. 'The necessary condition for an image is sight,' Janouch told Kafka; and Kafka smiled and replied: 'We photograph things in order to drive them out of our minds. My stories are a way of shutting my eyes.'[42]

The poem continues this oscillation between the particular (the detail or *punctum*) and the general, until, in the final stanza, Szirtes presents an image that clearly re-orientates the reader within recognisable historical events, though significantly even this is done implicitly through the use of a symbol:

> We are the poppies sprinkled along the field.
> We are simple crosses dotted with blood.
> Beware the sentiments concealed
> in this short rhyme. Be wise. Be good.

Taken in 1916, Kertész's photograph has thus become a record of the destruction of the First World War, and the re-drawing of Europe's maps. It was a war, and a peace settlement, that laid many of the foundations for the rise of communism in the East and fascism in the West, the twin forces that determined the lives of Szirtes' parents' generation.

Yet another way in which Szirtes allows language to enact Barthes' process of reorientation is through rhyme and pun. For while the poem creates a Barthian "blind field" within which the original photograph is radically disordered, rhyme and pun allow meaning to emerge not through the observable facts of the photograph but the textures of language itself. While pun serves to translate one word into another, one image into the next, allowing a word to emerge from out of the sound of another – accord from accordion, concert from concertina, tuba from tubercular – Szirtes uses rhyme to structure the poem's three quatrains and, in the final paragraph, draw the reader's attention to exactly the belief that makes any war possible: that "blood" and "good" are in some way inextricably linked. This is not to say that Szirtes invests language with any claims to absolute meaning. Rhyme, especially in sentimental verse, can trick the poet into saying things that are neither honest nor truthful; and 'Accordionist' closes on the ambiguous note of whether "Be wise. Be good" is another such platitude.

The relationship between text and image, word and sound is further developed in 'Hortus Conclusus'. Based on Kertész's 1924 photograph 'Tisza-Szalka' the photograph was taken – like each of the photographs used by Szirtes – before Kertész left Hungary for Paris in 1925. 'Tisza-Szalka' shows an elderly woman sitting on a chair in the shadow of a tree whose branches remain outside the frame. She is either preparing to or has just finished feeding five geese. The photograph, or rather its connotations, becomes a point of departure from where Szirtes launches into a re-telling of the annunciation.

There is still another kind of blindness/blind field implicit in the poem, one that leaves the woman unable to distinguish objects except by their name. Undifferentiated 'purity', or a goodness resulting in everything in the world becoming bleached white, leads to the dissolution of those language structures which, according to Structuralist linguistics, rely on systems of difference. The only way of seeing in such a world would be through shadows, which, as Andrew Benjamin says regarding Boltanski's use of them in his installations, serve not as sites of deception but of illumination. The relationship between shadows and photography is clear enough, with both relying on light being impeded by the presence of a physical object. The shadow, however, is not the same thing as the physical object. To quote Andrew Benjamin again:

As with any casting of shadows there is a transformation ...
Light works not only to present but to transform in the process
of presenting. The question that arises concerns the status of
the original and thus whether or not the transformation is a
transformation, and therefore a deceptive presentation of an
original which already had a singular and already determined
quality[.][43]

Benjamin's relentless logic offers a fascinating insight into the
relationship between Szirtes' poems and Kertész's photographs. I
have commented on the series of transformations that take place when
Kertész's image enters Szirtes' language, a transformation paralleled
by the miraculous birth announced by the angel's appearance to Mary.
The child in the poem emerges out of the gap between stanzas – is
born, in other words, out of the blankness of the page – in a process
akin to that which causes the photographic image to emerge when a
print is 'fixed' after immersion in a chemical solution. As with
'Accordionist', Szirtes presents a series of images that rely on their
emerging from places or details where they hadn't previously existed.
Ian McEwan, writing about the photographs of Harold Chapman
examines a similar perspective:

> In [Chapman's] hands, photography is not a matter of passive
> recording; the camera can make things happen. [B]ehind every
> innocent surface ... lies a secret which the art of photography
> is uniquely equipped to suggest. It would be tempting to write
> 'reveal' – but I suspect that Chapman does not believe in
> absolute truths. Nothing is finally revealed; behind every secret
> there is yet another glazed surface.[44]

As we have seen, Szirtes is also doubtful of 'absolute truths' – whether
presented in images or words.

A similar concern for the processes of revelation underpins the
two remaining poems in this sequence, 'Two Aunts Appearing' and
'The Voyeurs'. The latter takes as its starting point Kertész's 'The
Circus, Budapest' in which a couple, their backs to the viewer, are
shown peering through a hole in a wooden fence at something on the
other side. Only Kertész's title gives any indication as to what it is
they are looking at. In Szirtes' poem, the photograph becomes another
image in which significance lies not in what is seen, but in what is

hidden. At the poem's conclusion, photography is made an implicit player in this mystery:

> There must be a hole in the wooden slat
> and beyond it something perfectly new
> and terrifying that light will not let through.

Looking – or more specifically that kind of looking, voyeurism, which is to do with vicarious sexual pleasure – becomes associated with the couple's unconscious fears and desires, "that wealth of alien stuff/ of which half our minds are made,/leaving us lustful, lost and afraid."[45]

As Jacqueline Rose has pointed out, Freud related the "question of sexuality to that of visual representation", for which he took as his models:

> little scenarios, or the staging of events, which demonstrated the complexity of an essentially visual space, moments in which perception *founders* ... or in which pleasure in looking tips over into the register of *excess* ... Each time the stress falls on the problem of seeing ... The relationship between viewer and scene is always one of fracture, partial identification, pleasure and distrust.[46]

If, then, we see the photograph as another version of Freud's "little scenarios", Szirtes' investigation of the visual returns us once again to the processes whereby we attempt to establish a fixed and stable identity for ourselves. The irony of such a search is that it necessarily involves a process of fragmentation as well as integration. It also implicates a failure to recognise as well as an ability to identify. Rose's argument as regards the question of sexual identity, one that is implicit in Szirtes' title, 'The Voyeurs', sheds still more light on Szirtes' work.

Rose regards the "little scenarios" or "moments of disturbed visual representation" that mark the child's journey into adult life as exposing the fantasy that identity, as it appears in representation, is ever singular or fixed. She also associates this encounter, this 'staging' of psychoanalysis and artistic practice with the staging of something that has already occurred:

It is an encounter which draws its strength from that repetition, working like a memory trace of something we have been through before. It gives back to repetition its proper meaning and status: not lack of originality or something merely derived … nor the more recent practice of appropriating artistic and photographic image in order to undermine their previous status; but repetition as insistence, that is, as *the constant pressure of something hidden but not forgotten – something that can only come into focus now by blurring the field of representation where our normal forms of self-recognition take place* [My emphasis].[47]

Returning to 'The Voyeurs', it can be seen how the photograph has become for Szirtes a metaphor of how images are used, particularly photographs, to identify ourselves through an ongoing relationship with the past, biographical and/or cultural. A photograph shows a unique moment in time capable of being revisited and reinvested with a modified significance. This we know from Walter Benjamin, from surrealist experiments with photography, and from Barthes' model of how the *punctum* allows us to read an image (and ourselves) against the grain. And what each in their differing ways stress – as Szirtes' poem makes clear – is the release of the unconscious, "of which half our minds are made,/leaving us lustful, lost and afraid."

A photograph fixes only the external reality of an object, omitting the fact that individuals change, a fact that presents photography with its unique capacity to invoke melancholy or nostalgia.[48] In terms of the Kertész poems, this nostalgia is based on the fact that the world shown in each photograph no longer exists. This is of particular significance in these images because that world is one which contained traditions and beliefs eradicated by both Nazi and Soviet oppression. Kertész's snapshots of everyday life therefore take on the burden of remembering not only lost time but also lost lives. Such precariousness is re-staged in 'Two Aunts Appearing'. As with 'Accordionist', it is both the metaphoric and metamorphic power of the photographic image to which Szirtes draws our attention. The poem is all movement, but this movement disguises the fact of death. Once granted a kind of physical life, the static image appears to drain energy from the figures it represents. While 'Hortus Conclusus' alerts us to the fact that we can see nothing in a world of unmediated light, 'Two Aunts Appearing' is, as it were, a negative of that poem.

Here everything is seen as becoming a shadow of itself. It is a world of death and mourning. Though the two aunts appear, they do so only to disappear. It is a brittle world teetering on the edge of falling and breaking into splinters: "their legs are thin glass monuments that sway/with the gentle nudging of the wind".[49]

The example Barthes uses in *Camera Lucida* to clarify the relationship between photography and the object is that of the window-pane and the landscape: the photograph is merely the medium through which we observe a thing; it never asks the spectator that they look at it. And though Barthes does not refer to it directly, there is a photograph by André Kertész that captures perfectly both this aspect of Barthes' argument and the relationship between image and text in Szirtes' sequence.

When he left Paris for New York in 1936, Kertész left behind most of his glass plate negatives stored in crates. When he was later reunited with the negatives in 1963, he found that a large number had been broken. He discarded all the broken plates except one, which he chose to develop. The image, a view from above of the rooftops of Montmartre, is unremarkable in itself – indeed, Kertész has said that he only snapped it because he wanted to try out a new lens. What makes the subsequent photograph, 'Broken Plate, Paris', immediately memorable, is the bullet-hole-like fracture which punctures the centre of the image. The effect is to shift attention away from the view of Montmartre towards the shattered glass surface through which we see the objects 'outside'.

Discussing Kertész's work, and this photograph in particular, Charles Hagen, art critic for the *New York Times*, has commented on Kertész's ability to "bring out the metaphor of the photograph as a memory" and how this implicates the survival of memory in fragments.[50] Another photograph portraying this aspect of Kertész's work is 'Elizabeth, Paris'. Taken in 1931, it was originally intended as a rather traditional double portrait of Kertész and his second wife, Erzebét, showing her gazing at the camera and him looking at her, with his head turned in profile, his right hand holding her right shoulder. When, forty years later, Kertész returned to the negative and printed it, he chose to crop the image in such a way that only a detail of the original portrait remained: Erzebét's face is cut in half, and all that appears of Kertész is his rather menacing hand on her shoulder. The photograph, as it now exists, dramatises a form of dismemberment or separation, opening up a contradiction between how things actually were and how, subsequently, they can be 'staged' and made to appear. In the case of Kertész's art, this has been attributed to his sense of alienation, first in Paris, where he encountered Surrealism, then in America, where he emigrated in 1936 because of his Jewish family background. Leaving Hungary meant that Kertész, as any other émigré, would have had to reinvent himself, and a photograph such as 'Elizabeth, Paris' is a vivid example of just such a process.

Szirtes' interest in Kertész is not confined to this sequence of poems. Writing in *Modern Painters* in 1991, he commented that Kertész's is a photography that discloses a "coincidence of place-as-it-was and person" and that only an "unusually perceptive photographer will be able to discover this coincidence [and] locate the specific gravity of an image, time and again".[51] We might say, then, that Kertész's photographs allowed Szirtes access to this "coincidence", providing him with the opportunity of visiting the "place-as-it-was" of his parents' childhood and, confronting it with his own adult self, reinvesting it with an altered historical significance. Throughout 'For André Kertész', there is something of the same feeling that pervades *The Photographer in Winter* – a sense of Szirtes returning to a home that was never his, to a familiar that has become alienated. It is a nostalgia that comes very close to Freud's definition of *unheimlich*.

Certain objects or experiences, Freud said, can have the effect of prompting in us feelings of unease, of literally not 'being at home'. The *unheimlich* will always be associated with an experience of something "one does not know one's way around in"; for the better orientated to an environment a person is, the less susceptible to experiencing this unease in regard to objects and events. *Unheimlich*, Freud continues, "is the name for everything that ought to have remained … secret and hidden but has come to light".[52] The connection with Barthes' *punctum* is an interesting one, and becomes increasingly so when we read that one of the daily experiences in which Freud locates the unheimlich is seeing one's own face reflected in a window. The *unheimlich*, like Barthes' *punctum*, Kertész's 'Broken Plate, Paris' or Szirtes' coincidence of "place-as-it-was and person", depends for its effect on a certain ambiguity, something Freud saw as implicit in the word itself:

171

What interests us most … is to find that among its different shades of meaning the word '*heimlich*' exhibits one which is identical with its opposite, '*unheimlich*'. What is *heimlich* thus comes to be *unheimlich* … [O]n the one hand it means what is familiar and agreeable, and on the other, what is concealed and kept out of sight.

And this "what is concealed and kept out of sight" returns us to Benjamin's aesthetics of redemption, to Barthes' *punctum*, and to Boltanski's "small memory". Furthermore, in that the *unheimlich* is manifested most starkly in our experience of encountering a corpse, and given the close metaphorical parallels between photography and death, it returns us to the central concerns of 'The Photographer in Winter' and, as I now want to examine, 'For Diane Arbus'.

Famous for her disturbing images of twins, eccentric New Yorkers, circus people, and the mentally ill, Arbus herself defined photography as being "a secret about a secret. The more it tells you the less you know".[53] There are obvious parallels, then, between Arbus' work and Freud's theory of the *unheimlich*. Furthermore, for all its seeming matter-of-factness and documentary-style recording of daily life, Arbus' work can be regarded as a continuation of the Surrealist project – if, like Sherwood Anderson, we locate Surrealism in "the art of generalizing the grotesque and then discovering nuances (and charms) in *that*".[54] It is this aspect of Arbus' work to which Susan Sontag refers when she writes:

Buñuel, when asked once why he made movies, said that it was 'to show that this is not the best of all possible worlds.' Arbus took photographs to show something simpler – that there is another world. The other world is to be found, as usual, inside this one.[55]

Working primarily as a photojournalist, Arbus became notorious for seeking out characters from the shadier, more desperate side of the American Dream. Walker Evans called her a "huntress", commenting on her going "fearlessly into the underworld of New York". Likewise Szirtes' sequence of four poems is packed with references to literary journeys into various kinds of worlds-within-worlds. Chief among these are references to Lewis Carroll's Alice – "In a sudden fury Alice begins. She launches a volley/of clicks at the

mist and the leery disappearing/smiles of a hundred Cheshire cats" –
and to Dante. While the Carroll references may have been prompted
by Arbus' 'Auguries of Innocence', a sequence of child portraits
accompanied by captions from various riddles, including Carroll's,[56]
the references and borrowings from Dante's *Commedia* are of an
altogether different nature.

"Whoever does not, sometime or other," Rilke wrote, "give his
full consent, his full and *joyous* consent, to the dreadfulness of life,
can never take possession of the unutterable abundance and power
of our existence".[57] Throughout the *Inferno* Dante is encouraged by
Virgil to look unsparingly and objectively at the punishments meted
out to the dead, no matter how distressing this might be. Virgil dares
Dante to look in the knowledge that it is only by doing so that he will
be saved. The immediate parallel to this in Szirtes' work comes at
the close of 'The Photographer in Winter', when the poet, having
faced up to the worst aspects of the "Dear woman's" life, discovers
precisely this Rilkean form of redemption and with it the recognition
that "There's nothing to betray". But Arbus, too, dares us to look,
though rarely at anything where the subject matter is explicitly to do
with suffering.[58] Instead, her images show, as Susan Sontag has said,
"people in various degrees of unconscious or unaware relation to
their pain".[59]

These reasons alone would be sufficient to justify Szirtes'
references to Dante in the Arbus sequence, and are spelt out in
'Paragons', the opening poem:

> Distrust everything – especially the happy face,
> the successful face, the face with something solid
> stacked behind the eyes. Locate instead the scapegrace,
> the lost and squalid,
>
> those who have nothing to say with the eyes but the eyes
> are open and inward or are lost down a well
> where you look down the shaft to find them and their faces rise
> like your own in the circle[.][60]

The warning with which 'The Accordionist' concludes – "Beware
the sentiments concealed/in this short rhyme" – is here extended to
include the visual as well as the verbal. A representation of reality,

the poem says, is always capable of proving deceptive and thus of providing a shock. It has already been noted that one of the examples from everyday life that Freud cites as an example of the *unheimlich* is catching an unexpected glimpse of one's reflection. In 'Paragons', Szirtes adapts this to seeing one's reflection in a "circle of water", an image that evokes the circles of Dante's Inferno.

The process of imaginative empathy – what Szirtes calls locating the "scapegrace" – is one that leads to a point where the lines dividing the self from the other are no longer clearly defined: thus the observer and the observed merge into, in Eliot's words, "a familiar compound ghost". This loss of a substantive identity is paralleled in the final poem of the sequence by a list of some of the individuals Arbus tracked down and photographed, each of whom fascinated her because of their assumption of a fictional persona:

> The Mystic Barber teleports himself to Mars. Another carries
> a noose and a rose wherever he goes. A third collects string
> for twenty years. A fourth is a disinherited king,
> the Emperor of Byzantium. A fifth ferries
> the soul of the dead across the Acheron.[61]

With the possible exception of the third, each has adopted the persona of someone who mediates between opposing or contradictory states, specifically the living and the dead. This is most obvious with the fifth, whose persona is lifted directly from classical mythology via Virgil and Dante. But a further allusion to Yeats and another crossing into the afterlife, can be detected in the reference to a "disinherited king,/the Emperor of Byzantium". In 'Bichonnade', the fourth poem of the sequence, and in which there is a reference to yet another photographer, Jacques-Henri Lartigue, Szirtes describes Arbus in terms that suggest that, like the people she photographed, she too was ultimately unable to distinguish between reality and fantasy: "It takes courage to destroy the ledge you stand on,/to sit on the branch you saw through". And it is this, the poem suggests, that may have resulted in her suicide by drowning.

Szirtes is not alone in drawing a parallel between Arbus and Dante. Walker Evans mentions Arbus and the New York "underground", and Susan Sontag talked about her photographs in terms of their "Dantesque vision of the city".[62] What Szirtes appears to want to stress is the fact that Arbus' descent into this world of the marginalised – a society, as it were, within a society – is also a descent into her own unconscious fears and desires:

> ... There's a certain abandon
> in asking , Can I come home with you?
>
> like a girl who is well brought up, as she was, in a fashion,
> who seems to trust everyone and is just a little crazy,
> just enough to be charming, who walks between fantasy
> and betrayal and makes of this a kind of profession.

With the repetition of those two key words, "seems" and "betrayal", from 'The Photographer in Winter', Szirtes returns us to the central concerns of that sequence. It also signals, as will be discussed later, the parallels that exist in Szirtes' mind between Arbus and his own mother.

Photography, as all art, is not simply a mimetic record of an objective reality but is an intervention *into* that reality, recording not only external details but subjective fears and desires. Arbus, like Dante, is not a detached observer of suffering: the suffering she sees in others is a reflection of her own (un-)consciousness. There are, then, no easy divisions to be drawn between object and subject in a work of art. Indeed, 'For Diane Arbus' shows us how difficult it can be to draw any such distinctions. These difficulties are mirrored in the structure of Szirtes' poems, where the many layers of inter-textual meaning that run throughout the sequence complicate the search for a single overriding meaning.

In the third of the Arbus sequence, 'The Baths on Monroe Street', Szirtes describes how the photographer enters a women's sauna and begins to take photographs of the bathing women. The women then attack the photographer. At this point in the sequence it is increasingly difficult to separate the various strands of literary allusion from which Szirtes' constructs his poem. We are referred to the biblical Day of Judgement ("Like a reveille/the cry goes up to wake the dead"), Eliot's 'Gerontion' ("The walls are patched and blistered like Eliot's Jew"), Matthew Arnold's 'Dover Beach' ("Ah love let us be true to one another!"), and Carroll's *Alice in Wonderland*. Furthermore, there exists the ghost of another story in which the voyeur is punished by being torn to shreds: the myth of Diana and Actaeon, in which the hunter, Actaeon, is ripped to pieces by his own hounds because of his inadvertently having seen Diana bathing naked in a stream. Added to these literary allusions there is also, of course, the reference to Marilyn Monroe – a reference which not only brings into play notions of the 'male gaze' and voyeurism, but also Monroe's death by suicide.

It is clear, then, that as in 'The Photographer in Winter', Szirtes is refusing to present a straightforward biographical narrative. The reasons for this is that Szirtes, like Breton, is interested in questioning and disrupting the representation of reality as a seamless unity. What he does instead is to use the juxtaposition of literary texts in a way that is, in effect, a form of montage. We can go further and say that each quotation, removed from its original context, functions as the sort of 'found object' favoured by the surrealists in the construction of their artworks. We might even say that these techniques, in turn, are meant, in some way, to imitate the means by which memory salvages one or two details from a situation and, having forgotten the rest, must use these fragments in order to construct a record of the past. This obviously returns us to Walter Benjamin's critique of the edifice of Civilisation in 'Theses on the Philosophy of History', which in turn allows us another perspective on Arbus' work with society's marginalised:

> [W]ith whom [do] the adherents of historicism actually empathize? The answer is inevitable: with the victor. And all the rulers are the heirs of those who conquered before them. Hence, empathy with the victors invariably benefits the rulers … Whoever has emerged victorious participates to this day in the triumphal procession in which the present rulers step over those who are lying prostrate. According to traditional practice, the spoils are carried along in the procession. They are called cultural treasures, and a historical materialist views them with cautious detachment. For without exception the cultural treasures he surveys have an origin which he cannot contemplate without horror. They owe their existence not only to the efforts of the great minds and talents who have created them, but also to the anonymous toil of their contemporaries. There is no document of civilisation which is not at the same time a document of barbarism.[63]

Szirtes' comment that Arbus' work was balanced between "fantasy/and betrayal" can thus be seen as analogous to the dialectical arrangement of Benjamin's argument: art, or imagination, must tread a fine line between siding with institutionalised power and authority over the exploited and powerless. The means of doing so, Szirtes suggests, is to re-focus our attention on the "scapegrace,/the lost and squalid". Only in having done this can appearances "become something other/than imagined". And it is a construction of an alternative history made from fragments that provides Szirtes with an opportunity to memorialise not only Diane Arbus but his own mother, who, Szirtes has written, "shared many temperamental characteristics with Diane Arbus [and who] in a different world, a western Americanised world ... might well have been an Arbus."[64] It is a set of personal associations which, though never made explicit in the poems, certainly accounts for the oblique narratives and the sense of an uneasy truce between fact and fantasy, "fantasy/and betrayal" contained in the sequence.

In Canto Thirteen of the 'Inferno', Virgil leads Dante into a wood where, though he can hear voices, he cannot see who is making the sound. Virgil tells him to break off a branch from any tree:

> ... I reached my hand
> A little in front of me and twisted off
>
> One shoot of a mighty thornbush – and it moaned,
>   "Why do you break me?" Then after it had grown
>   Darker with blood, it began again and mourned,
>
> "Why have you torn me? Have you no pity, then?
>   Once we were men, now we are stumps of wood:
>   Your hand should show some mercy, though we had been
>
> The souls of serpents." As flames spurt at one side
>   Of a green log oozing sap at the other end,
>   Hissing with escaping air, so that branch flowed
>
> With words and blood together – at which my hand
>   Released the tip, and I stood like one in dread.[65]

The trees, as Dante discovers, contain the souls of those who have committed suicide. Thus Arbus' name, with its similarities to the Latin *arbour* – a tree – contains clues to her own life and death.

Szirtes' sequence radically re-constructs Arbus' biography through the juxtaposition of fragments which are then held together by the centripetal force of a recognisable narrative structure: Dante's journey into hell – a world-within-a world – where he talks and listens to the dead. But photographs, too, are fragments of a seemingly unified reality, capable, in Sontag's words, of "permit[ting] the mute past to speak in its own voice, with all its irresolvable complexity".[66] It is this multiplicity of textual voices and a refusal to offer any easy resolution to the historical, biographical and artistic complexities with which it is concerned, that means Szirtes' writings have much in common with the 'memory book' of recent Jewish history.

A photograph, said Jasper Johns, is an object, "that tells of loss, destruction, disappearance of objects. Does not speak of itself. Tells of other".[67] In other words, it is an elegy. This elegiac strain is also present in Szirtes' work, where its appearance no doubt owes something to what Marianne Hirsch defines as the "deep sense of displacement suffered by the children of exile, the elegiac aura of the memory of a place to which one cannot return".[68] In describing the experience of the "children of exile", Hirsch describes their attempts to reconstruct their missing past:

> None of us ever knows the world of our parents. We can say that the motor of the fictional imagination is fuelled in great part by the desire to know the world as it looked and felt before our birth. How much more ambivalent is this curiosity for children of Holocaust survivors, exiled from a world that has ceased to exist, that has been violently erased. Theirs is a different desire, at once more powerful and more conflicted: the need not just to feel and to know, but also to re-member, to re-build, to re-incarnate, to replace and repair. For survivors who have been separated and exiled from a ravaged world, memory is necessarily an act not only of recall, but also of mourning.[69]

That aspect of Szirtes' work which Sean O'Brien has described as offering "the feel and smell of life itself", making "the lives he recalls express the other, unknown lives, including the lucky ones", is clearly associated with the complex of desires described by Hirsch.[70] Hirsch goes on to locate this experience within a Jewish memorial tradition dating back to the waves of Jewish emigrations from Eastern Europe following the pogroms of the early part of the twentieth century. *Yizker bikher*, or memorial books, were prepared in exile in order to preserve the memory of a destroyed culture. These memorial books contained texts and images, and their influence can be seen in the Holocaust Museum in Washington, DC, where the exhibits, in Hirsch's words, "aim ... to get us close to the affect of the event, to convey knowledge and information without, however, attempting any facile sense of re-creation or reenactment".[71] Most of the Holocaust Museum's exhibits use photographs as the primary means of re-creating the pre-war lives of European Jews. By using photographs that show Jewish daily life rather than the better-known images of the death camps, the museum aims not only to present the variety and richness of a culture that has disappeared but to challenge that reading of Jewish history which insists on seeing what happened during the Holocaust as in any way inevitable.

If, as John Berger says, photographs "bear witness to a human choice being exercised in a given situation [and are] the result of the photographer's decision that it is worth recording that this particular event or this particular object has been seen",[72] then that same human choice extends to the decision that certain events or objects – and by extension individual lives and cultures – are not worth recording but, on the contrary, are to be eliminated. Read in this light, the photographs contained in the Holocaust Museum are survivors of Jewish culture's struggle with invisibility and silence. For so long regarded as the 'scapegraces' of European culture, it is to these fragile records to a vanished civilisation that we should look if we want to see, in Barthes' words, "Good and Evil, desire and its object: dualities we can conceive but not perceive".[73] In short, the invisible made visible; the vanished past made tangible.

In his poem 'Prodigy', Charles Simic – Serbian by birth, brought up under Nazi occupation and 'transplanted' to the United States at the age of 11 – speaks in the voice of someone for whom the veracity of what he has been told about the past has become an issue of doubt:

I'm told but do not believe
that that summer I witnessed
men hung from telephone poles.

I remember my mother
blindfolding me a lot.

She had a way of tucking my head
suddenly under her overcoat.[74]

History, rather than being an autonomous reading of objective events, has, for the poet, become displaced onto seemingly innocuous details. A cohesive narrative has thus been reduced to fragments. Simic's poem therefore reinforces the fact that memory does not exist in a vacuum: it does not exist as a purely subjective, psychological phenomenon. The poet's understanding of the historical past does not belong to him alone, but is mediated through his parents' subsequent re-telling of events. And while Ivan Lalic's poetry can be seen as being concerned with assimilation and synthesis, Simic and Szirtes stress the difficulties of this process. For them, history is as much a matter of what is not remembered as what is. Rather than being a retelling of objective events, history has become in Simic's poem the memory of subjective experience. The matter-of-fact record of "men hung from telephone poles" has given way to the matter-of-fact detail of the mother's overcoat. Meaning has been displaced; an otherwise innocent object has not only altered the poet's understanding of the determined relationship between past and present but brought about a condition where what is remembered is implicated in a conspiracy of silence. And as we have seen, photography, with its complex relationship to the past, shares in exactly this same displacement of major events onto the apparently innocent. Indeed, if we re-read Simic's poem alongside a passage from John Berger quoted earlier – "A photograph, whilst recording what has been seen, always and by its nature refers to what is not seen. It isolates, preserves and presents a moment taken from a continuum" – we can see the image of the mother "tucking" the child's head under her overcoat as a parallel to the early days of photography when the photographer would disappear beneath a black canvas hood.

Whether it is Boltanski's use of second-hand clothing and other people's photographs; Kertész's experiments with cropping images so as to produce a photographic print very different in form and content from the original negative; or Diane Arbus' descent into the marginal lives of the mentally ill or socially excluded – each, like Szirtes, investigates and draws their art, with all its complexities, from areas where what has been forgotten, overlooked or abandoned re-enters consciousness in such a way as to radically alter our perception not only of ourselves but our place within history, both familial and cultural. And in so much as he is a surrealist, Szirtes uses Surrealism, in Bataille's terms, to challenge and reconstruct history through a radical "politics of identity".[75] This does not mean, as some critics have said, that Surrealism retreats from the everyday into a world of the weird and bizarre but rather, as John Roberts argues, it means "a realist insistence on the power of photography to bring the contradictions of social reality into view. The document and archive are not incidental to 'convulsive beauty', but its dialectical partner".[76] Szirtes' achievement in 'The Photographer in Winter', 'For André Kertész' and 'For Diane Arbus' is precisely this: to reconcile the everyday with the 'convulsive', and to place the unacknowledged, the marginal, the silent and invisible back within a wider historical perspective.

IV

As should by now be clear, Szirtes' poetry is pre-occupied with a re-discovery and re-presentation of his biographical and cultural past as a means of understanding the relationship between these and aspects of his identity as a poet in Britain. The key word here, as Szirtes has himself signalled, is 'heritage', a word that for the exile is riddled with contradictions and ambiguities.

To discover one's roots is not the same as to discover a coherent identity. The danger, for the child of exiles or refugees, is that this sense of themselves in the present can too easily be determined by a past that they may not remember, a language they cannot speak, and a culture that leaves them isolated in the place where they now must live. The result, as Szirtes has expressed it in a number of poems, is a feeling of homelessness, of vague dis-ease:

The child I never was makes poetry
of memories of landscape haunted by sea.
He stands in an attic and shows you his collection
of huge shells, and with an air of introspection
cracks his knuckle bones.[77]

'The Child I Never Was' is typical of a number of Szirtes' poems
where he figures the relationship between his early childhood in
Hungary – "a country that is set in seas of land" – and his adult life
in England in terms of the double or doppelgänger. The theme is not
always as apparent as it is here. It often appears, as in 'Windows,
Shadows', in a modified form, such as the relationship between the
self and the reflection of that self in a mirror or a darkened window:

No companion could be more attached.
No brother show a greater sympathy
        than these black windows
making fiction out of fiction, and a body
out of nothing. Some windows may be touched
        only by shadows.[78]

But whenever – or however – it occurs, it bears a striking similarity
to aspects of Freud's *unheimlich*.

"The theme of the 'double'," Freud writes, "was originally an
insurance against the destruction of the ego, an 'energetic denial of
the power of death' ... This invention of doubling as a preservation
against extinction has its counterpart in dreams [and] led the Ancient
Egyptians to develop the art of making images of the dead in lasting
materials".[79] The connections between the *unheimlich*, photography
and memory have already been noted. The further significance of its
relationship to Szirtes' writings is that "the theme of the 'double'",
this self-preservation of the ego or a life-like representation of the
dead, is one that Freud associates specifically with childhood:

When all is said and done, the quality of uncanniness can only
come from the fact of the 'double' being a creation dating
back to a very early mental stage, long since surmounted – a
stage, incidentally, at which it wore a more friendly aspect.
The 'double' has become a thing of terror.[80]

Returning to 'The Child I Never Was' and 'Windows, Shadows', we might wonder whether the sinister 'double' cracking its knuckle bones "with an air of introspection" or the sympathetic "brother" might not also be connected in some way with retrospection, with that same kind of troubled looking-back or nostalgia running throughout Szirtes' sequences to do with photography. Here too, as in the image of the seashells the child collects, something significant has had to be lost. The photograph, like the shell, signifies absence. Just as the photographs in 'The Photographer in Winter' and 'For André Kertész' portray a Budapest and a Hungary that no longer exists, is no longer inhabited, so the shells too are vacant homes that speak of past occupants. Both photograph and shell function as a mnemonic, prompting the adult Szirtes, in Proustian terms, to rediscover lost time. And the importance attached to both, as in the detail of the mother's overcoat in Simic's poem, owes its existence to a process of displacement. They are, as Freud wrote in 'The Psychopathology of Everyday Life', "substitutes ... for other impressions which are really significant".[81]

Narratives of childhood are always in some way about adult experience. One reading of 'The Photographer in Winter', for example, is to see it as a *Bildungsroman*, the story of a young artist's struggle towards creative maturity. Certainly, there are comments in 'A Dual Heritage' that suggest the importance of the sequence to Szirtes' development as a writer. But for the children of Holocaust survivors, the burden of this responsibility is particularly heavy. As we have seen, this can become acute for an artist such as Christian Boltanski, concerned with the problems of language and representation. With this in mind, I want now to examine the way in which Szirtes approaches the narration of his own childhood experiences or memories, and how these operate within a wider historical framework.

The epigraph to 'Metro' – "What should they do there but desire" – is taken from Derek Mahon's 'A Disused Shed in Co. Wexford', a poem which impels us to find a means of allowing history's silenced and forgotten populations to speak. There are obvious comparisons here to Walter Benjamin's "optical unconscious" and Freud's *unheimlich*. Moreover, Szirtes has himself said that his own aim in writing was to show that "history [is] a fiction so powered by desire it felt like truth". Such might be the significance of Szirtes' use of Mahon's words. There is a further possibility, one that ties in with Szirtes' family history.

Mahon's poem begins "Even now there are places where a thought might grow –/Peruvian mines, worked out and abandoned/To a slow clock of condensation,/An echo trapped forever", lines which are strikingly similar to a passage from George Steiner's essay 'A Kind of Survivor':

> Somewhere the determination to kill Jews, to harass them from the earth simply because they *are*, is always alive. Ordinarily, the purpose is muted, or appears in trivial spurts ... But there are, even now, places where the murderous intent might grow heavy: in Russia, in parts of North Africa, in certain countries of Latin America.[82]

Steiner's essay is about 'self-definition', more particularly how the children of Holocaust survivors identify themselves in relation to European history and a culture that condemned their immediate family to death. Steiner describes this identification as being a "shadowy ... condition ... caught between two waves of murder, Nazism and Stalinism". It is a condition that precisely defines Szirtes' parents' experience, forming the historical basis of 'Metro'.

A long sequence of some sixty 13-line poems divided into ten sections, 'Metro' is arguably Szirtes' greatest achievement to date. It begins with the evocation of a now vanished past that locates the narrative in childhood experience: "My aunt was sitting in the dark, alone/Half-sleeping, when I crept into her lap." This scene immediately gives way to the narrator's adult self, trying to piece together the fragments of experience through memory:

> The smell of old women now creeps over me,
> An insect friction against bone
> And spittle, and an ironed dress
> Smoother than shells gathered by the sea,
> A tongue between her teeth like a scrap
> Of cloth, and an eye of misted glass,
> Her spectacles[.][83]

Like Simic's displacement of childhood memory onto details or Boltanski's use of second-hand clothing to memorialise the Holocaust dead, Szirtes builds up a picture of his aunt that might remind us of a painting by Arcimbaldo. Made as it is of fragments, scraps, odds-and-ends, it places the emphasis on a discontinuity of place and person, perhaps emphasising the child's partial understanding of the world of which he is a part.[84]

The poem is set in the Budapest of the immediate post-war years, when, as in many other communist countries, the persecution and suffering of the Jews came under the heading of Fascist atrocities; it was considered unnecessary, inappropriate even, to focus on the Jewish tragedy. There were no Jews, only victims of persecution. Such silencing of the Jewish experience was part of official culture. It also, as Szirtes shows, became part of everyday family life: "Her face glows like a lantern and she says/There is a God, the God of the Jews, of Moses and Elias,/But this is not the time to speak of him."

The ability to articulate recent history is driven underground, providing Szirtes with the central metaphor for the poem: the Budapest Metro. Other journeys become implicated in this: the deportation train that took his mother to the camp in Ravensbrück; his family's escape from Hungary to England; the other family members who left for North America or Argentina; Orpheus' quest for Eurydice; and, as in 'For Diane Arbus', Dante's journey among the dead. The result of this scattering and dispersal of those lives and significant objects that help us define ourselves in the present, evoking as they do our personal connections to the past, means that, as in the portrait of the poet's aunt in the opening lines, the past can only be made to speak through fragments.

> ... The earth gives up her worms and shards,
> Old coins, components, ordnance, bone and glass,
> Nails, muscle, hair, flesh, shrivelled bits of string,
> Shoe leather, buttons, jewels, instruments.
> And out of these come voices, words,
> Stenches and scents,
> And finally desire, pulled like a tooth.
> It's that or constancy that leads us down
> To find a history which feels like truth.

As with Homer's catalogue of the Greek ships that sailed for Troy, Szirtes' list of broken, damaged, useless objects evokes not only the individual lives that have been lost but the diminishment of a whole culture of feeling, remembering and, ultimately, truth-making.

Running parallel to this elegy for the Holocaust dead are Szirtes' own memories of the post-war years. It is a childhood dominated by the Big Brother-like presence of Stalin:

> The early fifties: Uncle Joe's broad grin
> Extends benevolently across the wall. ...
> Uncle Joe's moustache will shelter them.
> This is the era of benevolence.

It is a description reminiscent of Hans Magnus Enzensberger's poem, 'Dept. of Philosophy', where the omnipresence of Stalin's "inky moustache" is allowed to suggest the stifling atmosphere of Soviet Europe and the necessity of double-think:

> ... Our psyche
> calmly produces pertinent statements,
> and we agree that deep down in any given brutal pig
> a well-meaning public servant is found
> and the other way round. Abracadabra![85]

Both poems show how inextricably linked were the ideas of family and state, and how blurred the boundaries became between private and social. But in 'Metro', such a view also serves as a realistic representation of a child's view of the world, one where the child has absorbed the latest Party slogan and is able, parrot-fashion, to repeat that he is living in "the era of benevolence."

"No grown writer," Naomi B. Sokoloff has written, "can speak authentically in the name of childhood or in the voice of a child ... The sensations and perceptions of childhood are to some extent always irretrievable to memory and articulation".[86] Hence another reason why the world of 'Metro' is reconstructed out of fragments: it is in precisely this way that we remember things. Or is it? The defining feature of Szirtes' narrative technique in 'Metro' is that the sequence provides multiple perspectives on events: there is the child's voice, captured in its unquestioning acceptance of 'Uncle Joe'; there is the voice of the aunt, warning against the danger of re-telling the Jewish heritage; there is Paul Celan's voice, with snatches of his poems littering Szirtes' text; there is also the voice of Magdalena Szirtes – or rather, as in 'The Photographer in Winter', Szirtes' ventriloquising of her voice; and there is the voice of the adult poet, speaking about the past from the safety of the present ("In the benevolence of an August night/That smiles on our children").

The narrative, rather than being a linear account of events from Magdalena Szirtes' childhood in Kolozsvár in Transylvania, to her grandchildren's lives in England, moves between a number of points of reference. It is this, like the subterranean loops of the Metro, that gives the poem its structure, one which enacts Bergson's belief that memory, far from being a fragmented and discontinuous process of juxtaposition, is, in fact, continuous, involving as it does a constant to-ing and fro-ing between past and present:

> Whenever we are trying to recover a recollection, to call up some period of our history, we become conscious of an act *sui generis* by which we detach ourselves from the present in order to replace ourselves, first, in the past in general, then, in a certain region of the past – a work of readjustment, something like the focussing of a camera. But our recollection still remains virtual; we simply prepare ourselves to receive it by adopting the appropriate attitude. Little by little it comes into view like a condensing cloud; from the virtual state it passes into the actual; and as its outlines become more distinct and its surface takes on colour, it tends to imitate perception. But it remains attached to the past by its deepest roots, and if, when once realized, it did not retain something of its original virtuality, if, being a present state, it were not also something which stands out distinct from the present, we should never know it for memory.[87]

The defining feature of our memory of the past, says Bergson, is that we experience it as different from the present. And there exists, Bergson says, only one way of retrieving the past:

> [T]he truth is that we shall never reach the past unless we frankly place ourselves within it. Essentially virtual, it cannot be known as something past unless we follow and adopt the movement by which it expands into a present image, thus

emerging from obscurity into the light of day. In vain do we
seek its trace in anything actual and already realized: we might
as well look for darkness beneath the light.[88]

We can see, therefore, how Szirtes' narrative technique "follow[s]
and adopt[s] the movement by which [the past] expands into a present
image" by alternating between a number of narrative focalizers, each
of whom exists independently of the rest in a particular time and
place. Furthermore, Szirtes has placed 'himself' within this past, and
it is from this child's sensory perception from which, like Proust's
madeleine and cup of tea, the poem expands in an ever-widening
circle. It is this child focalizer whose perspective orientates the
narrative, as distinct from the adult narrator whose words make up
the text. The result, like a camera's zoom lens, is that this child's
view of the world, in Sokoloff's words, "encourages narrative
strategies that conflate perspectives, equivocation and duality".[89]

The relationship between these narrative strategies and other kinds
of photographic techniques can be taken still further. The
juxtaposition of narrating voices in the poem brings to mind montage;
and we might even see the process of retrospection which is signalled
by the poem's opening as being a kind of superimposition: with the
adult poet looking back and pretending to record the child's thoughts
and experiences. This merging of voices is given a figurative presence
in the poem when the adult narrator provides a self-portrait of himself
as a child: "A peculiar little old man of a boy,/A kind of dwarf,
benevolently wise/And puzzled, deep voiced, comic almost."

As was discussed earlier, one of the principal means by which
Szirtes constructs the internal structures of his poems is that of
montage. It is a technique which brings him into the orbit of Benjamin
and the Surrealists, for whom montage was, in Fredric Jameson's
words, "a reaction against the intellectualized, against *logic* in the
widest sense of the word, subsuming not only philosophical
rationality, but also the common-sense interest of the middle-class
business world, and ultimately reality itself".[90] In part a reaction to
the First World War and the application of reason and logic to bring
about the mechanised slaughter of millions, Surrealism rose out of
the geo-political instabilities following the Treaty of Versailles and
the subsequent displacement of civilian populations. To a critic such
as Hal Foster, the various forms of Surrealism are defined less by

their artefacts, than by a general concern with, and experience of, the *unheimlich* in a way that bears directly on the presentation of historical events in 'Metro'. Foster writes:

> If there is a concept that comprehends Surrealism, it must be contemporary with it, immanent to its field ... I believe this concept to be *the uncanny*, that is to say, a concern with events in which repressed material returns in ways that disrupts unitary identity, aesthetic norms, and social order.[91]

This last comment is important. Though sometimes perceived as apolitical, Surrealism did offer a challenge to the existing social order. That it did so in aesthetic rather than political terms should not diminish our recognition of the fact. Indeed, as far as Walter Benjamin was concerned, Marx, given his famous observation that "the world has long been dreaming of something of which it must only become conscious in order to possess it in reality" was a surrealist *avant la lettre*. What concerned Benjamin, however, was how he was to reconcile his own reliance on the small-scale with the wider necessities of a Marxist reading of history:

> The first step on this path will be to incorporate the principles of montage in the study of history. Thus, to construct the grandest edifices from the smallest, most precisely fabricated building-blocks. Thereby to discover the crystallization of the totality in the analysis of the small, individual elements.[92]

There are important parallels here to Szirtes' method in 'The Photographer in Winter', where Benjamin's "crystallization of the totality" takes the form of various references to a world made up of ice and snow. It is precisely these 'crystallized' details that capture and reveal the hidden significance contained in the present moment: "This winter is not metaphorical./The sun has broken into tiny pieces/ And goes on fracturing as it releases/ More and more light".

Szirtes is artistically and biographically the heir to those political and aesthetic upheavals that dominated the European continent after Versailles, continuing to rumble on, increasingly louder, throughout the 1930s and beyond. It was the failure of any coherent and sustained political alternative – at least on a governmental level – that enabled Hitler and Stalin to consolidate and then widen their ambitions, leading first to the deportation of Budapest's Jews, including Szirtes' mother, and eventually to the events of October 1956 and his family's exile from Hungary. Hardly surprising, then, that Szirtes' summary of his own approach to writing begins by stressing the vagaries of his biographical self. He then goes on to associate this with a poetics that explores precisely that terrain which intrigued the Surrealists:

> What the world lacks for the likes of me is stability. Form imposes an arbitrary stability that implies a continuity with the past ... Rhyme is arbitrary and at the same time provides a deliberate governance of the anarchic, dangerous sprawl and formlessness of the visual and psychological field.

What is immediately striking here is the relationship Szirtes perceives as existing between form and historical continuity. Arbitrary as it may be, form contains a link between the past and present. Just as every photograph, as Robert Hullot-Kentor writes, "is somehow equally old – even one snapped a second previously",[93] so poetic form, despite the essential instabilities of language and meaning, reconnects the writer and reader within a continuum of human experience. Again, Szirtes' locates his susceptibility to this aspect of poetry in terms of his own life:

> Language too is unstable ... It is not to be relied on ... Language only chases shadows. After all if you had to change languages at some stage you are more than usually aware of the thinness of the linguistic integument that covers the world. Poetry though is a way of reconnecting language to experience, signifier to signified. The sensation only lasts as long as you are reading – but then, that is all you have, so you'd better look after it.

We have seen how the lost world of 'Metro' is regained through an act of Proustian involuntary memory. The past is summoned through the particularities of the physical world. What also takes place is some kind of metamorphosis. Rather than appearing as a cohesive whole, the aunt becomes a series of verbal tropes. Furthermore, in becoming disconnected fragments the reader experiences the narrator's aunt as montage, as a series of still pictures by which the past is projected onto the screen of the present,[94] thereby locating the poem in that "crystallization of the totality" advocated by Benjamin.

There is a problem here. As we have seen, for Benjamin and the Surrealists, montage was a means of salvaging from the detritus of bourgeois culture those narratives that would otherwise be deemed valueless, and therefore be discarded. For Adorno, however, far from undermining bourgeois culture, such a process merely confirmed its omnipotence by fetishising it. In doing so, bourgeois culture was further allowed to dominate not only the material but also the imaginary world. And it is this that formed the basis of Adorno's criticisms of the movement in his 1956 essay, 'Looking Back on Surrealism'.

Taking issue with the accepted notion that Surrealism aimed to reproduce dream-like states – Adorno states that "surrealist constructions are merely analogous to dreams, no more" – he goes on to say that though Surrealism "suspend[s] the customary logic and the rules of the game of empirical evidence ... in doing so [it] respects the individual objects that have been forcibly removed from their context[.] There is a shattering and a regrouping, but no dissolution."[95] Such a process, as Richard Wolin has explained, accepts without criticism the material elements of bourgeois society. Wolin writes: "For this reason [Surrealism] remains 'inorganic and lifeless', since these elements remain untransformed ... that is, they are not reinstated in a new, conceptually integrated organic whole".[96]

The Surrealist image therefore betrays a libidinous desire that, rather than restructuring our understanding of social and historical reality, merely conforms it through a passive process of imitation. What is more, the Surrealist aesthetic – shock – lost its power when it came up against the authentic horrors of the Second World War. It is with a coded reference to this that Adorno's essay concludes:

> Surrealism salvages what is out of date, an album of idiosyncrasies in which the claim to the happiness that human beings find denied them if their own technified world goes up in smoke. But if Surrealism itself now seems obsolete, it is because human beings are now denying themselves the consciousness of denial that was captured in the photographic negative that was Surrealism.[97]

By using its own artworks to attack it (the reference to a photographic negative would seem to refer us to some of Man Ray's experiments with solarisation) Adorno refused to allow Surrealism – indeed, any art movement – an existence separate from political and economic realities. The success of the Surrealist movement, Adorno argues, is that it dealt in images which, rather than locating the fears and desires depicted in objective social reality, located them in a state analogous to dreams or, *pace* Freud, in childhood. Instead of liberating subjective experiences as a form of social revolution, as Breton had advocated, Adorno's reading of the movement accuses it of being complicit in maintaining the status quo. "The dialectical images of Surrealism," he writes, "are images of a dialectic of subjective freedom in a situation of objective unfreedom".[98] Thus, if we accept that the central thesis of Adorno's aesthetics is "that art becomes the unconscious writing of history through its isolation from society",[99] Surrealism becomes a symptom of other repressed or unacknowledged forces within society. These same forces can emerge as a Surrealist artwork or the "technified world" of the Final Solution. Read in this light, Surrealism becomes simply a reversed image – or negative – of other cultural forces.

Where, then, does this leave 'Metro' in relation to Surrealism? Clearly, Szirtes does utilise aspects of what can both loosely and more specifically be called Surrealist methods. One advantage he has over Breton and others, is, like Adorno, the benefit of hindsight. Breton et al could not have known the direction Europe was headed. As such, 'Metro' operates along two simultaneous but not analogous time scales. It is a point made by George Steiner in reference to all post-war attempts to write about and determine the continuing relationship between the Holocaust and our present selves:

> That, surely, is the point: to discover the relations between those done to death and those alive then, and the relation of both to us; to locate, as exactly as record and imagination are able, the measure of unknowing, indifference, complicity, commission, which relates the contemporary or survivor to the slain ... To make oneself concretely aware that the 'solution' was not 'final', that it spills over into our present lives is the only but compelling reason for forcing oneself to continue reading these literally unbearable records, for going

back or, perhaps forward, into the non-world of the sealed ghetto and extermination camp.[100]

Steiner's words can be used to sum up an aspect of Szirtes' narrative:

> … I place a woman
> On a train and pack her off to Ravensbrück:
> I send out a troop of soldiers to summon
> The Jews of this fair city.
> Off she goes,
> Repeating her unknown journey, and I must look
> To gauge the distances between us nicely.
> I see a voice, the greyest of grey shadows.
> Lead me, psychopompos, through my found
> City, down into the Underground.

Szirtes' is an essentially lyric voice that accepts the burden and responsibility of writing about historical events from the sanctuary of the present. To narrate is both to be a part of, and separate from, what it is one is telling. Such ambiguities are essential, as the woman is both guide to, and unknowing victim of, the past. Tenses switch and cross like railway tracks leaving a station. As such, we can say that Szirtes is conscious, to use Adorno's words, that he is writing about 'objective unfreedom' from a position of 'subjective freedom'. In many ways, then, Szirtes' narrative is built up of similar material to that used by the Surrealists when constructing their *objets trouvés*. It is to the abandoned and outmoded that he appeals in re-constructing a portrait of a lost culture.

'Metro' is driven by the struggle to salvage experience from the threat of silence. The poem aims to grant the fleeting moment a certain permanence and fulfilment in language. "One eroticises flesh in order to prevent it from dying and fading," Szirtes has written; "One eroticises language in order to emphasise its sensual consonance with the world." Ironically, given Szirtes' faith in the ability of language to reconnect us to experience, 'Metro' portrays a world in which the visible takes precedence over the verbal: "Her face glows like a lantern" and she says/"There is a God, the God of the Jews, of Moses and Elias,/But this is not the time to speak of him.'"

The poet's aunt inhabits a form of verbal exile. The past, the continuum of a living tradition, is forbidden expression. Language –

reason – induces not remembrance but sleep. The aunt's gradual lapsing into unconsciousness therefore begins to assume a more disturbing meaning: the translation of her subjective identity into the objective reality of mere bric-à-brac suggests, not Benjamin's aesthetic of the fragment as a dialectical image capable of redeeming the past from the forgetfulness of the present, but the systematic destruction of the sanctity of the human subject that was the aim of the Nazis. That this process culminates in the image of the aunt becoming a human lampshade only emphasises this.

What the poem also touches on in these early stages is the relationship between itself as artefact and the culture and traditions it memorialises. One of the ways in which 'Metro' mediates between these traditions is its refusal to present events from either a fixed perspective in time or place, thereby highlighting those cultural and historical forces that challenge us to define what is meant by, in Adorno's phrase, "universality through unrestrained individuation".[101] The danger of such an approach is acknowledged by Szirtes when he writes that the best he can hope to achieve is "To find a history which feels like truth."

In 'On Lyric Poetry And Society', Adorno proposed that in the 20th century the lyric was the only poetic form capable of expressing the disintegration and dissolution of social and historical meaning. It is the lyric poet, in his or her very isolation from society, that makes poetry most capable of articulating what would otherwise remain unconscious:

> The universality of the lyric's substance, however, is social in nature. Only one who hears the voice of humankind in the poem's solitude can understand what the poem is saying; indeed, even the solitariness of lyrical language itself is prescribed by an individualistic and ultimately atomistic society, just as conversely its general cogency depends on the intensity of its individuation. [102]

We have already seen how Szirtes associates a sense of the essential instability of language with his own refugee status and how, in turn, this can be seen as an explanation of his own attachment to a certain poetic tradition. Just as, in his early writings, he looked to pictures as a means of finding a subject "whose emotional centre was preserved in a kind of stasis", so his use of traditional metres and forms might equally be said to form an objective, impersonal framework within which to write about the personal. It is an attachment to form and rhyme, he says, that "might be traced back to exile, transplantation, displacement." What, then, are we to make of the form of 'Metro'?

Built as it is of individual sections, 'Metro' remains a series of fragments. Like the lozenges of sunlight in 'The Photographer in Winter', it "goes on fracturing as it releases/More and more light". We can also see each thirteen-line stanza as being somehow incomplete, just falling short of the formal coherence of a sonnet. Indeed, the poem's association with the sonnet sequence and its traditional subject matter of romantic love is something to which Szirtes alluded when he wrote that 'Metro' was planned as a kind of love poem.[103] As a result the poem can be read as we would a sequence by, say, Sidney or Spenser. If this provides one model for a formal understanding of 'Metro', there are others – acknowledged and otherwise.

Here as elsewhere, Dante provides the immediate model for his engagement with the problems of memorialising the dead. At various points in 'Metro', particularly in the sixth section, 'In Her Voice', the poet's mother speaks. The obvious parallel here is the souls throughout the *Commedia* who ask Dante to carry news of them back to the living. Their reported speech is always an act of ventriloquism on the poet's part. It is a deception which Szirtes himself acknowledges when he writes "I speak for another,/And buy my ticket for the underground." There remains, however, another possible reference to Dante in the structure of 'Metro'.

Canto Thirteen of the *Inferno* describes the circle of hell which houses those, like Magdalena Szirtes, who committed suicide. Like the souls of the *Commedia*, whether in Hell or Purgatory, she remains haunted by what happened to her while alive. Like many of the souls who approach Dante on his journey, she speaks with a similar mixture of authority and residual anger:

> … It was long ago
> And I have doubts whether such a truth
> Exists at all, as something we might know

Or understand, I have my hatred
Which is proof that something happened in my youth[.]

The poet's mother, however, is not the only suicide to haunt the poem.

Three times in the section entitled 'Stopping Train', which describes Szirtes' mother's experiences in the women-only camp at Ravensbrück, the narrator quotes lines that are in German: "Ich bin allein,/Ich stell die Aschenblume ins Glass voll/Reifer Schwärze"; and "das aschenes Haar". Like Auden in 'New Year Letter', Szirtes integrates German within the metrical and rhyming structures of his poem. But whereas Auden, though referring to a range of German sources, can be said to be speaking for himself, Szirtes incorporates the voice and presence of Paul Celan. What unites the two poems, is that Auden and Szirtes are both making profound statements about the relationship between language and experience. What Auden wants to express, of course, is his profound sense of alienation from England and his solidarity with the plight of German exiles and those aspects of European culture that were stigmatised by the policies of the Third Reich. Our cultural identity, Auden declares, is much more complex than we care to think in time of war. By including Celan among the many voices that speak in 'Metro', Szirtes is making a similar point.

Born at Czernowitz in Bukovina in 1920, Celan grew up in a Jewish community that, until the Treaty of Versailles, had been a part of the multi-ethnic Austro-Hungarian Empire. When the Empire was dissolved at the end of the war, Bukovina became independent and joined Romania as a province. In 1940, however, the area was occupied by Soviet troops. A year later these troops were forced to retreat and the town slipped into the hands of German and Rumanian forces who began herding the Jews into a Ghetto. What followed was similar to the experiences of Jews across Europe, including Budapest. Celan's parents were deported to an internment camp, where his father died of typhus and his mother, too exhausted to work, was shot dead. Celan himself was conscripted for labour service in Southern Moldavia, building roads for the advancing German army. After the war, Celan worked for a while in the Soviet Union before returning to Bucharest to work as a translator of Russian texts into Romanian. In December 1947 he travelled, illegally, to Vienna, and from there to Paris, where he began to study German literature. Paris remained his home until his suicide by drowning in 1970.

Despite his Eastern European heritage, Celan wrote in German. Both literally and metaphorically it was his mother tongue, the language he was later to call "a kind of homecoming".[104] And so to the writer in exile the language of his once oppressor became that which allowed him to revisit and memorialise aspects of the vanished past. All this is remarkable enough. But as Milan Kundera has commented, to be German or even speak German in the immediate post-war decades was to be associated with a defeated nation. "For the first time in history," Kundera writes, "the defeated were not allowed a scrap of glory: not even the painful glory of the shipwrecked. The victor was not satisfied with mere victory but decided to judge the defeated and judge the entire nation".[105] Celan's writings are therefore uniquely placed in that they speak to us about the experience of the Holocaust from within the very language which planned and executed it, while simultaneously acknowledging the subsequent pariah status of that language.

The phrases Szirtes quotes come from two early poems by Celan, published in *Mohn und Gedächtnis* (*Poppies and Memory*) in 1952. The shorter of the two – "das aschenes Haar" ("your ashen hair") – appears in what is not only Celan's best known poem but arguably the greatest single poem written about the Holocaust, 'Todesfuge' and which John Felstiner, in his critical biography of Celan, calls "the *Guernica* of postwar European literature". Felstiner continues:

> The prolonged impact that 'Todesfuge' has had stems partly from its array of historical and cultural signals – some overt and direct, some recondite or glancing. Practically every line embeds some verbal material from the disrupted world to which this poem bears witness. From music, literature, and religion and from the camps themselves we find discomforting traces of Genesis, Bach, Wagner, Heinrich Heine, the tango, and especially *Faust's* heroine Margareta, alongside the maiden Shulamith from the Song of Songs.[106]

It is this last reference in particular that Szirtes incorporates into 'Metro'. Shulamith, the "black and comely" princess of the *Song of Songs*, "the hair of whose head is like purple", becomes, in Celan's poem, ash blonde. She becomes, almost literally, a photographic negative along lines strikingly similar to the process described by

Adorno at the close of his essay on Surrealism. Everything about her is reversed: a figure of erotic power and sensuous beauty, she becomes a personification of death used by Celan to give an identity to the millions of faceless Holocaust dead. In 'Metro', however, Shulamith's features are projected first onto the poet's memory of his absent mother, then, in a final twist, onto himself:

> And if I attribute to you desire
> It is to replace what was voluptuous
> In bodies full of warmth, *das aschenes Haar*
> Which is also mine.

As at the close of 'The Photographer in Winter', the poet has been "exposed/And doubled ... /Become a multiple."

Celan now has a number of English translators. As such, his poems exist within the body of English Literature and are an indispensable part of our attempts to understand the continuing significance of the Holocaust. Why, then, when we have discussed how 'Metro', in Szirtes' words, functions as a way of "reconnecting language to experience", does Szirtes leave Celan's words untranslated? Why, if it is possible to discover a consonance between the experience of the Holocaust and the locating of that same experience in language and art, does 'Metro' stop short at providing an English version of Celan's testimony? One answer lies in the simple fact that for the vast majority of those who experienced the Holocaust, English was not their first language. In other words, the Holocaust is something that can be said to have occurred outside the history of the English-speaking world. As Susan Rubin Sulieman has said, this poses profound questions about how the Holocaust is to be represented, remembered or memorialised in English:

> [T]he first thing that strikes any viewer of videotaped oral testimonies by survivors ... is that almost all of them speak English with a heavy Eastern European, or occasionally French or German accent. In written texts, of course, one cannot actually hear an accent; but there exist written equivalents, and some writers have exploited them to great artistic effect.[107]

Read in this context, Szirtes' quotations from Celan's original German becomes a way of reproducing not only his words, or their translated meaning, but allows us, in the words of 'Metro', to "see a voice, the greyest of grey shadows". Celan's presence in the poem therefore becomes physically embodied in the actual sound of his voice, just as Dante allows the Troubadour poet Arnaut Daniel to speak from the flames of Purgatory in his own native Provençal, rather than the poem's Italian. There is a sense, then, in which we can see and hear Celan's voice, without necessarily being able to understand it. To the non-German speaking reader his words stand as a kind of semantic blank, a voice whose speech signifies nothing except sound and fury. In short, they represent what can be spoken about, but never understood.

This is not to say that Celan's poetry remains unaffected by its being incorporated into Szirtes' narrative. In the case of the lines taken from 'Ich Bin Allein', Szirtes establishes a tension between the metre of the original and the pentameter of 'Metro'. Celan's lines are therefore gradually modified by the line breaks and the change in stress: "Ich bin allein, ich stell die Aschenblume/Ins Glass voll reifer Schwärze" becomes first "Ich bin allein,/Ich stell die Aschenblume ins Glass voll/Reifer Schwärze", and then "Ich stell die Aschenblume ins Glass voll/Reifer Schwärze". The result, we might say, is that the German original is now given an English accent. The rhythms of the German have been modulated, or transposed into English, perhaps with the intention of, as Szirtes writes, "try[ing] to write the half dead a live song". If so, it is an intention which 'Metro' acknowledges the futility of. The poet is forever separated from the actuality of what his mother underwent:

Here's Ravensbrück. I stop dead at the gate,
Aware I cannot reach you through the wire,
I cannot send you poems or messages,
No wreath of words arranged across blank pages,
No art that thrives on distance and desire[.]

The result of these strategies and techniques is that 'Metro' becomes a text depending for a great deal of its effect on various kinds of caesura: between past and present; between the mother's direct experience of the war and the death camps, and the poet's attempts at reconstruction; between the adult narrator's and the child protagonist's understanding of events; and, perhaps most significantly of all, between the Hungarian and English languages. Just as a photograph, as Berger says, while recording "what has been seen, always and by its nature refers to what is not seen", so Szirtes is aware in 'Metro' that it is in the slippage between languages – what is lost in translation – where meaning resides. And this involves, as he says in the poem, "an odd sensation/Of belonging/not belonging, half and half./This half and half will always seem like truth". And these 'accidents' of time and place, of having to eat one's own words, brings us to a final determining aspect of Szirtes' work.

V

The articulation of the self in language and the determining part played in this by ideology is, Naomi Sokoloff argues, of "special resonance for Jewish literature, since instability of setting, periods of transition, and interpenetrations of language have been a staple feature of Jewish literary circumstances and subject matter in the modern period".[108] It is language, and the significant change in his relationship with it, that forms the basis of Szirtes' description of his arrival and earliest memories of the changed circumstances of his life in England. It is in this relationship with the English language that we again hear echoes of Freud's *unheimlich*, particularly that paradoxical element whereby "what is *heimlich* thus comes to be *unheimlich*":

> My first three English words were AND, BUT, SO:
> they were exotic in my wooden ear,
> like Froebel blocks. Imagination made
> houses of them, just big enough to hang
> a life on.[109]

This making a home within language means for the displaced child that "somehow it was possible to know/the otherness of people and not be afraid".[110] As the child grows older, however, this feeling of safety evaporates. Language, as a means of mediating between the self and this "otherness", is insufficient. Rather, language has *become* the other, developing, as Freud says, "in the direction of ambivalence, until it finally coincides with its opposite": "You say a word until it loses meaning/and taste the foreignness of languages,/ your own included."

We have seen how photographs, rather than simply recording a moment in time, can restructure and reorganise that moment. As such, photography can be regarded as having translated an event from one medium – time – into another – space. And this process of translation – the dispersal and subsequent loss of meaning as an experience is removed from one language to another – is implicit throughout Szirtes work.

For the seven-year-old Szirtes, the reasons for his parents abandoning their home and livelihood in Budapest were sudden and confusing. However, his memory of the days leading up to their leaving is shot-through with vivid details:

> As children we were of course not involved in our parents' plan for leaving the country, although one night, when it was being discussed with some close friends, a large map of Europe was left out and I spread it across the floor and pretended to step from country to country: one step to Austria, another into Germany, then Norway, Sweden. All one had to do was walk. Years later when I was asked what was the difference between living in England and in Hungary this was one of the terms in which I could express it. To an islander this thought is almost unthinkable.[111]

It is this sense of what is "unthinkable" to an island people that defines Szirtes' work in terms of contemporary British poetry. His great achievement has been to develop a formal technique able to meet the demands of speaking out clearly, giving witness to the horrors of the twentieth century. To those lucky not to have experienced these things, this is a matter of history; for Szirtes it belongs to memory, his own or his parents. This isn't to say that his work is mere biography. Far from it. As this chapter has shown, what Szirtes does is to bring history and biography imaginatively alive, and in doing so allows us, as Auden wrote in 'In Memory of Sigmund Freud', to "approach the Future as a friend/without a wardrobe of excuses, without/a set mask of rectitude."

The not inconsiderable difficulties involved in this return us to the question of translation in Szirtes' work. Though he had few problems learning English when the family arrived and settled in England, there remained tensions between his Hungarian and English identity. To his parents, he was practically English; but to English friends he remained Hungarian, a foreigner. These are tensions which repeatedly surface in the poems, almost always concerned with the relationship between experience and the possibility of expressing it in language. This must always imply some kind of translation in the loosest sense of the word; but it is an issue that has more profound ramifications in terms of the representation and memorialisation of the Holocaust.

Susan Rubin Suleiman has commented that students of Holocaust literature have long been aware of these problems of language and representation; what has received less attention is the added difficulties of doing so in translation. Jewish experience of the Shoah took place predominantly in languages other than English; what then happens, Suleiman asks, when that experience is translated into English?

> Anxiety about not being understood runs high among the writers of Holocaust memoirs, wherever they may be ... All the more so for the emigrant survivor writing in a foreign tongue: the abyss that separates his or her experience from the reader's is doubled by the difference in language, which is of course also a difference in worlds ... [T]he places and events she/he writes about, including those that preceded the radical break of persecution of deportation, are cut off from the 'adopted' reader by multiple separations: of language, geography, traditions, material culture – in short, of collective memory.[112]

Perhaps these difficulties are a further reason why, as I commented earlier, Szirtes chooses not to include precisely these kinds of references to geography or culture in his poetry, preferring to locate the experience of post-war Hungary in terms that evoke Orwell's *1984*, Carroll's *Alice In Wonderland* or Dante's *Commedia*. It is an issue that Szirtes confronts in 'The Looking-Glass Dictionary', the first of three sequences of Hungarian sonnets in *Portrait Of My Father In An English Landscape*.

Though he is writing about his family's early years in England, Szirtes has chosen to use a specifically Hungarian form,[113] thus highlighting the kinds of tensions between language and experience I have been discussing. Furthermore, the sequence's title alerts us to the fact that Szirtes is revisiting similar material to that which defines

'For Diane Arbus' and other poems: the illusion of normality; the presence of doubles in mirrors or in shadows; the difficulty of finding a definition for experiences that are in some essential way inexpressible; the entering of an alternative imaginary world; the relationship between the past and present, and the mediating role of memory; and, as in 'Metro' and elsewhere, the importance of reading between the lines:

> The language here blankly refuses to mean
> what it's supposed to. The signs are lost.
> If you could only read the space between
> or babble in fiery tongues at Pentecost. ...
> The world is what cannot be undone
> nor would you wish to undo it when it speaks
> so eloquently out of its dumbness, when
> its enormous treasury of hours and days and weeks
> resolves to this sense of now and never again.[114]

Overall, the sonnet sequence testifies to an acute form of defamiliarisation that is far from being a purely literary experience. As in 'The Photographer in Winter', it is Szirtes' mother and the isolation she experienced in England that is the hub of these difficulties – "The words my mother spoke were rarely home/to her, or moved at another, slower rate/which could not follow her" – bringing us close to what Suleiman defines as the transcendental homelessness experienced by Holocaust survivors unable to find a home in language.

What then, in conclusion, of Szirtes' attempt to make himself at home; to, in the words of one of his biographical essays, remake himself as an English poet?

Szirtes' *Selected Poems* (1996) is framed by poems that encapsulate the artistic as well as personal difficulties involved in exile. A poet without a clear sense of place or an identification with the cultural heritage of the language of that place is, Szirtes has said, "as light as a cork, at the mercy of the tides".[115] 'The Drowned Girl', the poem which opens both *Selected Poems* and *The Budapest File*, portrays the English language as only a child from another country could hear it. The sound of the sea and the sounds of a foreign speech become inextricably linked: "the spitting 'th',/'w' – the rolling silence of water,/the joyful crowned vowels". It is a vision of the language –

the 'Queen's English' – defined not just by geography but history, as signified by those "crowned vowels". But if the sea speaks of a certain restlessness and wandering, 'Soil', the final poem in the collection, looks to find a means of rooting oneself in a time and place:

> ... there is nowhere to go
> but home, which is nowhere to be found
> and yet
> is here, unlost, solid, the very ground
> on which you stand but cannot visit
> or know.

Read in conjunction with the lines quoted above from 'The Looking-Glass Dictionary', Szirtes can be seen as following in the footsteps of the Eliot of 'Little Gidding'. Transcendental homelessness is weighed against a kind of metaphysical homecoming. It is a precarious balancing act, difficult to achieve and to sustain, but one that is founded and renewed in a full acceptance of history as it appears in the quiddity of the everyday:

> And what you thought you came for
> Is only a shell, a husk of meaning
> From which the purpose breaks only when it is fulfilled
> If at all. Either you had no purpose
> Or the purpose is beyond the end you figured
> And is altered in fulfilment. There are other places
> Which also are the world's end, some at the sea jaws,
> Or over a dark lake, in a desert or a city –
> But this is the nearest, in place and time,
> Now and in England[.]

Notes

1   George Szirtes, *The Budapest File* (Newcastle-upon-Tyne: Bloodaxe, 2000), 12. Though it includes a number of new poems and sequences *The Budapest File* is essentially a collection of all Szirtes' poems on Hungarian themes up to the present.

2   Interestingly, Sontag firmly associates this aspect of photography with the European Old World:

> Fewer and fewer Americans possess objects that have a patina,
> old furniture, grandparents' pots and pans – the used things,

warm with generations of human touch, that Rilke celebrated in *The Duino Elegies* as being essential to a human landscape. Instead, we have our paper phantoms, transistorized landscapes. A featherweight portable museum (*On Photography*, 68).

The reason she gives for this is not without relevance to the role photography plays in Szirtes' poetry:

People robbed of their past seem to make the most fervent picture takers, at home and abroad. [In] certain countries ... the break with the past has been particularly traumatic (Ibid. 10).

3 Timothy Garton Ash, *History of the Present* (London: Allen Lane/The Penguin Press, 1999), 291.
4 George Szirtes, *The Budapest File*, 198.
5 Maurice Halbwachs, *On Collective Memory*, ed., trans. and with an Introduction by Lewis A. Coser (Chicago: University of Chicago Press, 1992), 40.
6 Letter to Matt Simpson, dated 5/11/83.
7 Roland Barthes, *Camera Lucida: Reflections on Photography*, trans. Richard Howard (London: Vintage, 1993), 5.
8 John Berger, 'Understanding a Photograph' in *The Look of Things* (London: Penguin, 1974), 293.
9 George Szirtes, *The Budapest File*, 110.
10 Unless otherwise stated, all quotes from George Szirtes are from correspondence with the author.
11 It is interesting to compare the relationship between the woman and narrator, and this question of betrayal, to what Garton Ash says about the experience of reading his own Stasi file:

More recently, I have been plunged still deeper into the labyrinth of memory by working on a book about the strange experience of reading my own Stasi file. To read a secret-police file on yourself is a Proustian experience. It brings back to you with incredible vividness many things that you had quite forgotten, or remembered in a different way. There is a day in your life twenty years ago, described minute by minute with the cold, clinical eye of the secret policeman. There are conversations recorded word for word. There are photographs taken with a concealed camera (Garton Ash, 1998, 288).

12 Walter Benjamin, 'The Work of Art in the Age of Mechanical Reproduction' (1950) in *Illuminations,* trans. Harry Zohn (London: Fontana Press, 1992), 229.

13 Walter Benjamin, 'A Small History of Photography' (1931) in *One-Way Street and Other Writings,* trans. Edmund Jephcott and Kingsley Short (London: New Left Books, 1977), 243.

14 Ibid., 243-244.

15 Ivan Lalic, *Fading Contact,* trans. Francis R. Jones (London: Anvil, 1997), 11.

16 Because of its strategic position on the route between Constantinople (present-day Istanbul) and Vienna, the city continued throughout the Middle Ages to be the prize of hard-fought contests; in addition, Belgrade occupied a commanding post on the Danube River. The Byzantine Greeks, the Bulgars, the Serbs, and the Magyars (Hungarians) were masters of Belgrade at various times from the 12th century to the beginning of the 16th century. The Turks captured the city in 1521 and called it *Darol-i-Jehad* ('home of wars of the faith').

17 See Michael Murphy, *After Attila* (Nottingham: Shoestring Press, 1998), 5-7.

18 Walter Benjamin, 'Theses on the Philosophy of History' (1950) in *Illuminations*, 254.

19 Helga Geyer-Ryan, *Fables of Desire: Studies in the Ethics of Art and Gender* (Cambridge: Polity Press, 1994), 16.

20 Ibid., 21.

21 Walter Benjamin, 'A Small History of Photography', 256.

22 Walter Benjamin, 'Theses on the Philosophy of History', 248.

23 Helga Geyer-Ryan, *Fables of Desire,* 21.

24 Ibid. 23.

25 See John Roberts, *the art of interruption: realism, photography and the everyday* (Manchester and New York: Manchester University Press, 1998), 128-135.

26 Andrew Benjamin, 'Installed Memory: Christian Boltanski' in *Object: Painting* (London: Academy Editions, 1994), 55.

27 Ibid. 56.

28 Tamar Garb, 'Tamar Garb in conversation with Christian Boltanski' in *Christian Boltanski*, ed. Didier Semin, Tamar Garb and Donald Kuspit (London: Phaidon, 1997), 19.

29 Walter Benjamin, *Illuminations*, 256.

30 Tamar Garb, *Christian Boltanski*, 22.

31 George Szirtes, *Bridge Passages* (Oxford: OUP, 1991), 40.

32 George Szirtes, 'On Being Remade As An English Poet' in *The New Hungarian Quarterly* (30:113), 151.

33 Letter to Matt Simpson, dated 23/11/93

34 John Roberts, *the art of interruption*, 102.

35 David Macey, *Lacan in Contexts* (London: Verso, 1988), 53.

36 In 'A Dual Heritage' he mentions Robert Desnos and Max Jacob (both Jewish, the latter, like Szirtes, was a poet and painter); and in 'Being Remade As An English Poet' he talks about art college and discovering "a new enthusiasm for the French surrealist poets". In both essays there is a clear sense that Szirtes sees these poets as in some way opposing the narrow insularities of English poetry in the 1960s and 1970s. What is interesting in relation to the concerns of this book is the fact that Szirtes regards Auden as straddling these two worlds of his reading experience. He writes:

> The whole question of the alternative to Modernism is answered in [Auden's] terms, rather than in Larkin's ... He is a world citizen in the English language [who] straddled two cultures. Perhaps in this situation a poet has to take certain things on trust: international form (rhyme, metre, etc. as agreed on the European model), and the common store of European imagery from history through to art and myth ('Being Remade As An English Poet', 156-157).

37 André Breton, 'Surrealist Situation of the Object' (1935) in *Manifestos of Surrealism*, trans. Richard Seaver and Helen R. Lane (Michigan: the University of Michigan Press, 1972), 269.

38 Roland Barthes, *Camera Lucida*, 53.

39 Quoted in Christian Meier, *Athens: A portrait of the City in its Golden Age*, trans. Robert and Rita Kimber (London: Pimlico, 2000), 89.

40 George Szirtes, *The Budapest File*, 28.

41 See *Fading Contact*. Jones is commenting on these lines from Lalic's 'Winter Sea': "We walk down the path towards the shore/Between yesterday's images, real only today/In our speech" (14).

42 Roland Barthes, *Camera Lucida*, 53.

43 Andrew Benjamin, *Object:Painting*, 65.

44 McEwan's essay, 'A spy in the name of art', appeared in *The Guardian* Saturday Review, April 29, 2000.

45 George Szirtes, *Blind Field*, 13.

46 Jacqueline Rose, *Sexuality in the Field of Vision* (London: Verso, 1986), 227.

47 Ibid., 228.

48 Johannes Hofer first used the word 'nostalgia' in 1688 in his medical thesis. Hofer was looking for a word that would translate the German Heimweh, meaning 'home hurt' or 'home ache' (the nearest English equivalent being 'homesickness') and which was "the familiar emotional phenomenon primarily associated at the time with exiles and [the] displaced ... into a medical term" (see Leo Spitzer, 'Persistent Memory' in *Exile and Creativity: Signposts, Travellers, Outsiders, Backward Glances*, ed. Susan Rubin Suleiman (Durham and London: Duke University Press, 1998), 375).

49 George Szirtes, *Blind Field*, 10.

50 André Kertész, *André Kertész: Photographs from the J. Paul Getty Museum* (Malibu, California: The J. Paul Getty Museum), 116.

51 George Szirtes, 'Kingdom of Shadows' in *Modern Painters* (4:1), 47.

52 Sigmund Freud, 'The Uncanny' (1919) in the *Penguin Freud Library, Vol. 14* (London: Penguin, 1990), 345.

53 Patricia Bosworth, *Diane Arbus: a Biography* (London: Heinemann, 1985), 47.

54 See Susan Sontag, *On Photography* (London: Penguin, 1979),74.

55 Ibid., 34.

56 In her biography of Arbus, Patricia Bosworth comments that "Carroll's blend of humour, horror, and justice always appealed to Diane; indeed, her own 'adventures' with hermits, nudists, carnival geeks, and midgets seemed almost inspired by Carroll." (219).

57 Rainer Maria Rilke, *Selected Poetry*, trans. Stephen Mitchell (London: Picador Classics, 1987), 317.

58 "One does not look with impunity as anyone knows who has ever looked at the sleeping face of a familiar person and discovered its strangeness. Once having looked [at Arbus' work] and not looked away we are implicated. When we have met the gaze of a midget or a female impersonator a transaction takes place between the photograph and the viewer. In a kind of healing process we are cured of our criminal urgency by having dared to look" (Marion Margid quoted in *Diane Arbus*, 248).

59 Susan Sontag, *On Photography*, 36.

60 George Szirtes, *Blind Field*, 16.

61 Ibid., 19

62 Susan Sontag, *On Photography*, 45.

63 Walter Benjamin, 'Theses on the Philosophy of History', 248.

64 After the war Magdalena Szirtes worked as a press photographer before joining the studio of Károly Escher, a Hungarian photo-journalist best known for his frank and unsentimentalised photographs of the urban poor in the 1930s, and his portraits of soldiers leaving and returning from the War.

65 Dante, *The Inferno of Dante*, trans. Robert Pinsky (London: J.M. Dent, 1996), 131.

66 Susan Sontag, *On Photography*, 77.

67 Ibid., 199.

68 Marianne Hirsch, 'Past Lives: Postmemories in Exile' in *Exile and Creativity*, 422.

69 Ibid., 419-420.

70 Sean O'Brien, review of *Metro* in 'Poetry Review' (78:3), 56

71 Marianne Hirsch, 'Past Lives: Postmemories in Exile', 426.

72 John Berger, 'Understanding a Photograph', 292.

73 Roland Barthes, *Camera Lucida*, 292.

74 Charles Simic, *Looking For Trouble: Selected Early and More Recent Poems* (London: Faber and Faber, 1997), 38-39.

75 See John Roberts, *the art of interruption*, 103.

76 Ibid., 112.

77 George Szirtes, *The Photographer in Winter*, 37.

78 George Szirtes, *Selected Poems 1976-1996* (Oxford: OUP, 1996), 50.

79 Sigmund Freud, 'The "Uncanny"', 356-357.

80 Ibid., 358.

81 Sigmund Freud, 'The Psychopathology of Everyday Life (1901) in the *Penguin Freud Library, Vol. 5* (London: Penguin, 1975), 83.

82 George Steiner, 'A Kind of Survivor' (1965) in *Language and Silence* (London: Faber and Faber, 1967), 164.

83 'Metro' is reprinted in *The Budapest File*, 43-73.

84 See n. 94 below.

85 Hans Magnus Enzensberger, *Selected Poems*, trans. by the author and Michael Hamburger (Newcastle-upon-Tyne: Bloodaxe, 1994), 149.

86 Naomi Sokoloff, *Imagining the Child in Modern Jewish Literature* (Baltimore and London: The John Hopkins University Press, 1992), 3.

87 Henri Bergson, *Matter and Memory* (1896), trans. N.M. Paul and W.S. Palmer (New York: Zone Books, 1988), 133-134.

88 Ibid., 135.

89 Naomi Sokoloff, *Imagining the Child in Modern Jewish Literature*, 29.

90 Fredric Jameson, *Marxism and Form: Twentieth-Century Dialectical Theories of Literature* (Princeton: Princeton University Press, 1971), 96.

91 Hal Foster, *Compulsive Beauty* (Cambridge, Massachusetts; London, England: The MIT Press, 1993), xviii.

92 Richard Wolin, 'Benjamin, Adorno, Surrealism' in *The Semblance of Subjectivity: Essays in Adorno's Aesthetic Theory*, ed. Tom Huhn and Lambert Zuidervaart (Cambridge, Massachusetts; London, England, 1997), 101.

93 Robert Hullot-Kentor, 'The Philosophy of Dissonance: Adorno and Schoenberg' in *The Semblance of Subjectivity*, 314.

94 In *Immortality*, a novel about the human longing for permanence and the desire to be remembered, Milan Kundera describes one of his character's attempts at reconstructing the history of his love life:

> But how is one to be obsessed with the past when one sees in it only a desert over which the wind blows a few fragments of memory? Does that mean [Rubens] would become obsessed with those few fragments? Yes. One can be obsessed even with a few fragments ... Rubens discovered a peculiar thing: memory does not make films, it makes photographs[... And when I say an album of pictures that is an exaggeration, for all he had was some seven or eight photographs: these photos were beautiful, they fascinated him, but their number was after all depressingly limited: seven, eight fragments of less than a second each, that's what remained in his memory of his entire erotic life to which he had once decided to devote all his strength and talent (London: Faber and Faber, 1991, 350).

95 Theodor W. Adorno, 'Looking Back on Surrealism' (1956) in *Notes to Literature, Vol. 1*, ed. Rolf Tiedemann and trans. Shierry Weber Nicholsen (New York: Columbia University Press, 1991), 87.

96 Richard Wolin, 'Benjamin, Adorno, Surrealism', 107-108.

97 Theodor W. Adorno, 'Looking Back on Surrealism', 90.

98 Ibid., 88.

99 Robert Hullot-Kentor, 'The Philosophy of Dissonance: Adorno and Schoenberg', 313.

100 George Steiner, 'A Kind of Survivor, 182.

101 Theodor W. Adorno, 'On Lyric Poetry and Society' (1957), in *Notes to Literature, Vol. 1*, 38.

102 Ibid.

103 ['Metro'] is the most serious attempt I have yet made to bring to some sort of synthesis certain elements of personal family history and that feeling of pastness and presentness about things that move me deeply: Central Europe, England. The main persona is again my mother but this time speaking as a young woman, as she is being taken away from Hungary to the concentration camp at Ravensbrück. It is absolutely full of city-scapes and is also a love poem on two levels. She very much loved her brother (who did not reciprocate her feelings), but he disappeared during the war, probably shot in a labour camp. I have

photographs of them as children. He was strikingly handsome. The hidden love poem is the fruit of my own love of the city of Budapest as it now is, and corollary to that, of the odd, sweet, slightly corrupt care and intelligence that produced it. I don't mean I planned things out this way. I began writing poems about mother/brother in Hungary this summer. Some came out as songs, some as fragments of something freer flowing. It is the fragments which have come together and were then added to and developed into something that I hope is a coherent whole (letter to Matt Simpson, dated 10/2/87).

104 Paul Celan, *Collected Prose*, trans. Rosemarie Waldrop (Manchester: Carcanet, 1999), 53.

105 Milan Kundera, *Immortality*, 27.

106 John Felstiner, *Paul Celan: Poet, Survivor, Jew* (New Haven and London: Yale University Press, 1995), 26-27.

107 Susan Rubin Suleiman, 'Monuments in a Foreign Tongue' in *Exile and Creativity*, 398.

108 Naomi Sokoloff, *Imagining the Child in Modern Jewish Literature*, 36.

109 George Szirtes, *Bridge Passages*, 33.

110 George Szirtes, *Selected Poems*, 227.

111 George Szirtes, 'A Dual Heritage', 6.

112 Susan Rubin Suleiman, 'Monuments in a Foreign Tongue', 401-402.

113 An Hungarian sonnet sequence consists of 15 sonnets, where the last line of the first sonnet becomes the first line of the second, and so on, until the 15th sonnet becomes the sum of all the first lines.

114 George Szirtes, *Portrait of my Father in an English Landscape* (Oxford: OUP, 1998), 46.

115 George Szirtes, 'A Dual Heritage', 12.

Bibliography

PRIMARY SOURCES
W.H. Auden
Collected Poems, ed. Edward Mendelson (London: Faber and
   Faber, 1976).
*The English Auden: Poems, Essays and Dramatic Writings 1927-
   1939*, ed. Edward Mendelson, 2nd printing (with corrections)
   (London: Faber and Faber, 1978).
Collected Longer Poems (London: Faber and Faber, 1974).
'Robert Frost' in *The Dyers Hand & other essays* (London, Faber
   and Faber, 1975), 337-53.
'Marianne Moore', ibid. 296-305.
'The Poet & The City', ibid. 72-89.
'American Poetry', ibid. 354-68.
The Enchafèd Flood (London: Faber and Faber, 1951).

Joseph Brodsky
Selected Poems, trans. and introduced George L. Kline (London:
   Penguin, 1973).
Collected Poems in English (Manchester: Carcanet, 2001).
Watermark (London: Hamish Hamilton, 1992).
'Less Than One' in *Less Than One: Selected Essays* (New York:
   Farrar Straus Giroux, 1986), 3-33.
'To Please A Shadow', ibid. 357-83.
'On "September 1, 1939" by W.H. Auden', ibid. 304-56.
'Footnote to a Poem', ibid. 195-267.
'The Child of Civilisation', ibid. 123-44.
'The Condition We Call Exile', *On Grief and Reason: Essays*
   (New York: Farrar Straus Giroux, 1995), 22-34.

George Szirtes
The Slant Door (London: Secker & Warburg, 1979).
November And May (London: Secker & Warburg, 1981).
Short Wave (London: Secker & Warburg, 1983).
The Photographer in Winter (London: Secker & Warburg, 1986).
Metro (Oxford: Oxford University Press, 1988).

Bridge Passages (Oxford: Oxford University Press, 1991).

Blind Field. (Oxford: Oxford University Press, 1994).

Selected Poems 1976-1996 (Oxford: Oxford University Press, 1996).

Portrait of My Father In An English Landscape (Oxford: Oxford University Press, 1998).

The Budapest File (Newcastle-upon-Tyne: Bloodaxe, 2000).

An English Apocalypse (Newcastle-upon-Tyne: Bloodaxe, 2001).

'Being Remade as an English Poet', *The New Hungarian Quarterly* (30:113), 149-59.

'A Dual Heritage' in *Poetry Review* (75:4), 5-12.

'A Dual Heritage: On Being a Hungarian-Born English Poet' in *The New Hungarian Quarterly* (26:99), 71-82.

'Kingdom of Shadows' in *Modern Painters* (1991 4:1), 46-8.

'Losing Our Identities' in *The Independent on Sunday*, 28/5/2000, 16.

SECONDARY SOURCES
Adorno, Theodor W.

Minima Moralia: Reflections from Damaged Life (1951), trans. E.F.N. Jephcott. (London: Verso, 1978).

'On Lyric Poetry and Society' (1957) in *Notes to Literature*, vol. 1, ed. Rolf Tiedemann and trans. Shierry Weber Nicholsen (New York: Columbia University Press, 1991), 37-54.

'In Memory of Eichendorff' (1958), ibid. 55-79.

'Looking Back On Surrealism' (1956), ibid. 86-90.

'On the Final Scene of Faust' (1959), ibid. 111-29.

'Words from Abroad' (1959), ibid. 185-99.

'On the Use of Foreign Words' (1920) in *Notes to Literature*, vol. 2, ed. Rolf Tiedemann and trans. Shierry Weber Nicholsen (New York: Columbia University Press, 1991), 286-91.

Adorno, Theodor W. and Horkheimer, Max

Dialectic of Enlightenment (1944) (London: Verso, 1997).

Alexander, Michael (trans.)

The Earliest English Poems (London: Penguin, 1966).

Alter, Robert

Necessary Angels: Tradition and Modernity in Kafka, Benjamin and Scholem. (Cambridge: Harvard University Press, 1991).

Arendt, Hannah

'Walter Benjamin: 1892-1940' in *Illuminations* (London: Fontana Press, 1992), 7-58.

Ascherson, Neal

Black Sea: The Birthplace of Civilisation and Barbarism (London: Vintage, 1996).

Bal, Mieke

The Mottled Screen: Reading Proust Visually, trans. Anna-Louise Milne (Stanford, California: Stanford University Press, 1997).

Barthes, Roland

Camera Lucida: Reflections on Photography, trans. Richard Howard (London: Vintage, 1993).

Benjamin, Andrew

'Installed Memory: Christian Boltanski' in Object Painting (London: Academy Editions, 1994), 54-69 and Peter Osbourne, 'Destruction and Experience' in Walter Benjamin's *Philosophy: Destruction and Experience* (London: Routledge, 1994), x-xiii.

Benjamin, Walter

Illuminations, trans. Harry Zohn (London: Fontana Press, 1992).

'Theses on the Philosophy of History' (1950) in *Illuminations*, 245-55.

'The Task of the Translator' (1923), ibid. 70-82.

'On Some Motifs in Baudelaire' (1939), ibid. 152-96.

'The Work of Art in the Age of Mechanical Reproduction' (1950), ibid. 211-44

'A Short History of Photography' (1931) in *One-Way Street and other Writings*, trans. Edmund Jephcott and Kingsley Short (London: New Left Books, 1977), 240- 57.

Reflections: Essays, Aphorisms, Autobiographical Writings, trans. Edmund Jephcott (New York: Harcourt Brace Jovanovich, 1978).

Berger, John

Success and Failure of Picasso (London, Penguin, 1965)

'Understanding a Photograph' in *The Look of Things* (London: Viking Press, 1974), 291-4.

Bergson, Henri

Matter and Memory (1896), trans. N.M. Paul and W.S. Palmer (New York: Zone Books, 1988)

Bethea, David M.
Joseph Brodsky and the Creation Of Exile (New Jersey: Princeton University Press, 1994).
Bhabha, Homi K.
The Location of Culture (London and New York: Routledge, 1994).
Bishop, Elizabeth
Complete Poems (London: Chatto & Windus, 1991).
Bloom, Harold
The Western Canon (London: Macmillan, 1995).
Borges, Jorge Luis
'Notes on Germany & The War' in *The Total Library: Non-Fiction 1922-1986*, ed. by Eliot Weinberger, trans. Esther Allen, Suzanne Jill Levine and Eliot Weinberger (London: Allen Lane/The Penguin Press, 1999), 199-213.
Bosworth, Patricia
Diane Arbus: a Biography (London: Heinemann, 1985).
Boym, Svetlana
'Estrangement as a Lifestyle: Shklovsky and Brodsky', in Suleiman (1996), 241-62.
Breton, André
Nadja (1928), trans. Richard Howard (New York: Grove Press, 1960).
'Surrealist Situation of the Object' (1935) in *Manifestos of Surrealism*, trans. Richard Seaver and Helen R. Lane (Michigan: The University of Michigan Press, 1972), 255-78.
Buck-Morss, Susan
The Origin of Negative Dialectics: Theodor Adorno, Walter Benjamin, and the Frankfurt Institute (Hassocks, Sussex: The Harvester Press, 1977).
The Dialectics of Seeing: Walter Benjamin and the Arcades Project (Cambridge Massachusetts, London, England: The MIT Press, 1991).
Budick, Sanford and Wolfgang Iser (ed.)
The Translatability of Cultures: Figurations of the Space Between (Stanford, California: Stanford University Press, 1996).

Burt Foster, Jr., John
Nabokov's Art of Memory and European Modernism (Princeton: Princeton University Press, 1993).

Calhoun, Craig (ed.)
Habermas and the Public Sphere (Cambridge, Massachusetts and London: The MIT Press, 1992).

Callan, Edward
'Disenchantment With Yeats: From Singing-Master to Ogre' in *Modern Critical Views: W.H. Auden,* ed. Harold Bloom (New York: Chelsea House Publishers, 1983), 161-76.

Carpenter, Humphrey
W.H. Auden: A Biography (London: Unwin Paperbacks, 1983).

Celan, Paul
Selected Poems, trans. Michael Hamburger (London: Penguin, 1996).
Ausgewählte Gedichte, Zwei Reden, Nachwort von Beda Allemann (Frankfurt am Main: Suhrkamp Verlag, 1968).
Collected Prose, trans. Rosemarie Waldrop (Manchester: Carcanet, 1999).

Chénieux-Gendron, Jaqueline,
'Surrealists in Exile: Another Kind of Resistance' in Sulieman (1996), 163-79.

Coote, Stephen
W. B. Yeats: A Life (London: Hodder and Stoughton, 1998).

Craft, Robert (ed.)
Stravinsky: Selected Correspondence, Vol. 1 (London: Faber and Faber, 1982).
'Music and Words' in *Stravinsky in the Theatre*, ed. Minna Lederman (New York: Pellegrini and Cudahy, 1949).

Cunningham, Valentine
Spanish Front: Writers on the Civil War. Oxford: OUP, 1986).

Czerniawski, Adam
Scenes From A Disturbed Childhood (London: Serpent's Tail, 1991).

Dante
The Inferno of Dante, trans. Robert Pinsky (London: J.M. Dent, 1996).

Davenport-Hines, Richard
Auden (London, Minerva, 1996).

Donne, John

The Complete English Poems of John Donne, ed. by C.A. Patrides (London: J.M. Dent & Sons Ltd, 1985).

Dowling, William C.

The Epistolary Moment: The Poetics of the C18th Verse Epistle (Princeton, New Jersey: Princeton University Press, 1991).

Dunn, Douglas

'Back and Forth: Auden and Political Poetry' in *Critical Survey* (ed. Stan Smith), 6:3 (1994), 325-35.

Eliot, T.S.

The Complete Poems and Plays of T.S. Eliot (London: Faber and Faber, 1969).

Ellmann, Richard

Ulysses On The Liffey, 3rd printing (with corrections), (London: Faber and Faber, 1984).

Enzensberger, Hans Magnus

Selected Poems. trans. the author and Michael Hamburger (Newcastle upon Tyne: Bloodaxe, 1994).

Felstiner, John

Paul Celan: Poet, Survivor, Jew (New Haven and London: Yale University Press, 1995).

Forster, E.M.

Two Cheers For Democracy (London: Edward Arnold & Co., 1951).

Foster, Hal

Compulsive Beauty (Cambridge, Massachusetts, London, England: The MIT Press, 1993).

Freud, Sigmund

'The 'Uncanny" (1919) in *The Penguin Freud Library,* vol. 14 (London: Penguin, 1990), 339-76.

'The Psychopathology of Everyday Life' (1901) in *The Penguin Freud Library*, Vol. 5 (London: Penguin, 1975), 37-344.

'The Future of an Illusion' (1927) in *The Penguin Freud Library*, Vol. 12 (London: Penguin, 1991), 183-241.

Fuller, John

A Reader's Guide to W.H. Auden (London: Thames and Hudson, 1970).

Garb, Tamar
'Tamar Garb in conversation with Christian Boltanski' in
Christian Boltanski, ed. by Didier Semin, Tamar Garb and
Donald Kuspit. London:
Phaidon, 1997), 8-40.

Garton Ash, Timothy
History of the Present (London: Allen Lane/The Penguin Press,
1999).

Geyer-Ryan, Helga
Fables of Desire: *Studies in the Ethics of Art and Gender*
(Cambridge: Polity Press, 1994).

Gibson, Ian
Federico García Lorca (London, Faber and Faber, 1990).

Goya, Francisco y Lucientes
Los Caprichos, with an Introduction by Philip Hofer (New York:
Dover Publications, 1969).

Grennan, Eamon
'American Relations' in *Irish Poetry Since Kavanagh*, ed. Theo
Dorgan (Dublin: Four Courts Press, 1996), 95-105.

Griffiths, Paul
Modern Music: A Concise History (London: Thames and Hudson,
1994).

Gumpert, Lynn
Christian Boltanski (Paris: Flammarion, 1994).

Haffenden, John (ed.)
W.H. Auden: The Critical Heritage (London: Routledge and
Kegan Paul, 1983).

Halbwachs, Maurice
On Collective Memory, ed., trans. and with an Introduction by
Lewis A. Coser, (Chicago: University of Chicago Press, 1992).

Hamilton, Ian
Robert Lowell: A Biography (London and Boston: Faber and
Faber, 1982).

Heaney, Seamus
Beowulf (London; Faber and Faber, 1999).
'Osip and Nadezhda Mandelstam' in *The Government of the
Tongue: The 1986 T.S. Eliot Memorial Lectures and Other
Critical Writings* (London: Faber and Faber), 71-88.

Heaton, John M.
Wittgenstein and Psychoanalysis (Cambridge: Icon Books, 2000).
Hirsch, Marianne
'Past Lives: Postmemories and Exile', in Suleiman (1996) 418-46.
Hobsbawm, Eric
Uncommon People: Resistance, Rebellion and Jazz (London: Weidenfield & Nicolson, 1998).
The Age of Empire: 1875-1914 (London: Weidenfeld & Nicolson, 1987)
Age of Extremes: The Short Twentieth Century 1914-1991 (London: Weidenfeld & Nicolson, 1994)
The New Century (London: Little, Brown and Company, 2000).
Hollander, John
The Work of Poetry. New York: Columbia University Press, 1997).
Hullot-Kentor, Robert
'The Philosophy of Dissonance: Adorno and Schoenberg' in *The Semblance of Subjectivity: Essays in Adorno's Aesthetic Theory*, ed. Tom Huhn and Lambert Zuidervaart (Cambridge, Massachusetts, London, England: The MIT Press), 309-19.
Iser, Wolfgang
'Coda to the Discussion', in Budick and Iser (1996), 294-302.
Isherwood, Christopher
Christopher and His Kind (London: Methuen & Co., 1977).
Jakobson, Roman
'Two Aspects of Language and Two Types of Aphasic Disturbances' (1956) in *Language in Literature*, ed. by Krystyna Pomorska and Stephen Rudy (Cambridge, Massachusetts: Harvard University Press, 1987), 95-114.
'Marginal Notes on the prose of the Poet Pasternak', ibid. 301-317.
Jameson, Fredric
Marxism and Form: Twentieth-Century Dialectical Theories of Literature (Princeton: Princeton University Press, 1971).
Late Marxism: Adorno, or, The Persistence of the Dialectic (London: Verso, 1996).
'Postmodernism, or The Cultural Logic of Late Capitalism' in *Postmodernism:*

A Reader, ed. Thomas Docherty (Hemel Hempstead: Harvester
Wheatsheaf, 1993), 62-92.

Jarrell, Randall
Kipling, Auden & Co.: Essays and Reviews 1935-64 (Manchester:
Carcanet, 1986).

Jarvis, Simon
Adorno: a Critical Introduction (Cambridge: Polity Press, 1992).

Kelly, Catriona, (ed.)
Utopias: Russian Modernist Texts 1905-1940 (London: Penguin,
1999).

Kertész, André
André Kertész: Photographs from The J. Paul Getty Museum
(Malibu, California: The J. Paul Getty Museum, 1994).

Kramer, Lloyd
'Habermas, History, and Critical Theory' in *Habermas and the
Public Sphere* (Cambridge, Massachusetts and London: The
MIT Press, 1992), 236-58.

Kristeva, Julia
Proust and the Sense of Time, trans. and with an Introduction
Stephen Bann (London: Faber and Faber, 1993).
'The Ethics of Linguistics' (1974) in *Modern Criticism and
Theory: a Reader*, ed. David Lodge (London and New York:
Longman, 1988), 230-9.

Kundera, Milan
Testaments Betrayed (London: Faber and Faber, 1995).
Immortality (London: Faber and Faber, 1991).

Lacoue-Labarthe, Philippe
Poetry As Experience, trans. Andrea Tarnowski (Stanford,
California: Stanford University Press, 1999).

Lalic, Ivan V.
Fading Contact, trans. Francis R Jones (London: Anvil, 1997).

Lehmann, John
Poems From New Writing: 1936-1946 (London: John Lehmann,
1946).

Lohmann, Hans-Martin
'Adorno's Aesthetic Theory', *Adorno: an Introduction*
(Philadelphia: Pennbridge Books, 1992), 73-81.

Lorca, Federico García

Selected Poems, trans. Merryn Williams (Newcastle-upon-Tyne, Bloodaxe, 1992).

'Play and Theory of the Duende' (1933) in *Deep Song and Other Prose,* trans. Christopher Maurer (New York: New Directions, 1980), 42-53.

Poet in New York, trans. Greg Simon and Steven F. White, ed. and with an introduction by Christopher Maurer (London: Penguin, 1988).

Lowell, Robert

Life Studies (London: Faber and Faber, 1972).

Robert Lowell's Poems: A Selection, ed. with an Introduction and notes by Jonathan Raban (London: Faber and Faber, 1974).

Macey, David

Lacan in Contexts (London: Verso, 1988).

Macneice, Louis

The Poetry of W.B. Yeats (1941) (London, Faber and Faber, 1967).

Collected Poems, ed. E.R. Dodds (London: Faber and Faber, 1979).

Mahon, Derek

Collected Poems (Loughcrew: The Gallery Press, 1999).

Mandelstam, Nadezhda

Hope Abandoned (1972), trans. Max Hayward (London: Collins Harvill, 1989).

Mandelstam, Osip

The Collected Critical Prose and Letters, trans. Jane Grey Harris and Constance Link (London: Collins Harvill, 1991).

'Journey To Armenia' (1933) in *The Collected Critical Prose and Letters,* 344-96.

'Conversation About Dante' (1933), ibid. 397-451.

'On The Nature of the Word' (1922), ibid. 117-32.

'The Word and Culture' (1921), ibid. 112-16.

Stone (1913), trans. with an Introduction and Notes by Robert Tracy (London: The Harvill Press, 1991).

'The Noise of Time' in *The Noise of Time and Other Prose Pieces,* collected, translated and with an Introduction by Clarence Brown (London: Quartet Books, 1988), 69-117.

Mann, Thomas
Essays of Three Decades, trans. H.T. Lower-Porter (London: Secker & Warbourg, n.d).

Marvell, Andrew
Complete Poetry, ed. George deF. Lord (London: Everyman, 1984).

Mazower, Mark
Dark Continent: Europe's Twentieth Century (London: Penguin, 1988).

McDiarmid, Lucy
Auden's Apologia for Poetry (Princeton, New Jersey: Princeton University Press, 1990).

Meier, Christian
Athens: A Portrait of the City in Its Golden Age (1993), trans. Robert and Rita Kimber (London: Pimlico, 2000).

Mendelson, Edward
Later Auden (London: Faber and Faber, 1999).

Miller, Tyrus
Late Modernism: Politics, Fiction, and the Arts Between the World Wars (Berkely/Los Angeles/London: University of California Press, 1999).

Mitchell, Donald
The Language of Modern Music, with an Introduction by Edward W. Said (London: Faber and Faber, 1993).

Motzkin, Gabriel
'Memory and Cultural Translation', in Budick and Iser (1996), 265-81.

Murphy, Michael
'Honoured Guests: The Elegy as Homecoming in W.H. Auden and Joseph Brodsky' in *Symbiosis* (3.1), 13-25.
'Auden's Jeremiad: *Another Time* and Exile From the Just City' in *Miscelánea: A Journal of English and American Studies*, vol. 20 (1999), 303-28.

Nabokov, Vladimir
Speak, Memory: An Autobiography Revisited (London: Penguin, 1969).

New Verse
nos. 26-27 (November 1937).

Novick, Peter

The Holocaust and Collective Memory (London: Bloomsbury, 2000).

O'Brien, Sean

'*Metro* by George Szirtes' *Poetry Review* (78:3), 56.

Ovid

The Poems of Exile, trans. Peter Green (London: Penguin Books, 1994).

The Erotic Poems, trans. Peter Green (London: Penguin, 1982).

Patterson, D.

'From Exile to Affirmation: The Poetry of Joseph Brodsky' in *Studies in C20th Literature* (1993: 17:2), 365-83.

Piette, Adam

Imagination at War: British Fiction and Poetry 1939-1945 (London: Papermac, 1995).

Polukhina, Valentina

Joseph Brodsky: A Poet For Our Time (Cambridge: Cambridge University Press, 1989).

Pope, Alexander

Alexander Pope: A Critical Edition of the Major Works, ed. Pat Rogers (Oxford and New York: Oxford University Press, 1993).

Proust, Marcel

In Search of Lost Time, general ed. Christopher Prendergast, 6 vols. (London: Penguin/Allen Lane, 2002).

Pushkin, Alexander

After Pushkin, ed. with an introduction by Elaine Feinstein (Manchester: Carcanet, 1999).

Rilke, Rainer Maria

Selected Poetry, trans. Stephen Mitchell (London, Picador Classics, 1987).

Roberts, John

The art of interruption: realism, photography and the everyday (Manchester and New York: Manchester University Press, 1998).

Rochlitz, Rainer

The Disenchantment of Art: The Philosophy of Walter Benjamin (London: The Guildford Press, 1996).

Rose, Jaqueline
Sexuality In The Field Of Vision (London: Verso, 1986).
Rushdie, Salman
Imaginary Homelands: Essays and Criticism 1981-1991 (London: Granta, 1991).
Said, Edward W.
Culture and Imperialism (London: Chatto & Windus, 1993).
Scott, Bonnie Kime (ed.)
The Gender of Modernism: a Critical Anthology (Bloomington and Indianapolis: Indiana University Press, 1990).
Simic, Charles
Looking for Trouble: Selected Early and More Recent Poems (London: Faber and Faber, 1997).
Smith, Stan
'Auden's Oedipal Dialogues with W. B. Yeats' in *W. H. Auden: The language of learning and the language of love*, eds. Katherine Bucknell and Nicholas Jenkins (Oxford: Clarendon Press, 1994), 155-63.
W.H. Auden (London: Writers and their Work, 1997).
Sokoloff, Naomi B.
Imagining the Child in Modern Jewish Fiction (Baltimore and London: The John Hopkins University Press, 1992).
Sontag, Susan
On Photography (London: Penguin, 1979).
Spitzer, Leo
'Persistent Memory' in Suleiman (1998), 373-96.
Squiers, C. (ed.)
The Critical Image: Essays on Contemporary Photography. (London: Lawrence & Wishart, 1990).
Steiner, George
After Babel: Aspects of Language and Translation (Oxford: Oxford University Press, 1975).
Language and Silence. (London: Faber and Faber, 1985).
Stravinsky, Igor and Robert Craft
Conversations with Igor Stravinsky (London: Faber and Faber, 1979).
Suleiman, Susan Rubin (ed., with an Introduction)
Exile and Creativity: Signposts, Travellers, Outsiders, Backward Glances (Durham and London: Duke University Press, 1998).

'Monuments in a Foreign Tongue', ibid. 397-417.

Sutherland, James,
English Literature of the Late C17th (Oxford: Clarendon Press, 1969).

Terras, Victor
A History of Russian Literature (New Haven: Yale University Press, 1991).

Thomas, Hugh
The Spanish Civil War (London, Eyre and Spottiswoode, 1964).

Tippett, Michael
Those Twentieth Century Blues: An Autobiography (London: Hutchinson, 1991).

Trachtenburg, A. (ed.)
Classic Essays on Photography (New Haven, Connecticut: Leete's Island Books, 1980).

Volkov, Solomon
Conversations With Joseph Brodsky: A Poet's Journey Through the Twentieth Century, trans. Marian Schwartz (New York: The Free Press, 1998).

Walcott, Derek
'Magic Industry: Joseph Brodsky' in *What the Twilight Says: Essays* (London: Faber and Faber, 1998), 134-52.

Warren, Rosanna
'Alcaics in Exile: W.H. Auden's "In Memory of Sigmund Freud"' in *Philosophy and Literature* (20:1), 111-21.

Wat, Aleksander
My Century: The Odyssey of a Polish Intellectual, ed. and trans. Richard Lourie (New York and London: W.W. Norton & Company, 1990).

Weber Nicholsen, Shierry
Exact Imagination, Late Work: On Adorno's Aesthetics, (Cambridge, Massachusetts, London, England: The MIT Press, 1997).

Wellmer, Albrecht
Endgames: The Irreconcilable Nature of Modernity (Cambridge, Massachusetts, London, England: The MIT Press, 1998).

Wolin, R.
Walter Benjamin: An Aesthetic of Redemption (Berkeley: University of California Press, 1994).

'Benjamin, Adorno, Surrealism' in *Semblance of Subjectivity: Essays in Adorno's Aesthetic Theory*, ed. Tom Huhn and Lambert Zuidervaart (Cambridge, Massachusetts, London, England: The MIT Press), 93-122.

Yeats, W.B.

The Poems, ed. Daniel Albright (London: Everyman's Library, 1992).

Essays and Introductions (London: Macmillan and Co. Ltd, 1961).

Zaret, David

'Religion, Science, and Printing in the Public Spheres in Seventeenth-Century England' in *Habermas and the Public Sphere* (Cambridge, Massachusetts and London: The MIT Press, 1992), 212-35.

Index

A

Adorno, Theodor W., 39, 40, 57, 191
Minima Moralia by, 44
on the aphorism, 43
Adorno and Horkheimer, 41
African-Americans, W.H. Auden and, 30
Akhmatova, Anna, 89, 99
Brodsky on, 100
Alcaeus and Auden, 44
Alcaic stanza, 44
Alienation, 4
Auden on, 37
Marx on, 37
Allegory, 157
'American Poetry' by W.H. Auden, 1
Another Time by W.H. Auden, 22
Aphorism, Theodor Adorno and Walter Benjamin on the, 43
Ash, Timothy Garton, 144
Auden, W.H., and Adorno, 40
and African-Americans, 30
and Alcaeus, 44
and the economic condition of the 1900s, 5
and the Just City, 35
and Modernism, 27
and the role of the poet, 35
and the Spanish Civil War, 6-7
in the *Daily Worker*, 8
and Yeats, 2-3
cities and towns in the work of, 11-12
decision to leave England of, 30
distrust of Utopias by, 12
George Szirtes on elegy for W.B. Yeats by, 13
indebtedness of to Marianne Moore, 44
influence of Lorca on, 15

C

D

E

F

G

Grippius, V.V., 85
Grynspan, Herschel, 33
Guernica by Picasso, 9, 22
Gumpert, Lynn, 159
The Gypsy Ballads by Lorca, 23

H

Hagen, Charles, 1 73
Halbwachs, Maurice, 144
Hamilton, Ian, 116
Heisenberg's Uncertainty Principle, 56
Hirsch, Marianne, 178
Hitler, Adolph, 189
Hobsbawm, Eric, 32
Hollander, John, 113
Holocaust, 43, 192, 198
    Auden's attitude on the, 34
    Peter Novick on the, 34
Holocaust literature, 202
Holocaust Museum in Washington, D.C., 179
Home, meanings of in Brodsky's 'Lithuanian Nocturne', 113
Horace, 44
Hungary in 1926, 143, 190
Hybridity, Mandelstam's idea of, 82, 89

I

Illusion and Reality: A Study of the Sources of Poetry by Christopher Caudwell, 10
'In Memory of W.B. Yeats' by Auden, 2
    Brodsky on, 17
Isherwood, Christopher, 12

J

Jacob, Max
Jakobson, Roman, 109
    on Boris Pasternak, 120
Jameson, Frederic, 104

GREENWICH EXCHANGE BOOKS

Greenwich Exchange Student Guides are critical studies of major or contemporary serious writers in English and selected European languages. The series is for the student, the teacher and 'common readers' and is an ideal resource for libraries. The *Times Educational Supplement* praised these books, saying, "The style of these guides has a pressure of meaning behind it. Students should learn from that ... If art is about selection, perception and taste, then this is it."

(ISBN prefix 1-871551- applies)
The series includes:
W.H. Auden by Stephen Wade (36-6)
Honoré de Balzac by Wendy Mercer (48-X)
William Blake by Peter Davies (27-7)
The Brontës by Peter Davies (24-2)
Robert Browning by John Lucas (59-5)
Samuel Taylor Coleridge by Andrew Keanie (64-1)
Joseph Conrad by Martin Seymour-Smith (18-8)
William Cowper by Michael Thorn (25-0)
Charles Dickens by Robert Giddings (26-9)
Emily Dickinson by Marnie Pomeroy (68-4)
John Donne by Sean Haldane (23-4)
Ford Madox Ford by Anthony Fowles (63-3)
The Stagecraft of Brian Friel by David Grant (74-9)
Robert Frost by Warren Hope (70-6)
Thomas Hardy by Sean Haldane (33-1)
Seamus Heaney by Warren Hope (37-4)
Gerard Manley Hopkins by Sean Sheehan (77-3)
James Joyce by Michael Murphy (73-0)
Philip Larkin by Warren Hope (35-8)
Poets of the First World War by John Greening (79-X)
Laughter in the Dark – The Plays of Joe Orton by Arthur Burke (56-0)
Philip Roth by Paul McDonald (72-2)
Shakespeare's *Macbeth* by Matt Simpson (69-2)
Shakespeare's *Othello* by Matt Simpson (71-4)
Shakespeare's *The Tempest* by Matt Simpson (75-7)
Shakespeare's Non-Dramatic Poetry by Martin Seymour-Smith (22-6)
Shakespeare's Sonnets by Martin Seymour-Smith (38-2)
Tobias Smollett by Robert Giddings (21-8)
Dylan Thomas by Peter Davies (78-1)
Alfred, Lord Tennyson by Michael Thorn (20-X)
William Wordsworth by Andrew Keanie (57-9)

LITERATURE & BIOGRAPHY

Aleister Crowley and the Cult of Pan *by Paul Newman*
Few more nightmarish figures stalk English literature than Aleister Crowley (1875-1947), poet, magician, mountaineer and agent provocateur. In this groundbreaking study, Paul Newman dives into the occult mire of Crowley's works and fishes out gems and grotesqueries that are by turns ethereal, sublime, pornographic and horrifying. An influential exponent of the cult of the Great God Pan, his essentially 'pagan' outlook was shared by major European writers as well as English novelists like E.M. Forster, D.H. Lawrence and Arthur Machen.
Paul Newman lives in Cornwall. Editor of the literary magazine *Abraxas*, he has written over ten books.
2004 • 223 pages • ISBN 1-871551-66-8

The Author, the Book and the Reader *by Robert Giddings*
This collection of essays analyses the effects of changing technology and the attendant commercial pressures on literary styles and subject matter. Authors covered include Charles Dickens, Tobias George Smollett, Mark Twain, Dr Johnson and John le Carré.
1991 • 220 pages • illustrated • ISBN 1-871551-01-3

John Dryden *by Anthony Fowles*
Of all the poets of the Augustan age, John Dryden was the most worldly. Anthony Fowles traces Dryden's evolution from 'wordsmith' to major poet. This critical study shows a poet of vigour and technical panache whose art was forged in the heat and battle of a turbulent polemical and pamphleteering age. Although Dryden's status as a literary critic has long been established, Fowles draws attention to Dryden's neglected achievements as a translator of poetry. He deals also with the less well-known aspects of Dryden's work – his plays and occasional pieces.
Anthony Fowles was born in London and educated at the Universities of Oxford and Southern California. He began his career in filmmaking before becoming an author of film and television scripts and more than twenty books.
2003 • 292 pages • ISBN 1-871551-58-7

The Good That We Do *by John Lucas*
John Lucas' book blends fiction, biography and social history in order to tell the story of his grandfather, Horace Kelly. Headteacher of a succession of elementary schools in impoverished areas of London, 'Hod' Kelly was also a keen cricketer, a devotee of the music hall, and included among his friends the great Trade Union leader, Ernest Bevin. In telling the story of his life, Lucas has provided a fascinating range of insights into the lives of ordinary Londoners from the First World War until the outbreak of the Second World War. Threaded throughout is an account of such people's hunger for education, and of the different ways government, church and educational officialdom ministered to that hunger. *The Good That We Do* is both a study of one man and of a period when England changed, drastically and forever.
John Lucas is Professor of English at Nottingham Trent University and is a poet and critic.
2001 • 214 pages • ISBN 1-871551-54-4

In Pursuit of Lewis Carroll *by Raphael Shaberman*
Sherlock Holmes and the author uncover new evidence in their investigations into the mysterious life and writing of Lewis Carroll. They examine published works by Carroll that have been overlooked by previous commentators. A newly discovered poem, almost certainly by Carroll, is published here.
Amongst many aspects of Carroll's highly complex personality, this book explores his relationship with his parents, numerous child friends, and the formidable Mrs Liddell, mother of the immortal Alice. Raphael Shaberman was a founder member of the Lewis Carroll Society and a teacher of autistic children.
1994 • 118 pages • illustrated • ISBN 1-871551-13-7

Liar! Liar!: Jack Kerouac – Novelist *by R.J. Ellis*
The fullest study of Jack Kerouac's fiction to date. It is the first book to devote an individual chapter to every one of his novels. *On the Road, Visions of Cody* and *The Subterraneans* are reread in-depth, in a new and exciting way. *Visions of Gerard* and *Doctor Sax* are also strikingly reinterpreted, as are other daringly innovative writings, like 'The Railroad Earth' and his "try at a spontaneous *Finnegans Wake*" – *Old Angel Midnight*. Neglected writings, such as *Tristessa* and *Big Sur*, are also analysed, alongside better-known novels such as *Dharma Bums* and *Desolation Angels*.
R.J. Ellis is Senior Lecturer in English at Nottingham Trent University.
1999 • 295 pages • ISBN 1-871551-53-6

Musical Offering *by Yolanthe Leigh*

In a series of vivid sketches, anecdotes and reflections, Yolanthe Leigh tells the story of her growing up in the Poland of the 1930s and the Second World War. These are poignant episodes of a child's first encounters with both the enchantments and the cruelties of the world; and from a later time, stark memories of the brutality of the Nazi invasion, and the hardships of student life in Warsaw under the Occupation. But most of all this is a record of inward development; passages of remarkable intensity and simplicity describe the girl's response to religion, to music, and to her discovery of philosophy.

Yolanthe Leigh was formerly a Lecturer in Philosophy at Reading University.

2000 • 57 pages • ISBN: 1-871551-46-3

Norman Cameron *by Warren Hope*

Norman Cameron's poetry was admired by W.H. Auden, celebrated by Dylan Thomas and valued by Robert Graves. He was described by Martin Seymour-Smith as, "one of ... the most rewarding and pure poets of his generation ..." and is at last given a full length biography. This eminently sociable man, who had periods of darkness and despair, wrote little poetry by comparison with others of his time, but always of a consistently high quality – imaginative and profound.

2000 • 221 pages • illustrated • ISBN 1-871551-05-6

Poetry in Exile *by Michael Murphy*

"Michael Murphy discriminates the forms of exile and expatriation with the shrewdness of the cultural historian, the acuity of the literary critic, and the subtlety of a poet alert to the ways language and poetic form embody the precise contours of experience. His accounts of Auden, Brodsky and Szirtes not only cast much new light on the work of these complex and rewarding poets, but are themselves a pleasure to read." *Stan Smith, Research Professor in Literary Studies, Nottingham Trent University*

"In this brilliant book Murphy strives to get at the essence of 'poetry in exile' itself and to explain how it is at the centre of the whole political and cultural experience of the turbulent 20th century. His critical insight makes it one of the most important recent books on poetry in English." *Bernard O'Donoghue, Wadham College, Oxford*

Michael Murphy teaches English Literature at Liverpool Hope University College.

POETRY

Adam's Thoughts in Winter *by Warren Hope*
Warren Hope's poems have appeared from time to time in a number of literary periodicals, pamphlets and anthologies on both sides of the Atlantic. They appeal to lovers of poetry everywhere. His poems are brief, clear, frequently lyrical, characterised by wit, but often distinguished by tenderness. The poems gathered in this first book-length collection counter the brutalising ethos of contemporary life, speaking of and for the virtues of modesty, honesty and gentleness in an individual, memorable way.
2000 • 47 pages • ISBN 1-871551-40-4

Baudelaire: Les Fleurs du Mal *Translated by F.W. Leakey*
Selected poems from *Les Fleurs du Mal* are translated with parallel French texts and are designed to be read with pleasure by readers who have no French as well as those who are practised in the French language.
F.W. Leakey was Professor of French in the University of London. As a scholar, critic and teacher he specialised in the work of Baudelaire for 50 years and published a number of books on the poet.
2001 • 153 pages • ISBN 1-871551-10-2

'The Last Blackbird' and other poems by Ralph Hodgson *edited and introduced by John Harding*
Ralph Hodgson (1871-1962) was a poet and illustrator whose most influentialand enduring work appeared to great acclaim just prior to and during the First World War. His work is imbued with a spiritual passion for the beauty of creation and the mystery of existence. This new selection brings together, for the first time in 40 years, some of the most beautiful and powerful 'hymns to life' in the English language.
John Harding lives in London. He is a freelance writer and teacher and is Ralph Hodgson's biographer.
2004 • 70 pages • ISBN 1-871551-81-1

Lines from the Stone Age *by Sean Haldane*
Reviewing Sean Haldane's 1992 volume *Desire in Belfast*, Robert Nye wrote in *The Times* that "Haldane can be sure of his place among the English poets." This place is not yet a conspicuous one, mainly because his early volumes appeared in Canada and because he has earned his living by other means than literature. Despite this, his poems have always had their circle of readers. The 60 previously unpublished poems of *Lines from the Stone Age* – "lines of longing, terror, pride, lust and pain" – may widen this circle.
2000 • 53 pages • ISBN 1-871551-39-0

Shakespeare's Sonnets *by Martin Seymour-Smith*
Martin Seymour-Smith's outstanding achievement lies in the field of literary biography and criticism. In 1963 he produced his comprehensive edition, in the old spelling, of *Shakespeare's Sonnets* (here revised and corrected by himself and Peter Davies in 1998). With its landmark introduction and its brilliant critical commentary on each sonnet, it was praised by William Empson and John Dover Wilson. Stephen Spender said of him "I greatly admire Martin Seymour-Smith for the independence of his views and the great interest of his mind"; and both Robert Graves and Anthony Burgess described him as the leading critic of his time. His exegesis of the *Sonnets* remains unsurpassed.
2001 • 194 pages • ISBN 1-871551-38-2

Wilderness *by Martin Seymour-Smith*
This is Martin Seymour-Smith's first publication of his poetry for more than twenty years. This collection of 36 poems is a fearless account of an inner life of love, frustration, guilt, laughter and the celebration of others. He is best known to the general public as the author of the controversial and bestselling *Hardy* (1994).
1994 • 52 pages • ISBN 1-871551-08-0

BUSINESS

English Language Skills *by Vera Hughes*
If you want to be sure, (as a student, or in your business or personal life), that your written English is correct, this book is for you. Vera Hughes' aim is to help you remember the basic rules of spelling, grammar and punctuation. 'Noun', 'verb', 'subject', 'object' and 'adjective' are the only technical terms used. The book teaches the clear, accurate English required by the business and office world. It coaches acceptable current usage and makes the rules easier to remember.
Vera Hughes was a civil servant and is a trainer and author of training manuals.
2002 • 142 pages • ISBN 1-871551-60-9